The
Book
of Dog

Celebrating
30 Years of Publishing
in India

The Book of Dog is a project to which the editor and all the authors have contributed for free. All royalties will go to the following registered animal welfare charities.

Friendicoes SECA

271 & 273, Defence Colony Flyover Market

(Jungpura side)

New Delhi 110024

The Welfare of Stray Dogs

2nd Floor, Yeshwant Chambers

B. Bharucha Marg

Kala Ghoda

Mumbai 400 033

Voice of Stray Dogs

4062, 19th Main Rd

HAL 2nd Stage

Indiranagar

Bengaluru 560008

Praise for *The Book of Dog*

'This collection is a printed version of the hours people spend absorbed in talking of their dogs ... a celebration of a bond that is full of fun, and moments comic or poignant. A relationship with a beloved dog is among the most passionate, intimate and powerful that any human being experiences, and in describing it these essayists delve into the deepest parts of themselves. ... Reading this book I felt I was in the company of friends who were Labradors and Retrievers, Road Asians and Bhimtailians, all of whom were making me smile for no reason other than their infectious instinct for happiness.'

—**Anuradha Roy,** *Biblio*

'An ode to canine companionship ... an interesting compilation, with each author bringing a unique perspective to the relationship between man and canine. The book is like a bag of Bertie Bott's Every Flavour Beans, perfect for dipping into, with each visit giving a different experience.'

—***The Book Review***

'This isn't just another pet book. It is a book of relationships ... about the love, affection and fondness between dogs and humans that have existed forever. Nuances of this bond have been brought to life through personal accounts of dog owners and dog lovers—rich with anecdotes. ... A labour of love. The character, charisma and the fuzziness of all the canine protagonists of *The Book of Dog* may convert you into a dog lover even before you hit page 100.'

—***Outlook***

'*The Book of Dog* is an ode to all the wonderful times that dogs have gifted us and changed us for the better. ... Remarkable, funny, introspective ... [It] chronicles the lives of man's best friend through personal essays, poems, haikus, and photo essays. Written by dog lovers (who also happen to be some of India's popular public figures), each piece is a celebration of the deep abiding love between canines and their humans.'

—*Scroll*

'Some of the country's leading writers, new voices as well as individuals who have dedicated their lives to animal welfare, write movingly about the dogs that have in big and small ways changed their lives ... [T]houghtful pieces that make up this delightful collection.'

—*Mid-Day*

'In the pages of [this book], I found people who laughed at their pets' silly antics, shed tears when they fell sick, indulged in their every whim, wrote them poetry, and treated them better than they did themselves. ... This collection, edited by Hemali Sodhi, has 45 pieces from writers whose work I have enjoyed reading: Ashok Ferry, Jerry Pinto, translator Arunava Sinha, Nilanjana Roy [whose book on cats is delightful], Anita Nair, and Gulzar. Each of them writes reverently about their dogs.'

—*Firstpost*

'Funny, sad and sometimes astonishing ... [a] must-have. Written by people whose lives have been fundamentally altered by the sometimes absurd but often unbearable sweetness of furry, four-footed creatures.'

—*India Today*

'Sometimes funny, sometimes sad, but always touching, *The Book of Dog* celebrates a love that can never be measured.'

—*HT Brunch*

'Just like two dogs, no two essays in the book are alike. But they all deliver on emotions and will either leave you smiling or sniffling ... *The Book of Dog* is a book about love that has been made with lots of it too.'

—*The Deccan Herald*

'Anyone who has had a pet would instantly connect with the tales of old soul Simba, mango bhakt Kafka, uppity Pali, wondrous Anokhi, sweet Kishmish and sensible Laika and their delightful canine buffoonery ... The journey through this book of magnificent tales unravels the incredible man-dog bond.'

—*The Tribune*

'Loving an animal opens up corners of your heart you never suspected existed. ... *The Book Of Dog* [does] a wonderful job of putting some of these stories together. Each essay and story brings alive a special relationship, and not always one of joy and humour and unconditional love—though there is all that too. Each piece ... is to be savoured, re-read and shared, for even though they may not all be perfect, they all come from a true and honest place.'

—*MintLounge*

'Engaging, personal, interestingly written … [this book] will make rewarding reading: there's literary merit, originality, some very interesting characters (canine, feline and human) and an insight on how these animals can insert themselves into, and change, our lives and hearts forever, usually in the best, happiest way possible.'

—***Open***

'*The Book of Dog* is a celebration of the bond dogs form with us and [how they] make us feel alive even in our darkest hours. An ode to a never-ending friendship.'

—**The Chakkar**

'[The book] captures profound moments of life with dogs.'

—**PTI**

The
Book
of Dog

Edited by

Hemali Sodhi

HarperCollins *Publishers* India

First published in hardback in India by HarperCollins *Publishers* 2022
4th Floor, Tower A, Building No 10, DLF Cyber City,
DLF Phase II, Gurugram, Haryana – 122002
www.harpercollins.co.in

This edition published in paperback by HarperCollins *Publishers* 2023

4 6 8 10 9 7 5 3

The quote on p. xxvii is by W.R. Purche. The quote at the beginning of the
Introduction is unattributed.

P-ISBN: 978-93-5489-462-6
E-ISBN: 978-93-5489-364-3

For sale in the Indian subcontinent only.

The Book of Dog is a project to which the editor and all the authors have contributed
for free. All royalties will go to registered animal welfare charities.

Hemali Sodhi asserts the moral right
to be identified as the editor of this work.

Cover and text design: Gavin Morris
Cover and endpaper illustrations: Tarang Maheshwari
Photos of the dogs are reproduced courtesy of the individual authors.

Printed and bound at
Replika Press Pvt. Ltd.

 HarperCollinsIn

CONTENTS

INTRODUCTION

'If you're lucky, a dog will come into your life, steal your heart, and change everything.'

I have a confession. Growing up, I was terrified of dogs. It was an entirely irrational fear—I'd never been bitten by a dog or had an unpleasant experience, but I was a timid child, fearful of many things I didn't yet understand.

Social gatherings were a traumatic affair if the hosts had a canine member in the house—all hell would break loose, and everyone's attention would be focused on keeping me calm and keeping the curious dogs away. For as anyone with a dog will know, one of the unwritten rules of the dog world is that the more you avoid them, the more they'll come sniffing around you, puzzled by this strange presence in their territory that seems to be displaying highly questionable behaviour: which surely calls for a thorough investigation.

Life continued the way it was, with dogs and I maintaining a respectable distance from each other, occasionally coming close to curiously sniffing around the contours of these invisible but firmly drawn lines, but never crossing them—till (the irony!) I got married into a family of devoted dog lovers. Since my partner's family lived in another city, this did not pose any immediate threat to my carefully constructed dog-free existence. But slowly, softly, dogs began to enter into conversations, and to hear dogs being spoken about with such affection stirred the first beginnings of curiosity in me. These weren't just alien, scary beings any more; Chikky, Kellie and Brandy all became real characters, with defined personalities of their own.

And I began to wonder. What, really, would it be like to befriend a dog? Had I missed out on something special all these years? And I slowly came around to the idea of giving myself a chance to see what could happen.

Around this time, a friend in another city sent out a distress signal—he was moving and needed to rehome his pup—would we know anyone who might want to give little Simba a home? After days of intense discussions I hesitantly said yes, with all 'fallback' safety nets in place—if I couldn't adjust to this startling change, we would have friends who would take in the pup, we'd get a trainer to make the adjustment smoother, it wouldn't be the end of the world—and really, how much harm could a little pup do? The monumental decision was taken: a pup would enter our home and our lives. And thus began a period of intense preparation as we (anxiously, in my case) awaited the arrival of this new member.

But fate clearly had something else in mind. Due to a variety of circumstances, little Simba could not be sent to Delhi, and his family decided to keep him with them. And suddenly, it was unbearable that after all that anticipation and all that preparation, we weren't going to have a dog! This was the biggest anti-climax, if there ever was one—we *had* to have a pup now, one we could call Simba since we had grown so accustomed to the name! We began asking around and found there was a family in our own neighbourhood that was looking for homes for their Labrador litter—would we want to take a look? We went across; I sat in the car, a bundle of nerves, while my partner went inside the house to see the pups.

Minutes later, this round, chubby, golden-white ball of fluff was put into my arms. And so, on a perfect day in February many years ago, little Simba came into our lives.

And completely changed my world.

I have always been at a loss for words when it comes to talking about Simba. It is said that there are life-altering instances that change everything about you and every belief or pre-conceived notion you've held on to. Simba was just that—a moment of falling completely, irrevocably, unquestioningly in love. With the sweetest temperament and the kindest heart, Simba was an old, old soul in a young body. There was dignity and kindness, a gentleness in him, which put everyone at ease (oh how I wish I had Simba in my life in my growing-up years!). If someone at home had a challenging day, Simba would pick up on that immediately and come sit next to them. He had many nicknames, each sillier than the next, and he'd respond to each of them. He patiently listened to the tuneless loud singing I subjected him to every morning, with a huge grin on his face, tail slowly thumping in support (appreciation may be taking it too far). He loved car rides and travelled with us everywhere, heading to the door automatically when he heard the word 'drive'. He had a favourite blanket he carried around everywhere—including on his walks! He loved muffins, and was perhaps the only dog who recognized a café on sight, his tail immediately wagging in anticipation.

Simba completely won over my parents, who ended up loving him unreservedly; early mornings saw Simba and my father sit with each other in companionable silence, my father sipping tea and Simba lost in his own thoughts. Everywhere Simba went, he left a trail of smiles—people would stop and stare or give a pat to this calm and gentle dog with the kind, brown eyes, whenever we took him anywhere.

Simba's arrival also opened up an entirely new world for me; from being scared of dogs, I now plunged headlong into a world inhabited by dogs and dog lovers. I made friends with other dog parents. I gradually became invested in issues around animal welfare, and those of animals in shelters desperately looking for someone to adopt them, abandoned dogs, and dogs living on the streets. I learnt about unethical backyard breeding, and about the many dogs who were given up by their families who couldn't—or didn't want to— take care of them. My heart sank on hearing stories of horror and mistreatment, and celebrated stories of rescue and hope.

Eventually, when Simba turned five, we got more dogs—to give Simba company, we told ourselves. But honestly I think we just loved the idea of being dog parents so much that we just had to expand our family. And so more dogs entered our heart and our home—the delightfully crazy brothers Jack Sparrow and Carlos; Cooper, who was rescued from a shelter; the tenacious Nikki, king of our street, who adopted our home after he was run over by a car; and more rescues: Junior and Muffin, and Custard. Our house became full of the most incredible, loving, amazing dog children (each of them with their individual, delightful personalities, and deserving a chapter and story of their own—but one I won't get into here).

Simba did all that.

But there is a heartbreaking reality that every dog parent is aware of—one we skirt around and don't put into words, but which lurks constantly at the back of our minds. Dogs have short lives. You will see them grow older, the gait become slower, the muzzle greyer. You will see the crazy zoomies turn into a slow and painful limp, and you will see that beloved face turn old. It is devastating, and even though it was something I knew would eventually happen, I wasn't prepared for it—with Simba, or with any of the other dog children we had.

It is said that dogs come into our lives to teach us about love and depart to teach us about loss—and eleven years and one month after he entered our lives, Simba left us after a brief illness. And even though I knew that parting was inevitable at some point, losing him meant losing a part of myself. I know that I am now lesser. Something has changed irrevocably, and even the happiest day of the rest of my life will not be perfect, for it will be a day without Simba.

But dogs also teach you some of the most profound lessons of life. They teach you to live in the moment, to live for the moment. They teach you unconditional love, given so freely it sometimes makes you tear up and wonder what you did to deserve this. They teach you to love unreservedly, and never let the child die in you. And they teach you kindness.

In 2020, when Covid hit unexpectedly and the world went into lockdown, the dogs at home were probably the only ones not unhappy with this strange new world—their humans were home and spending time with them for longer periods: it was like hitting the jackpot! And it was the dogs who kept many of us sane and provided comfort—in a world where everything was uncertain, here were our dogs, delighted with this change of circumstance and making the most of it. And that's when an idea I had thought about earlier slowly started taking shape—a book of essays and stories on these funny, furry, four-legged companions, an ode and a tribute to all the wonderful dogs from their devoted humans.

And that's when another extraordinary truth about the effect of dogs came into play—dogs bring us together in a way few things can, and bring out the most remarkable side of us. When I started reaching out to writers I knew were pet parents, I was making a huge imposition and a demand on highly regarded authors and accomplished professionals who led busy lives—and I didn't have much to offer: no money (in fact from the beginning I was keen that the royalties should go to animal welfare charities), no sight of a publisher at that stage—just a heartfelt request to these remarkable individuals to send in an essay on life with a dog.

And the messages and words of encouragement came pouring in from each one of them.

The first person I contacted was the wonderful Shobhaa De, having heard some fantastic stories of her beautiful dog Gong Li. And the always generous Shobhaa instantly responded with a yes, which was encouragement enough for me to reach out to some of the other writers and pet parents featured here: the dazzling Anuja Chauhan, whose very entertaining adventures with Chhabbis I had been reading about with immense interest; the wonderfully evocative Tishani Doshi, who had met some of our dogs and I knew was crazy about dogs herself; Rajdeep Sardesai, whose trusty companion Nemo was well known in circles in Delhi; the always kind Ashwin Sanghi—pet parent to the wonderfully named Simba; and friend of many years Jai Arjun Singh, with whom most of my conversations have been around dogs.

In this book, you will see accomplished translator Arunava Sinha's dog Tingmo wielding the pen to write some haikus about a typical day in his life, while Cyrus Broacha turns his humorous gaze on the dogs (and accompanying humans) in his building. Ashok Ferrey talks about his ever-expanding dog family with affectionate humour and resignation (we've been there, Ashok), and in a lovely piece, the immensely gifted Mahesh Rao talks about the fictional dogs who were his companions when he was growing up, since he was unable to have dogs of his own owing to a medical condition in the family.

Siddharth Dhanvant Shanghvi pens the experience of his early years as a dog trainer in exquisite prose as only he can, and in a poignant piece the talented Anindita Ghose writes about her Kafka's obsession with mangoes, and how that was to be the final moment of truth. Jerry Pinto's unnamed dog protagonist takes it upon himself to school a younger pup on the unpredictable ways of the world, while Fiona Fernandez turns her gaze to Jim Brown, a dog from her childhood she remembers and misses to this day. Manjula Narayan talks about some precious moments of solitude with her soul dogs for company, and in a moving piece, Keshava Guha turns the light on his relationship with his dog Pumba, during a particularly difficult period in his life.

In these pages, you will also meet the delightfully named Sunderapandi and Nachimuthu, Anita Nair's beautiful pups; and in a wonderfully charming and nostalgic piece, Mark Tully, a devoted dog lover, reminisces about all the wonderful dogs in his life.

Nilanjana Roy has written elegantly and memorably on her cats, but I knew she was a compassionate dog lover as well (our lovely children Jack and Carl came into our lives thanks to a phone call from her, for which I am forever in her debt), and I was so grateful when she agreed to write a piece for the book. I discovered that the academician Ananya Vajpeyi was a devoted dog parent through her beautiful, evocative posts on her lovely dog children Anokhi and Kishmish. I reached out and was delighted when she agreed to write a piece, despite her intensely busy schedule at the time.

I have always been a fan of Gillian Wright's writing and have known her to be a passionate dog lover; her piece on the dogs of a lifetime makes for wonderful reading. Paro Anand is another devoted dog parent, and I have had several conversations with her around her rescue dogs—I'm so happy to make the acquaintance of her two children Gia and Nadia through her piece. And it's delightful to meet the loyal Gaddies (mountain dogs) in Bulbul Sharma's piece—I have met a few Gaddies and have always been struck by their air of independence combined with unwavering devotion to those they love and protect. Manu Bhattathiri's piece on Yippee will make you smile—he sounds like such a delightful character, and I so wish I had had the opportunity to meet him!

I was also very fortunate to get contributing pieces from the peerless Gulzar—his love for his Boxer Pali is well known, and here he shares a poem and a note on Pali (translated into English by Udayan Mitra, also the publisher of this book). And everyone's beloved writer Ruskin Bond delights us as always with a tender piece on a dog who could see a spirit—it is something that only he could write.

Acclaimed mythologist Devdutt Pattanaik contributes a wonderful piece about dogs in Hindu myth, while historian Aanchal Malhotra has a fascinating and very informative essay on dogs deployed in World War I. Sumita Mehta writes a lovely, entertaining and nostalgic piece on one of the most famous dogs in the country—Editor. Prerna Bindra's love for her wonderful Doginder has been documented by her earlier; in her new piece she beautifully captures an inimitable conversation with Doginder. And Amitava Kumar turns his gaze at his younger self as he finally finds a chance to say goodbye to a faithful friend.

The visual essays in the book are all gorgeous. Leading filmmaker, screenwriter and photographer Sooni Taraporevala beautifully captures the free spirits of Marine Drive—these photos will make you smile; the highly accomplished Sarnath Banerjee does a brilliant piece on the life of Shehzada Ozu, the postcolonial Pekingese; and Divya Dugar, who leads the ideal life travelling with her dogs around the country and runs the very entertaining and popular Chaos in a Coupe on Instagram, talks about the joys and travails of travelling with three dogs and a baby in trains, and we get to see some lovely photos of their adventures as well.

One morning, a friend sent across the unforgettable image of a beautiful older dog bathed in sunlight, eyes closed—and there was an indescribable peace in that one photograph. Reading up on him I realized this was Kaju, the dog adopted by the tremendously talented graphic artist Orijit Sen. Orijit was kind enough to share Kaju's story—a sad beginning but a happy ever after, and I'm delighted Kaju features in this book.

There are also some astounding standout pieces from new voices. Naomi Barton writes with astonishing clarity in her stunning piece about Melody and Angel—bringing to mind that old saying: In reality, it is dogs who rescue us, rather than the other way round. Meenakshi Alimchandani, who opens up her home and her heart to give retired Greyhounds a second chance (Greyhounds are unfortunately used in dog racing in the US, and often put down once they outlive their 'purpose' on the track), writes about these incredible dogs with an aristocratic lineage. And Shrutkeerti Khurana writes about the challenges and joys of parenting a toddler and a small dog, in a very sensitive and heartfelt piece.

The wonderfully multi-talented Vikas Khanna has been busy with a new role—that of a parent to his dog child Plum. He writes about how Plum has changed his life dramatically—and as a bonus, gives us a recipe for what sounds like a delicious dog treat (clearly extending his culinary fan following into the canine world).

I have been following Abhishek Joshi for many years on social media and have always marvelled at his tireless energy in trying to find homes for dogs in need; in his poignant piece, he writes about the passing of his beloved dog Kaali. Geetan Batra's daughter is also a 'serial rescuer'—and Geetan's purported air of weary acceptance is actually a cover for a compassionate heart which is always open to giving shelter to animals in need—her lovely piece is an indication of that.

One of the pieces closest to my heart (though who am I kidding—they're all close to my heart) is my friend Sian Morton's piece on the draconian Breed Specific Legislation (BSL), and her beloved dog Alex's desire to live a normal life after being seized (the horrors we inflict, and the many ways we devise to make lives miserable for dogs could make for another—long—book). Sian and I met many years ago on a campaign we worked together on to help rescue Lennox, a dog seized under BSL—we lost that campaign, and Lennox was tragically put down under the law. It is fitting that Sian's wonderfully compassionate piece is about another dog—her lovely Alex—another victim of BSL, who finally found his forever home with her. Sian has devoted her life to spreading awareness about BSL and I'm tremendously grateful to her for writing this piece, which is as informative as it is engaging.

My role models in the past few years have been animal rescuers. It takes the highest form of compassion, combined with a great degree of selflessness, to devote your life to animal welfare, with its many heartbreaks and challenges. I just had to feature stories from some of the rescuers I have had the honour of knowing personally, and I'm so very grateful and delighted to feature pieces by Atul Sarin—the founder of Welfare of Animals in Goa (Atul gave up his career as a barrister in London to move to India to start a shelter)—Tandrali Kuli, who works tirelessly at Friendicoes in Delhi to rescue dogs and find them homes, and Maneka Gandhi, who actively put the spotlight on animal welfare in the country, and is one of the most passionate advocates of animal rights I have met.

My deepest gratitude to all these wonderful contributors—and all their marvellous dogs—who have made these pages come alive.

A heartfelt thank you to my wonderful agent, friend and fellow dog lover Mita Kapur of Siyahi, who agreed immediately to take on representation for this book and championed it passionately; Mita also very generously agreed to waive her fee since all royalties from the book are being donated to animal welfare. And gratitude to the wonderful team at HarperCollins India for taking this book on and sharing our vision for it—in particular to Udayan Mitra, a devoted dog lover himself who worked tirelessly on the book and gave the most insightful feedback, Bonita Vaz-Shimray, the art director who had several brilliant inputs, Shatarupa Ghoshal and Ujjaini Dasgupta, the editors on the book, and Shivendra Singh and

Rahul Dixit. Thanks also to Tarang Maheshwari for his evocative illustrations, and to the wonderfully talented Gavin Morris, who made the book come alive with his design.

So much gratitude to my parents who cheerfully accepted—and wholeheartedly loved—all the dogs who joined our ever-expanding family, and to Savita, who brought that little decorative blue bell for Simba the day he came home—he adored that bell, just as he adored her.

No words will ever be enough for Ananth, who showed me what I had been missing all these years, and opened my heart to the indescribable joys of life with dogs.

These are stories of love, and stories of loss—for that is the nature of being a dog parent. But there is also tremendous joy and laughter, silliness (everyone should be silly once in a while—nothing to beat an old-fashioned bout of silliness to get some perspective), and the sheer, simple happiness that dogs bring into our lives.

Dogs make our world better. As you go through these pages and read these stories, you will share in some of the best moments and adventures of what it is like being a dog parent.

And if you haven't yet, I hope you will meet your Simba one day.

December 2021   Hemali Sodhi

Everyone thinks they have the best dog ... and none of them are wrong.

The Average
Sri Lankan Family
ASHOK FERREY

Not so long ago we were the perfectly average Sri Lankan family—
father, mother, son, daughter, one dog, half a cat. (Almost every other
family in Sri Lanka has a cat, so that means every family has half a
cat; or a little less if you want to split cats.)

Oh, how I long for those days!

So when did the rot set in, I hear you ask. When did the decline begin?

One morning, after my daily toil of many, many minutes at the unfinished novel, I came downstairs for a break.

'There's a dog in the front room,' I informed the Wife.

'Oh?' she replied with casual insouciance. (She does casual insouciance very well, the Wife.)

'It has lots of hair,' I said. Our normal dog has very little. It is an average Sri Lankan dog, remember.

'That's lucky,' said the Wife.

'Really? I never knew long hair was a sign of luck.'

'No, I mean that's her name. Lucky. Anyway,' she pointed out, '*you* don't have much hair. Could that be why you never sell any books?'

Pretending not to hear this, I began to pet Lucky. A car had run over her front paws and somebody had dumped her at the vet's. She was now recovering and the Wife (naturally) felt she had to give her a home. Lucky sat on the Persian carpet, looking at us with the most enormous, beautiful eyes. Kind eyes.

A day later she had chewed a hole in the Persian carpet the size of a dinner plate. She obviously had an eye for fine things, and felt the design needed improvement. The Wife rolled up the carpet and put it away. 'She'll get over it,' she reasoned. 'Just give her time to forget about the carpet.'

Next day Lucky began on the cushions. The Wife put these away too, what was left of them. 'I'm a great fan of minimalism,' she explained.

'So I noticed,' I shot back, 'last time I looked in your shoe cupboard.' (The Wife has a humongous almirah groaning with shoes, mostly unworn. She is the uncrowned Imelda Marcos of Colombo.)

Our other dog ignored Lucky, the cat ran rings around her, and life returned to normal. Till the Wife next came back from the vet's. Now, the Wife goes to the vet to spend any free time she has, the way other people go to the British Council library. She always returns with something.

'There's a dog in the front room,' I said. (It is so satisfying when you have rehearsed the script, and you're more or less word-perfect.)

'That's Crisco,' the Wife said.

I would have preferred a little more casual insouciance in her delivery but there you are. Nobody's perfect.

'Crisco?' I exclaimed. '*Crisco?*'

'They found her outside the Crisco factory in Ratmalana, so she's called Crisco. She has cancer. Only weeks to live, I'm afraid, so let's make them her best.'

Crisco looked at us with the most enormous, beautiful eyes, etc. etc., and life settled back to normal. As much as it can with a cancer patient in the house. Meaning regular visits to the vet for chemo, radio, tomo and many other treatments ending with the letter 'o', all costing in the thousands-o.

Weeks turned to months and before you knew it a full year had passed. Crisco continued to flourish. Meanwhile, my hair had begun to fall out. With worry, I think.

'Well, it's a good thing *I'm* the one who's paying,' said the Wife, trying hard not to stare at the bald patch on my crown. 'Otherwise just imagine *how many books* you'd need to sell!' She gave me a withering look. I withered.

This is not where this story ends, though.

After that came Jools, jolly Jools with the appetite of a smallish elephant. Followed by Fritz, of the two differently coloured eyes and (I suspect) half a brain, so called because he came from a German rescue home in Galle. Then there was Popeye, snarling ferocious Popeye who took one look at a visiting British High Commissioner and squirted all over his handmade nut-brown brogues. I never knew he felt so strongly about Anglo–Sri Lankan relations—the dog, I mean, not the envoy. And then Paloma, who diligently dug up and chewed her way through the entire sprinkler system laid at great expense under the front lawn. The garden is now as dry as Outer Mongolia.

'Just think of all those water bills we're saving,' the Wife sang out joyfully.

'Just think,' I sang back.

The Wife fed and took care of all these canines ceaselessly, selflessly. A sort of Florence Nightingale in killer heels. And the rest of us? Well, you know the famous saying—behind every successful woman there's an average family? That is us.

It isn't all bones and roses in this canine dream world either. There are strict laws governing their behaviour. Some are downstairs dogs; some upstairs; yet others—a favoured few—are allowed on the bed. At this point the story begins to get murky, so anyone who doesn't own a dog, please stop reading right away, before I offend your delicate sensibilities. Dogs on the bed can only mean one thing: tiny patches of damp on the sheets when they get excited and lose control, or when it's raining and they simply cannot be bothered to go outside and get their paws wet. In the tropics you naturally expect damp patches on the ceiling and rising damp in the walls. On the mattress, however? But the Wife is a very forgiving sort.

I only wish I were. 'Do you know there are certain homes,' I began bravely, 'where dogs are only allowed on the bed for a few hours during the day? And that at night they have to go downstairs to sleep?'

'Really?' said the Wife icily. 'I suppose *you* could always go downstairs to sleep if it bothers you so much.'

And so we carry on—in that age-old war between Canine and Man. Or more accurately, Canine and the Average Sri Lankan Family. No prizes for guessing who's winning. If there's ever a fire in this house at night, and they form a dramatic human chain (as they do in films) to rescue the valuables, with the Wife directing operations in her booming—sorry, I mean dulcet tones, I know it won't be the artwork or the antiques or even the Average Family Members that are taken out first. As for me, I will be fast asleep in bed, I suppose, done to a turn on both sides, nice and crisp and even.

The Bow-Wow Years

FIONA FERNANDEZ

Prologue

It's Christmas, and Jim Brown's sharp nose detects the heady whiff of the aromas emanating from the kitchen. It's a typical festive day filled with canine tomfoolery, chasing unsuspecting squirrels and cats, and where food is always the centre of attention. Except this is doggie heaven. And for Jim Brown, it is a day to remember his happy life—the thirteen years on earth that were spent with a loving middle-class family in a quiet suburb of Mumbai.

CHRISTMASTIME was always special in the Fernandez household. Mrs F, my favourite hooman, would start prepping for the big day at least a week in advance. Did I tell you that she was the one who gave me this wonderfully different name? Brown, because according to her, I had the best brown coat she'd ever seen on a doggie. And Jim? Well, Jim Reeves was her favourite singer. She would say I was a '*pukka* Anglo-Indian bugger' who loved his '*khana-peena*', his afternoon siestas and music (yes, I was all ears each time she played a few catchy tunes on their home system). Thank goodness I wasn't named Bingo or Rocky or Chickoo.

Many moons ago, one rainy morning, I showed up at their doorstep, trembling with fear and soaking wet. My mother had been run over by a speeding train as we—she, my brothers, sisters and I—tried to cross the railway tracks. It was night-time, and I could not locate my siblings in my hour of grief. The universe led me to this home that was a stone's throw away from the railway line. Mrs F found me curled up in the daily newspaper. She wrapped me up in a towel and offered me some bread and warm milk. I became family that day, and the next year onwards, that very same day was celebrated as my birthday.

But let's get back to those wonderful memories around Christmas. Mrs F ensured that delicacies like Country Captain Chicken, Beef Devil Chilli Fry and Fish Curry were always part of the spread for the big day. It meant I too could tuck into every part of that excellent meal. Let me tell you something right away. I'd always hear my doggie pals in the neighbourhood, Sheru and Hero, whine about how they'd have to fight for leftovers from their caretakers. But not me. I always had a bowl filled with all the best cuts and juicy bones, and I ate both my meals at the same time as the family. It made me feel blessed. Often, during teatime, when Mrs F played her favourite music, including Jim Reeves's classics, she would call out to me for a quick snack. I could never refuse a few biscuits or banana chips. And if I paid real close attention as I sat by her feet near the doorstep, I'd be able to hear her hum the notes of the songs too. Those evenings, while everyone else was away, were so relaxing. Around noontime, if she spotted me from her kitchen window, all I had to do was give her one of my warm, fuzzy looks and her heart would melt. And a little treat would be passed to me over the windowsill! Now don't get me wrong; though Mrs F loved dogs to a fault, I swear I never took advantage of her generosity.

I remember that one time, when Mr F (he worked in some really far-off place) had returned home for Christmas after a long time, the feasting never seemed to end. Mr F would shower his family with gifts during these short visits. Even I got lucky with treats whenever he spotted me nosing around the courtyard! During one of those humongous luncheons, Mr F's younger brother—a lanky, good-for-nothing fellow who would hang around their home hoping to feed off their generosity—poured a colourless liquid in my water bowl. I sniffed at it and took a few laps, and before I knew it I began to sway from side to side while he danced around me like a circus clown, mockingly suggesting that I was as fat as a sausage. How rude! Luckily for him, it took me a while to regain my bearings, or else it would not have been such a funny ending for him. As I recovered and sat up, I could hear Mrs F yell at that 'rascal' (the loudest she had ever raised her voice), 'How dare you trouble my dear Jim Brown!' She was clearly annoyed with her brother-in-law's antics. A bowl of warm chicken soup acted like a soothing balm to me. Fortunately, that was the last I saw of that mean man.

When Mr F was at home, our wrestling games, especially with a handkerchief, would be such fun, you know—the man-to-man kind. But just as we would get used to a routine, it would be time for him to leave again. Mrs F would become really quiet for the next few days. As it was, she was a soft-spoken soul, and in the weeks after Mr F's departure, I'd barely hear her call me for my meals—until Small F would shout out to me from a distance in her sing-song drawl, 'JimBraaauun, come faaaast! Your food'll get cold!'

Pint-sized with a mop of curly hair, Small F was my second most favourite person in the world. She was Mr and Mrs F's younger daughter. Small F would talk to me about her day, complain about her struggles with learning Marathi, and sometimes even cry to me when she got a poor report card at school or had a fight with her class friends. She probably thought I was a hooman with four legs. Each time Mrs F gifted her a new eraser, a raincoat or a cricket bat, she would bolt out of the front door, call out to me from the gate, or come looking for me in my cosy sandpit under the tamarind tree, kneel down and say, 'JimBraaauun, see what Mama gave me today because I came first in class. You like it, no?' I would nod and give her my paw. It was my way of congratulating her. Thrilled, she would giggle, flash one of her wide grins and hop across to play with her friends. Sometimes, when Mrs F wasn't watching, she and I would harass the neighbour's plump, pure-bred cat, Sundari: I swear she was a witch in a furry avatar. She imagined herself to be the queen of the colony. She had this impossibly white coat, but I was pretty sure she had it secretly painted or dyed by her owners every month. Small F and I loved pulling pranks on her, like tricking her with make-believe food, and then leading her into a big, slushy puddle.

Small F was a tomboy; her friends were the older boys of the colony who played cricket or badminton. I loved hanging out with her gang. After school, they'd all gather in the playground. And the best part? They let me be the umpire during a game of cricket! And if it was badminton, I was the imaginary net that divided the court. They had a music band too that would come to life during the school vacations. Oh, not the kind you would imagine. Mrs F called it a 'rut-put band', a tin-pot-sounding outfit because all the instruments—from the two guitars to the drums and the keyboards—

were toy versions. But it was fun! They sang (off-tune) covers of songs
from hit films or chosen from the enormous audio-cassette collection
owned by the Fs. When those tapes went bad, they'd give them to me
to chew on. What an interesting pastime that turned out to be! How
Mrs F endeared herself to that gang, egging them on to sing encores,
and feeding them snacks after every 'concert'. Those entertaining
summer evenings were the best.

Small F had an older sister, Big F. I was a bit wary of her in the
beginning. Well, it was partly my fault that she wasn't as indulgent
with me as the rest of the family was. We didn't get off to the best
of starts. See, this one time, I spotted a bright-looking piece of cloth
hanging on their clothesline. I was tempted to have a closer look,
test my agility and stuff. I darted towards it and jumped up to grab
it. But in my excitement, I ripped apart the fabric that happened to
be part of Big F's important school project. I received a thunderous
earful from her. I imagined I would be banned from entering their
lovely courtyard after that day. When Big F had cooled off and left
in a huff, Mrs F came by to my sandpit. 'Son, you mustn't be a bad
boy now; don't behave like one of those other junglee strays, okay?'
she whispered in her typically gentle tone.

Big F eventually grew to like me, though not in an obvious way.
What can I say! Clearly, the swag and the charm finally won her
over! Still, I kept a safe distance after that scolding, and definitely
stayed away from the clothesline. Then, one day, as I lazed under
the mango tree, I realized that she had been observing me for a
while. She was sitting by their doorstep, balancing a board of some
sort on her lap. Gingerly, I headed towards her. 'Jim Brown,' she
called, 'come here … don't worry, I won't bite.' (Ha, now that
would have been fun!) She chuckled; she was always cheeky in her
comments. And that's when I saw it with my own eyes: Big F had

drawn a sketch of me. 'This is how you look, Jim Brown. You like it?' she asked. Until then, I had no clue about my appearance, but my goodness, I must admit I did like what I saw in front of me. She earned a paw-shake that day.

My average day would fly past except for the bad, bad rainy season, when water would accumulate everywhere and there would be no cats to chase and no dry spaces for a quick snooze. On such days, Mrs F would create a temporary warm bed for me by their doorstep. Otherwise, my day began with a pretty important chore: seeing Small F and Big F off to school. We would wait near the gate for their school bus. Once they hopped aboard, they would turn around to wave back at me from one of the windows as the bus sped off. I never missed that routine. Of course, the petting from the other kiddos was a bonus. Some of them would even treat me with a biscuit or a toffee. Others would call me 'Brownie' and admire my handsome coat.

Then one day, Rajah arrived. He was this overfed, 'high-class' dog with shampooed hair. He would accompany his master's daughter and pretend to lord over the place. He even had an attendant. Rajah would park himself in my seating area but I chose to be the cool guy and ignored his attempts to irk me, because I had a reputation. Then one day, the smart fella tried to dare me to enter the school bus. Aha! I was not going to tolerate any of this bunkum. It was against the rules. So I darted into the bus to show him who was the boss: 'Get out of the bus, you big bully; this is only for schoolchildren!' I barked my head off to make him see sense but he wouldn't budge. Idiot. All I could hear were a range of shrieks from the kids, and a lot of commotion. An umbrella swung in Rajah's direction and was accompanied by a booming yell. Tail between his legs, he meekly scampered off the bus. This intervention was courtesy of another 'huge' fan: Small F's rotund class teacher who took the same bus to school. It was a no-contest. Rajah had lost—both the dare and his pride.

Following Mrs F around for her daily errands was another activity that I thoroughly enjoyed and, might I add, took very seriously. I felt I had to keep her safe at all times, what with Mr F away. She worked so hard all week and kept the home in such good shape; most importantly, she fed me and was kind to me—it was the least I could do in return. Whether it was her many trips to the veggie or fish markets (I could smell that bag from a mile away!), the circulating library or the post office—all of which were within a short radius—I would tail her by a safe distance to ensure she was fine. On one occasion, I spotted a scruffy-looking man walking suspiciously close to her. It made me uncomfortable. I was about ten paces behind her when I realized that he was aiming to snatch her handbag. She was an easy target since her arms were occupied carrying groceries. I lunged from behind and pounced on him. I'd never felt so athletic in my life. He shouted in agony because I had inflicted sufficient damage with my claws. I was angry. How dare he attack Mrs F! 'Let him go, Jim Brown,' I could hear her plead with me. After a menacing growl, I loosened my grip on him and allowed him to dash off. I hope I taught him a good lesson to never repeat such an act. It took Mrs F a few moments to collect herself. Poor thing, she was shaken by what had just happened. I'll never forget the gratitude in her eyes that day. Oh, and that afternoon's lunch was epic.

My life was a collection of happy, warm memories and a lot of love from the Fs. Though, over the years, I noticed Small F couldn't spend as much time with me as before because she had more homework. 'I have to go for so many tooshins. Sorry, JimBraaauun, we can't play,' she bawled one afternoon while telling me about her school problems. Big F was hardly around as she had to go to some place called college (some far-off land, I guess) and Mr F's trips home now happened after even longer intervals. Mrs F was the only constant in my life. My second mother. My guardian angel. My friend.

Every summer, it would be a struggle to find cool corners for my afternoon siesta as it got too warm to snooze under the mango or tamarind trees. I had my eye on this minivan that would always park above a large dug-out. There was still some time before Small F would hop off the school bus. I loved how we did this little jig all the way back home; it was our thing. That morning, as I waited with her at the bus stop, she had told me excitedly that it was her last day before school closed for the holidays. 'No toooshins, JimBraaauun. Yay!' she squealed in delight. I was excited too. Soon we'd be back to having more masti and playing cricket with the gang. Did I imagine it would be our last meeting?

Lunch that day was an unusually grand affair. Mrs F outdid her own levels of generosity, topping my feast with the most delicious mutton mince cutlets, chicken legs and—the Anglo-Indian staple— beef roast. The bowl was laced with some of her super-yum broth as well. A nap was essential for all of this to settle.

I found the minivan parked in that same spot and slipped into the sandpit below it. Soon I was in slumber land, chasing Sundari until her fat self fell into another puddle. A loud, jarring screech and the head-spinning, whirring sound of turning wheels jerked me out my snooze. I was in excruciating pain—as if two buses had rammed into me from either side. The drunken driver hadn't bothered to check underneath his vehicle, and had started to back out the minivan while I was fast asleep under it. Silly me, I must have rolled over closer to one of the wheels to cushion myself.

Within moments, I felt a lightness envelop my body. I found myself floating over the scene below, actually able to see what was happening. Mrs F, Small F and some of her gang were sobbing uncontrollably as they stared at my motionless body. Even Sheru and Hero had showed up; both looked confused and began to wail in an odd-sounding symphony. I understood that my time on earth was up.

I was blessed with a happy, fulfilling life because my hooman family treated me like their own—from ear tip to tail end. Simply put, they made me feel extraordinary. I hope I was able to return the favour in my own, Jim Brown-kinda way.

When Gong Li Speaks to Me

SHOBHAA DÉ

Gong Li is a lady. I am not. A lady-lady, I mean. I can be rough, uncaring, boisterous, coarse and an *asli tapori*. Gong Li? Never! She is the most feminine person I have ever known. And being all woman, she can be pretty unpredictable too. Which makes her the perfect BFF. It's boring being around predictable people. With her, I am never sure which avatar it is going to be. I love the Diva avatar the most. That one comes on right after her bath, when she is fluffed up, fragrant and frisky—ready to flirt and go beyond just a kiss, should she encounter a worthy suitor. So far, no one has been good enough for her. She responds with utmost disdain to the lovelorn overtures of local swains. Which pleases me immensely, of course. That has always been my big concern: What if Gong Li falls madly in love and runs off with the first scoundrel she swoons over during her walk? I am possessive and protective about this little lady, with her fancy airs and graces. I watch with an eagle eye if a swaggering lothario approaches her as she ups her little Pekingese nose and turns her face away. Many are they who have tried and failed to woo her!

Gong Li keeps me insecure. Until her, insecurity was a trait unknown to me. Now, it has become a constant, playing on a loop. Each time she steps out, I am left wondering whether she will come back to me. To me, not the home we share. There's a huge difference. I like her aloofness. It adds to her allure. Had she been the typical lapdog she was born as and was meant to be, I would have been bored after the first few months of cuddling this snow-white ball of fur. But no! Gong Li arrived with attitude intact. She was more cat than dog, in that way. Even when she was just a few weeks old, she displayed a healthy sense of self-sufficiency. Aah! An aristocrat, I concluded, when she turned down bread and milk, favouring bits of buttery croissant instead.

But wait, let's back up to the '*jab we met*' scene.

Location: Pune. Setting: an al fresco restaurant run by a dishy Italian chef. Supporting cast: Mandakini, my Pune-based sister, my daughter Anandita, and local friends. We had just polished off a creamy fettuccine and a bottle of a crisp white wine. The plan was to head back to Mumbai after the tiramisu. One of our friends mentioned casually that her adored pet Skittles had delivered a litter and she was looking for a home for the last pup, a female. 'Nobody wants a female ...' she said. And we laughed. Don't we know that! Nobody wants a female! Hah! Time to show them, I say! She said her driver had offered to take care of the last pup. Maybe it was the wine talking, but I got all militant and impassioned and declared, 'I want her!' Glances were exchanged. 'Those' sort of glances. I repeated slowly, 'I want the female pup.' After a short discussion, it was decided the pup and I should meet first, before committing. Agreed. We waited for the pup to show up, and took our time over the superb Italian coffee. I wanted to reach Mumbai before sundown. And if we were to have one more passenger in the car, a few arrangements needed to be urgently made.

She arrived like a mini-empress in a palanquin. Well, it was a wicker basket, but not the usual doggy one. It was elegant and kitted out in pink hand towels. She was sitting up and staring at the world like she owned it. Can't speak for her, but for me it was instant love. She captured my heart on the spot. There was no way I was going to leave Pune without her.

Then came the challenge of breaking the news to Mr De.

We had taken a family decision not to look for another house pet after losing our beautiful Kiara, the Irish Setter whose graceful lines inspired painters and poets. Strangers would stop dead in their tracks and stand mesmerized, jaws dropping, gazing at her breathtaking beauty. I had been heartbroken by her tragic passing and was pretty sure I would never love another. Isn't that how it always happens? And boom! I was gone! Smitten.

That still left an unsuspecting Mr De in Mumbai, who had zero idea at this point that Anandita and I would be bringing our newest family member home from Pune. Hmmm. An inspired brainwave struck halfway down the treacherous ghats. Out of nowhere, as it were, I decided on the name 'Gong Li'. Confession: Apt though the name was for this beauty, I was being sly. Mr De's movie heart-throb at the time was the divine Chinese actress, the original Gong Li. I called him and said sweetly (I can be sweet … sometimes), 'Just thought I should let you know that I am bringing Gong Li home. We should be there for dinner.' Pin-drop silence. Had he fainted from the excitement? I could almost hear his heart going thud-thud-thud. Maybe the anticipation of meeting his senior-citizen crush

was getting to be a little excessive? He stuttered, 'What? Gong Li?
Don't be ridiculous.' I imagined him disconnecting the call,
rushing into the shower, hastily shaving and splashing on a bucket
of Terre D'Hermès … No. This was getting cruel. I paused and
said evenly, 'Umm … this Gong Li has four legs and is a beautiful
Pekingese pup.'

Mr De was not amused. But even he could not resist Gong Li's
abundant charms when they met.

So, when and why did Gong Li become Ganguly? For that's how
she is known in our residential complex. Ganguly! It happened on
the Pune Expressway, when I was sheepishly telling Mr De about
the surprise guest who'd soon be sharing her home with us. Our old
faithful behind the wheel overheard the conversation and chipped
in when we made a pee stop for our tiny fluff ball at Navi Mumbai.
He congratulated me for choosing the perfect name for our newest
family member. Said Choudhary, beaming happily, '*Bahut badhiya
naam rakkha—Ganguly—India ka best cricket captain.*'

He introduced her to all his buddies in the complex as
Ganguly—and Ganguly she remains to them.

It's been seven years. And no seven-year-itch so far. At least
not from my side. As for Gong Li, she has grown into a supremely
poised monarch and continues to intrigue me with her petulance
and picky palate. She is fastidious about everything! People, food,
ambience, music. She is adorably anti-social and dislikes everybody.
She listens in on all my conversations—and that's not polite. Her
monumental ego makes her believe she can take on beasts ten
times her size … and win. It must be something about her body
language and sharp bark—I see hulks and bullies cowering in her
presence before turning tail and fleeing. Hmmm … what is it that

they say about certain traits running in families? Don't look at me! Compared to Gong Li, I am Minnie Mouse.

Her personality overwhelms the unwary, those foolish humans who approach her thinking, 'Oh … she's just a little doggie … so sweet!' Ooops! Wrong doggie! Gong Li is many things, but sweet she ain't! Even though her breed makes the best lap dogs—Chinese empresses bred Pekingese to keep themselves warm during the long, cold winters; four or five little ones would snuggle in the flowing, deep cuffs of the empresses' sleeves, or be held close to their bosom while the good ladies rested against silk bolsters in their magnificent palaces—I prefer to leave her alone. Not being a Chinese empress, I dare not cuddle Gong Li. I would rather tell her secrets. She keeps them well!

I understand Gong Li. She understands me. Possibly better than my closest family members. We have our own language and it isn't flowery. In fact, there are no filters. I don't need to be politically correct when I tell her what she needs to hear. And she puts me in my place often enough—one glare, one sharp bark is enough. We share sunsets and never skip having evening tea together. She has strange taste when it comes to tea-time snacks, preferring spicy upma or poha to butter biscuits. A few treats drive her nuts with impatience—bits of coconut, for example, before we start making coconut chutney for Sunday dosas. Nagpur oranges and chilli chicken, mangoes and cheese omelettes. Being a lady and a very classy one, Gong Li does not beg for food. She waits to be served. I appreciate good manners, and often end up overfeeding her.

But of all her avatars, it is Gong Li the Confidante whom I love the most. Especially when I am feeling low and believe I have nobody to talk freely to. You know the mood? 'The world does not love me'—that mood. She senses it, and hangs around more than usual, often staring soulfully into my eyes. I whisper into her perked-up ears, and I know she 'gets' every word, minus judgement. She tells me stuff too. But we don't overload one another with our respective angst. Another exceptional quality I deeply admire in Gong Li is that she never whinges and whines unnecessarily—like most of us do. Not even when I leave on a trip. No guilt is thrown at me when the suitcase is rolled out of the front door. Nor do I have to deal with accusations when I return. She is as overjoyed to greet me as I am to see her, her eyes shining with excitement and her little pink tongue hanging out while her tail wags and wags and wags. And I coo and coo and coo.

Gong Li, remember this: We are soul sisters. I will willingly pledge a lifelong supply of your favourite chewy sticks if you promise to stay you—so that I can stay me too!

Till Death Do Us Part

ANANYA VAJPEYI

Mama was a mother to her dogs long before I came along. When my parents were newly wed, she had Bhaloo, who ran away. Then she had Billi, who counts as the first dog in my life, though I have no memory of the dog whose name meant 'Cat'. After a long stay overseas, my parents returned with me to India in time for me to begin school. One day my mother and I were on our way back from a visit to my grandparents. Along the road we saw a pair of Lhasa Apsos walking with a stern-looking gentleman. My mother pulled over the white Fiat and got out of the car. She knelt down and patted and played with the fluffy little creatures, who were introduced to us as Laika and Rufus.

The gentleman looked on politely. I watched from the car window. In no time, my mother's obvious delight enveloped the dogs, the gentleman and me. 'Would you like to take them?' the man said. My mother looked completely surprised. 'I am an army man,' he said, 'and about to be posted out of Delhi. If you will take care of them, you are welcome to keep them.' My mother clapped her hands and shouted for sheer joy. She had just cut her beautiful thick shiny black hair short, in a fit of pique whilst waiting for me to stop wailing through my first week at school. The light bounced off it in the hot Delhi sun, and Laika and Rufus were brought home the next day.

Oh, adorable pups! Laika, named after the Russian dog, the first to be sent to space—India was still friendly with the USSR in those days—was black and white, silky to the touch and somewhat cat-like in her independence. Rufus was sable and had rickets, which made it difficult for him to run, though he tried valiantly every day to dash out whenever the front gate or the back door were accidentally left open. Laika basically minded her own business. But Rufus gave chase to all the neighbourhood dogs, cats and children, to the occasional ass or pig or cow that wandered over from the urban village abutting our colony, to moles and mice and geckos and sparrows that shared our small house and tiny garden with us. How thinly urbanized our locality must have been that so many domestic animals were about, vegetation overran the back alleys, and nature was always near, with all its pleasures and dangers. Rufus was fierce in intention but utterly ineffective. Everyone adored him.

My best friend Sonu, who lived a few houses down the street, offered to swap her younger sister Monu for Rufus. We would scoop him up into our arms and adorn him with our hair clips and give him parts in all our games of make-believe (a privilege firmly denied to the long-suffering Monu). Once, in the back lane, a large pregnant sow sat on Rufus, almost killing him—with her weight, if not with fright. 'Memsahib ji, PIIIIG!' screamed Pushkar, our young Kumaoni cook whom my mother was treating for TB, terrified that Rufus would not emerge alive from under his filthy tormentor.

When my mother came home after teaching her classes she would honk the car horn and I would rush to open the gate for her, still in my blue school uniform. Laika and Rufus would tumble out after me. The white Fiat had to pull into the small driveway without the canines scrambling out of the gate or getting run over. My mother would laugh and laugh as she got out of the car, the dogs hurling themselves at her, a mad flurry of fur and love and squealing and barking, a daily ritual that had the ecstatic quality of reunion after a long parting of years. I locked the gate and we all came indoors for lunch, Mama carrying Rufus, Laika jumping alongside, and me bearing Mama's attendance registers, her shapeless oversized tan American handbag with far too many things in it, most of them of questionable utility, and her books of poetry and fiction that she had taught from that morning.

So we were the welcome committee, the triumphant homecoming procession, our queen's entourage. My poet father, who wrote all night and slept in all morning, resigned to living with dogs since he had married my mother, referred to it as the '*hahakaar band*'. Sometimes he would call out, like a puppet master setting up a show on a street corner in his native Lucknow, '*Gulabo Sitabo ke tamaashe—Rangeeli Chhabeeli ke tamaashe.*' We were all crazy with excitement, despite the absolutely routine nature of this lunch-hour gathering of the three Vajpeyis and their two Lhasa Apsos. After lunch it was my dad's turn to take the car and go teach his classes. By then girls and dogs were all in siesta mode.

Once, a boy from one of the two or three villages that surrounded our bourgeois enclave made so bold as to kidnap Rufus. Remembering the long-lost Bhaloo, my mother became frantic with worry. The press-wallah and the sabzi-wallah and various other neighbourhood informants told us that Rufus had been seen being carried away on a bicycle that was heading towards the flour mill in the back of the colony. We jumped into our car, although it was not far to go. I think my father drove, because my mother was hysterical with anxiety. I sat in the back seat, Mama's alert lieutenant, and scanned the streets for the slightest sign of escapee sable fur, a rickety gait, a Rufus lost, unstable on his little legs, trying to find his way home or fruitlessly giving chase to some prey far larger, nimbler, faster and more sure-footed than himself.

Finally we arrived in the village behind the flour mill. Lo and behold, our hostage was tied with a thick rope to a jute charpoy, happily drinking creamy buffalo milk out of a tin bowl. Cow dung, threshed grain and wood stoves gave to the air that rustic smell I now associate with childhood, old India, gone forever. The villagers surrounded Rufus, utterly smitten with his miniature perfection and his toy-like appearance. They were not openly belligerent but were clearly unwilling to return him to us. The village headman—the kidnapper's father—shamelessly offered my mother money for the cuddly dog. She was livid with indignation, even though everyone else seemed very amused. She untied her errant pet, hoisted him up unceremoniously with milk still dripping from his whiskers, and ran back with him to the waiting car, while my father expertly backed us out of the scene of crime.

'When Rufie was stolen and found drinking buffalo milk' became part of street lore for all the years we lived in that house. We would roll with laughter remembering the whole escapade. 'Such a little fool!' my mother would say. 'That buffalo could have knocked him down with a flick of its tail. Where did he think he was going?' Laika would never have been lured away by uncouth strangers to gambol in cow dung. Rufus routinely got his fluffy head stuck in the flowery pattern on our iron gate, or got stuck in the storm-water drain that ran under the driveway. Perhaps memory is playing tricks, but I could swear that his twin rolled her long-lashed eyes and puckered up her button nose at his ridiculous antics.

At some stage, the sweet, civilized, sensible Laika died prematurely: She had swallowed a dead gecko. Decades later, I found a window display about Laika, the first dog in space, at Orhan Pamuk's Museum of Innocence in Istanbul. I did not know that she had met a sad end as a result of her cruel, impossibly lonely expedition away from our planet. As a child I had been impressed by her pioneering role in exploring the last frontier, but it had never struck me that she was just a small, bewildered earthling hurled into trackless oblivion. Rufus lived until he could barely walk, his brave and feisty spirit undimmed till his last breath. How we loved those two. I still do, long after they, and my parents, have all gone to a happier place.

My mother continued to have dogs, throughout my childhood and adolescence and youth. When I went away to study, to work and to live my itinerant life, I would return periodically to my parental home to find one dog or another, often two at the same time—Sufi the dervish, undoubtedly a highly evolved soul in a canine body, according to my father, who knew little about dogs but a lot about souls; Shabana, pretty and vain but incorrigibly quarrelsome, whose bad manners my mother defended to the bitter end because she was deaf and hence paranoid; Zulfi the dandelion dog, who pirouetted about in a blur of weightless white fur, lithe, affectionate and devoid of meanness; Roger the obese Dachshund, rescued from a friend of my mother's, together with his silly name, his diabetes and his proverbial propensity to bite my mother's hand; and last but not least, Kolaveri (née Cleopatra), who came to be babysat but was never returned to her original owners, much to their chagrin. My mother disapproved of the way in which she was banished to a kennel in the garden and not allowed into the house. She simply refused to send her back. Cleo was renamed for the Tamil hit song that went viral that year.

But I will cut to the year my father died. Mama was left alone then with Kolaveri, the very naughty, absolutely gorgeous and thoroughly self-willed Beagle. My father used to call her '*Lady Gunda*', since she regularly played havoc inside the house or further afield. Once, she got into a spat with the monkeys who came to raid my mother's mango tree, swallowed a mango whole in the middle of their inter-species argument and had to be operated on to have the mango seed removed from her gut after several weeks, during which nobody could figure out what was wrong with her.

'Why is there a mango seed in the dog's intestine?' the irate vet asked my mother. 'Who feeds their dogs mangoes?' Poor Kolaveri had to wear one of those conical collars until her stitches healed, but she never quite regained the oomph to take on the troops of monkeys who continued to ravage the tree of its sacks and sacks of small, sweet fruit—as indeed they still do, all these summers later. Mama waited a few months after losing my father, and then began to say that she wanted another dog. I was on the lookout, once again, as my mother's loyal lieutenant.

A publisher friend put out a desperate message on Facebook. She and her family wanted to go away to Goa over the Christmas holidays; apart from their other dogs, they had a small puppy at home they didn't want to leave behind. Barely had I finished reading out the post to my mother, than she asked for my friend's address, got into her car—now driven by a chauffeur, since Mama had grown old—and went to fetch the pup. She came home in an hour or two with an adorably winning, golden Cocker Spaniel. His parents, Nawab and Bella, stayed where they were, having bid a fond farewell to the runt of their litter.

Mama proposed he be called 'Christmas', since he had arrived during the holidays. Puniya, my parents' trusted housekeeper—a Christian herself—said 'Kishmish?' So Kishmish he was, a tiny golden bundle of sweetness, like his name, which means 'raisin'. Kolaveri—snooty, imperious and singularly devoid of maternal instinct—was bemused by this intruder in her domain. But he attached himself to her from day one, and thereafter they were inseparable, a sight to see, if ever there was one. My beloved father was gone, but Gulabo-Sitabo were back.

My mother's house once again descended into its familiar doggone anarchy. Until a few months ago, people had trooped in to offer their condolences at my father's demise. Now they came to see the dogs. Ramin, a philosopher friend of mine, an Iranian in exile, brought home a Cocker Spaniel puppy of his own to entice his young daughter into visiting him in India. She was given to Mama to foster for a while. Naturally there was absolute mayhem in the house, with Kolaveri, Kishmish and little L—whose name was either Lennon or Laila, nobody was quite sure—trooping and tumbling about with their respective attitudes of annoyance (K.veri), adoration (K.mish) and peskiness (L.). Daddy had departed, but the *hahakaar band* that my mother was accustomed to had returned.

One day Kishmish, who had been playing in the winter sun on the roof, was nowhere to be found. It turned out he had run so fast that in his jump he had sailed right over the low parapet, and landed two floors below on an asbestos sheet covering our laundry shed. The asbestos had cracked, but Kishmish was unhurt. He lay there, splayed in a furry daze, until someone saw him and rescued him. My mother and Puniya were mortified. They had the parapet on the roof rebuilt, higher than ever before. Thankfully the puppy was safe and none the worse for his short airborne journey. 'Not the brightest bulb in the chandelier,' I said to my mother, but she didn't appreciate my wry humour at the pup's expense and hugged him closer to herself.

L eventually left for Canada with Ramin's daughter. Kolaveri took ill for unknown reasons and dropped dead, leaving us, especially Kishmish, devastated. Then my mother went out to a dog-adoption drive being held in the mall near her house and came home with a sleek, smoky, leggy cur, her eyes deep, dark and lined as if with kohl, her howl strange, her ears snipped, her front paws encased in white fur like long, elegant gloves, the tip of her tail white as though dipped in a can of paint, her antecedents unclear. 'She wouldn't take her eyes off me,' Mama explained. 'I had no choice but to bring her back.'

She wailed like no dog we had ever known. Kishmish, enchanted but puzzled, cocked his head until his ear touched the ground. Kishmish has long ears and curly bleached hair atop his golden head, giving him the overall look of a judge in a wig. ('A blond barrister,' laughed my friend Ravit, 'or Farah Fawcett.') 'Maybe you should call her Ms Hyena,' I said to my mother when I first saw the unlikely new arrival. Mama was incensed.

'She's such a beauty,' she insisted. 'I will call her Nainsukh.' I objected, pointing out that it made absolutely no sense to name a contemporary creature of unknown descent (fox? hound? jackal?) after a great Pahari master painter of the eighteenth century.

'Naintara then,' Mama said, beaming. Both words mean 'apple of my eye', more or less, and I doubt highly that they have ever been applied to dogs. The certificate from the adoption agency noted her name as 'Tiger', which was even less apt, given both her silvery colour and her nightly baying. We settled on 'Anokhi', since she was strange, wondrous and quite unique.

But Kolaveri's untimely death had been a premonition, a warning of things to come. Hardly three months later my mother was diagnosed with last-stage lung cancer. She had the healthiest lifestyle imaginable and had shown no symptoms, except a cough that ran for a few weeks and which no one had noticed, given that it was peak pollution season in Delhi.

My husband and I had just left for England when this terrible news brought us back home. The next months passed in a nightmarish daze. I realized I was going to lose my mother hardly two years after I had lost my father. Neither of them had been in bad health or given any signs of the impending end. My mother stayed at home, refused treatment or hospitalization, and clearly wanted to live as normally as possible.

About thirty-six hours before she died, Mama got herself off the medical bed we had installed in her room, disconnected her respiratory mask from the oxygen tank, asked her nurses and Puniya to step away, and walked by herself to the dining table sans wheelchair or walker. She pulled out her usual chair, sitting on which she had eaten her meals for forty years (the dining table had come with us from the earlier house to this one). There she sat, silently, for about half an hour, communing and conversing with Kishmish and Anokhi.

She patted their heads, stroked their fur, held the paws—one narrow, dainty and white-gloved and the other wide, furry and golden—that they each offered her. My mother's beautiful hair was discoloured and straggly now, after a lifetime of bounce and light. Yet she blazed brightly, like a flame before it is extinguished. The dogs were rapt. They looked into her eyes and she into theirs. They were saying goodbye to one another. I felt my heart give way inside my chest at that moment—not a day and a half later, when Mama stopped breathing. She did not speak again after she took leave of her dogs.

Unbeknownst to me, the daughter of a friend of my mother's, who ran an animal shelter, had put up a photo of Kishmish and Anokhi on social media, saying their owner had terminal cancer and that they were up for adoption. She also added my mobile number, without my permission or knowledge. Through my mother's death and funeral, and for days afterwards, I was inundated with calls and messages, random people asking to adopt the dogs—or rather, Kishmish, 'golden wala dogie', but not both. Indians are caste-conscious even about animals, it turned out.

I didn't know what to do. I allowed some people to come and see them—others I turned away. I had no understanding of the difference between breeders, trainers, adoption agencies, private parties, dog enthusiasts, do-gooders, people in different cities in India, foreigners spending a few years in Delhi, batty women who droned on about my mother's spirit, and the sort of unsavoury characters who call any number they find circulating on WhatsApp.

One day I spoke to a pair of sisters—one a schoolteacher, the other a doctor, both unmarried. They said they had recently lost their own mother and wanted to get our dogs for their old father, who was lonely. I invited them to visit us. They came in their car and brought collars and chains and muzzles with them. They said they had taken the day off from work to drive all the way across town to us, and had come to pick up Kishmish and Anokhi. I was horrified, frozen with disbelief and shock. I had thought they were coming to meet the dogs, not to take them away.

We haven't bathed them, I said, in rising desperation. My husband is not around and he would like to meet you. They've never lived away from this house. Puniya held back briefly, but then burst into tears. The two women were unperturbed and waited patiently till we collected ourselves. The dogs were oddly subdued and submissive. I carried them both, one large bundle and the other small, and set them down on the back seat of the car. They made not a sound of protest. Their tails were down, like flags of a defeated army. They looked at me with those soft round eyes, two brown, two black, absolutely trusting, absolutely helpless: sentient beings, orphaned like I was. I felt viscerally the bond between us, of love, of loss, of suffering, of pain.

I wanted to die. I wished it had been me that had died over those miserable years, rather than Mama or Kolaveri or Daddy. The women drove away with my mother's dogs, and I experienced a grief so profound that I cannot type these words even today, years later, without crying out of guilt, remorse and sheer agony. It was the worst day of my life. I know that it will always be that, no matter how little or how long I live.

My husband returned from wherever it was he had gone. He had grown up being at best indifferent to and for the most part frightened of dogs. He enjoyed visiting my parents, but the dogs had to be sent away upstairs or outside for the duration of his visit. He did not know how we could handle my parents' dogs after them and assumed we had no choice but to give them up for adoption. But when he came back to find them actually gone, he was, to my surprise and his own, not happy. 'Are you sure those women were all right?' 'Where do they live? Did you take their address?' 'Can they send us photos and videos every day to show us how they're doing?' He goaded me into calling the adoption service from which Mama had brought Anokhi.

I found myself talking to lawyers, to animal rights activists, to veteran dog-shelter volunteers, and I got an earful from them, saying it was irresponsible of me to give away dogs traumatized by their owner's recent death. I spoke to one person who actually looked up Anokhi's records, found my mother's name and remembered her. 'Professor Vajpeyi?' he said. 'We were so happy she took Tiger! Older women who live alone are the best caregivers for rescued animals,' he explained, 'and your mother was a force of nature. We knew the dog would be in safe hands.'

He sent me a photo of Mama with Anokhi at the mall where they had first met; I hadn't seen this one before. They seemed to belong together from the get-go. Nothing in my mother's confident demeanour, her short-sleeved red kurta, her chin set in the determination to take on this ungainly creature, suggested she would die within six months, leaving the unfortunate Ms Hyena homeless yet again.

I rang the women—whom I had taken to calling the Evil Sisters in my head—every day. They were fed up with me and wouldn't always answer my calls. One day they said they had three other dogs—a Dalmatian, a Rottweiler and an Alsatian. I was taken aback. Why did they need five dogs? How did their widower father manage so many? And why take our little ones, when they had such huge, ferocious breeds already? They said Anokhi was not adjusting with the others, while Kishmish was very friendly with them—because they were all females. Never mind that they were all twice his size, if not larger. And the most dreadful thought of all: They weren't trying to get Kishmish to father puppies, were they?!

They sent alarming pictures of Anokhi and Kishmish in full harness, looking lost among these gigantic animals. We never tied or locked up our dogs—it wasn't good to see them thus restrained in unfamiliar and potentially hostile surroundings. They were being fed dog food—a big no-no in my health-conscious, low-fat, all-natural, organic-only, yoga-practising, waste-recycling, vegetarian mother's house. I called up Anokhi's adoption agency. 'If she's never behaved aggressively, they're probably lying,' the man chided me. 'They want to keep the pedigreed Cocker Spaniel and get rid of the Indie. Or they want the male, not the female. They're just making excuses to abandon her.'

That very day, while I was still agitated and upset, the schoolteacher called me. 'Every time a car passes by, Kishmish runs out to the gate,' she said. 'I think he expects you to come and fetch him.' I told my husband and Puniya about this. 'That's enough,' my husband said. 'They're coming back.' I hesitated. How would we look after them? How would we go overseas, leaving them behind? But Puniya was having none of it. Without waiting for a second, or asking for our opinion, she jumped into the car and set off with the driver (whom I had retained after my mother's death because I didn't want the man to lose his job as abruptly as he had lost his employer). They were on a mission to bring Kishmish and Anokhi home.

My husband told me quite recently something he had neglected to mention at the time of my mother's illness. 'The dogs came to me,' he said, 'when your ma was about to die. They asked me to take care of them. They said, "We are going to be orphaned, please don't abandon us."' I looked at him, doubtful, not to say sceptical. 'Why didn't they come to me?' I asked. 'Oh you were in no state,' he said. 'They knew they had to come to someone who would listen.'

'How did you know what they were saying?' I asked. 'They made it very clear,' he said. 'They sat at my feet and they cried. They knew your mother was leaving them.'

That evening, on their return from Purgatory, the dogs were half mad with excitement and relief. Both Puniya and the driver wore the air of conquering heroes back from battle, bearing trophies. They reported that the women lived in a part of town that no dog of ours would ordinarily deign to visit; that their house was small and their street narrow; that our dogs were miserable there, like prisoners; that there were no parks and trees, and there were all those other wretched dogs, crammed into the same space. And the odious loathsome pet food! Puniya declared that she would have to spend weeks getting the dogs back to their proper diet and their regular weight. Despite this highly biased and probably unfair report, I felt awash with the blessing of forgiveness, the miracle of a second chance. In fact, hardly ten days had passed since they had left. But this time, we all knew our reunion was forever.

I told my friend Rani about this. She's a beautiful writer, a passionate dog person and had lost all her parents—her father, her stepfather and her mother—tragically early. 'They didn't want to leave because they didn't want to abandon you,' she explained to me. 'I think your mother had instructed them to stay with you no matter what, and to take care of you after she was gone. You know that last time when they all spoke? They promised her they would stick by you.' Rani was right, of course. I thought I was saving Kishmish and Anokhi. But in fact, it was they who saved me.

And now, for the first time in my life, nourished and chequered and brightened by my mother's boundless capacity for care, for nuisance and for delight, I have my own dogs—my children and my siblings, fellow inheritors of my mother's house, my nearest and dearest—and I will never let them go.

Coda

When we first moved from the house where we had Rufus and Laika to the house my parents built (the house from which they left only on their biers), we got a video cassette recorder. My mother and aunts all liked to rent new Hollywood and Bollywood films to watch on the VCR; my father, however, watched the same few videos again and again. One of his favourites—and I have no idea where he got it from—was a Peanuts cartoon film, titled *Come Home, Snoopy*.

In this we hear Snoopy's back story, which is that he was brought from the Daisy Hill Puppy Farm, via a previous owner called Leila, who had him when he was a puppy, before Charlie Brown. Somehow Snoopy gets word that Leila is sick and in hospital, and he decides to go see her. Charlie Brown can't take him, I forget why, so Snoopy goes away on his own. Charlie Brown and his crew are all frantic. Meanwhile, Snoopy and Woodstock—who goes with Snoopy, naturally—have a series of adventures on the road, after which they arrive at the hospital. Charlie Brown follows, hot on the heels of his runaway pet. There are teary reunions on all sides. The details escape me, even though my father and I must have watched this film at least two hundred times. Finally, of course, Snoopy goes home with Charlie Brown, where he belongs.

It's possible I have forgotten some of the plot twists because my father cried so much through the film. He sang along with all the songs—despite their American accents—and burst into tears every few minutes. The song that really broke his heart, though, each and

every time, was Charlie Brown's lonely dirge, staying up sleepless
nights eating cereal and milk, going out to Snoopy's kennel forlorn
under the moon, and missing his dog like mad:

Just when you think
That you know
Where you stand
You've got the world
In your hand.

Just when you're sure
Of a dream
That you planned
That's when the scenery changes
It changes.

Just when you think
That you know
All the facts
You hold the whole
Ball of wax
You've got it made
You can start to relax
That's when your world rearranges
It changes.

Someone that you really cared about
Someone that you couldn't live without
Severs all ties.

Suddenly you're all alone and scared
All the happy hellos that you shared
Change to goodbyes.

Just when you're sure
That you're safe and secure
That's when it happens to you
It changes.

Why must we pay
For hellos that we say?
Pay when we sigh an 'Adieu'?
Why,
Oh why?

The age of the VCR is long gone, but the film is easily found on the internet. I should watch it again to reconstruct the storyline accurately and confirm the mid-century American lyrics. But I dare not. Like my father, I stay up all night, knitting my brows, roiled by memories. Like my mother, I hold on to my dogs through thick and thin, to anchor me in a turbulent world with their constant presence, tiny heartbeats encased in warm furry sheaths—unconditional, unwavering, undying love. Nainsukh and Naintara. Now I know why Daddy cried, and I don't want to cry any more.

Let's say this is what happened: Snoopy and Woodstock came home, and they all lived happily ever after.

The Way of Sunlight

JERRY PINTO

Now listen up, young feller, and listen well. Tomorrow those kind people who came to see about a puppy are going to take you home. Is this a good thing or a bad thing? I don't know … I've done it all: I've lived on the street and I've been part of a human pack. And now, here I am in the Welfare of Stray Dogs Kennel. It's a decent place—the food is regular, the folk are loving. Some nice people come and take me for walks. They feel good and it's nice to get out once in a while and see the sights. There's lots of company, warm snoozes in the sun on a winter day and in the cool shade in the summer.

When you're an old hound dog, that's more than enough. Sixteen times I've watched the sonchafa carpet the streets with gold. It's good to sleep for as long as I want.

So you're joining a new pack tomorrow. You're going to a 'forever home', as they say. I wish I could give you some advice about humans but from what I've discovered, they …

No, perhaps I should just tell you what happened to me and you can make up your mind.

My first real memory isn't of my mother or my brothers and sisters. I must have had a mother—we all do—and siblings, since we rarely come alone. So, there must have been a mother ... but time is short and my story is long, so I'll cut to the chase.

Two little boys. They seemed friendly. I was happy to play with them and they seemed happy to play with me. We like people. It is our strength. And our weakness. They had a ball and I wanted to play with it. The ball flew down the road, and I ran after it and brought it back. The boys laughed and threw it again. I ran after it again and they ran after me. An hour later, I was hungry and tired and thirsty. And the boys took their ball and left.

I looked around. I had no idea where I was. I had run and run and run and I had not looked where I was going because I was having fun and following the ball.

You will say: Why didn't you use your nose?

I did. I turned on my own smell and tried to follow it back. I finally came to the place where I had left the others, but they were gone. Perhaps the dog van had come there and picked them up. Perhaps the dog van had come and they had run away. I don't know what happened but there I was, alone, and it was getting dark.

I wandered around until I came to a row of huts. A little girl was washing the dishes from the evening meal. She saw me and raised her arm. For a moment, I thought she was trying to drive me away but then some food flew through the air. It was not much but I ate it ... so fast that she giggled and scraped some more food together and threw it at me. I went and settled down at her feet. Later, she came out with a bowl of water and I drank it and went to sleep outside her hut.

But the next day the municipality came and began to break down the huts. The girl was running around, trying to gather her things, wrap them up and take them away.

An hour later there was nothing left.

This is the thing about people. They need houses to live. We don't. You are going to live in a house with your forever people. But it may not be your forever house. People move all the time. Sometimes they go to another, bigger house. And sometimes to a smaller house. Sometimes they go to another city. That's because they have this thing called money. I think it's like food. Or maybe a promise of food. Or something. If you ever figure out what money is, you must tell me. I still don't understand it but it's very important to human beings.

I was sitting there, looking around at the rubble when the television cameras arrived. One of the journalists was a young man who was fond of dogs.

'Poor mutt,' he said when he saw me. 'Have they abandoned you?' He picked me up and offered me a biscuit. Now I don't really like biscuits but I ate it to be polite and so he took me home. But his parents were not happy.

'Will you bring home every waif and stray you meet on the road?' his mother asked.

'I don't understand you at all,' said his father.

'Only for a few days, until we find a foster home for him,' he said and took me to his room. There was a cat on his bed. She had only one eye; I tried to be friends but she almost scratched my nose. There was a turtle under the bed but every time I went to sniff it, it withdrew into its shell.

I found a quiet spot under his bed and went to sleep. The next morning the journalist forgot about me and left for work. I needed to pee pretty desperately, so I found a suitable tree trunk. It was a bit thin but all the tree trunks there seemed thin.

'Oh! Look what this stupid dog has done!' the old lady shouted.

'Give me that puppy,' said the old man as he advanced on me. I could see he was angry, so I ran for the door. He opened it and I dashed out on to the road. I was free again.

I wonder what would have happened if I had stayed. What would have happened if I had been taken for a walk in the morning and had done my business beside a real tree. I suppose I would have become a house dog. There is nothing wrong with being a house dog. It's just that they have a different life. They only go out when they are allowed to and when the human being they live with wants to go home, they must go home too.

But I didn't stay.

I wandered around for a bit and found a park. I thought I might sleep under a bench there. Only, two dogs came up and began to snarl at me. I rolled over and showed them my belly. They sniffed me all over and then left me alone. Later in the day, a nice lady came along and fed the dogs.

'You're a new one here,' she said. She found a small bowl and put it out for me.

I have always relied on the kindness of strangers and for the next year or so I lived at the park. It was a good place. When the ticks began to worry us, we simply sat down in the red mud. There was cool grass for the hot afternoons. The nights, when the humans all went home, belonged to us. The two older dogs in the park taught me everything I know. One of them didn't like boys much. He had been hurt by a boy. But the other one said, 'You can't judge all boys by one boy. You can't judge all human beings by one human being.' I thought this made sense. You can't judge all dogs by one dog either.

But that is generally what human beings do. A little boy came to the park and began to trouble a dog. He pulled his ears. He pulled his tail. He kicked him. The dog snapped at him. He only meant to warn him: Stop that! But he got too close and his teeth nicked the boy. The boy ran back to his mother, screaming.

I wanted to tell everyone: He started it. But if you bark, human beings think you're trying to frighten them.

Later, the dog van came. The woman must have gone to the police station. We hate the van. It smells of fear. It smells of death.

We ran, the three of us, all in different directions.

I ran and ran and ran until I was near the sea. The dog catchers had given up by then. I spent the night by the sea. In the morning, I thought about going back, but I decided I couldn't.

It was time to leave the park. It was time to move on.

I ran for a while and then walked for a while until I came to a spot that looked nice. It was near a market. But there was already a dog there who thought that was his area. He came up and barked. I considered rolling over but suddenly I didn't want to. It's different when you're a puppy; it's different when you're a fully grown dog.

We fought. It was quick and at the end of it, I was bleeding a little but I was the winner. I found a good patch near the market. I should have driven the other fellow away but I couldn't.

'We'll share,' I said.

He was surprised but quite happy not to have to find another place. He rolled over on to his back to show he trusted me and I gave him a good sniffing so I should know him later. He might have been here with me if a stupid human in a car had not decided to feed the dogs in the middle of the road. I was tempted to go and eat but I'd had a good meal that evening so I didn't bother to run into the street. The other dog did and got run over by another car. Don't look sad. Life isn't life if death isn't death. No, I'm not going to explain what I mean. One day, if you remember these words, you'll figure out what I mean. And if you forget the words, their meaning won't bother you, right?

Okay, so where was I? Yes ... human beings are like that. Some of them are stupid. You see a human mother with her child. The child is hurting a dog. You'd think she would stop the child, but she doesn't. Yet, when the dog tries to stop it, she gets angry. That is stupid.

Some are cruel. There are two kinds of cruel. There's the cruel that gives pain to find pleasure. Humans know so much about dogs that they have invented a dog whistle which only we can hear because our hearing is so much better than theirs. Now, when they know that our hearing is so good, why would they let off loud crackers during their festivals? Even many people who love dogs will do this, without thinking about it.

Then there's the cruel that is unthinking. You be very careful about what you eat. Stay away from the chicken bones humans throw out so casually. I have lost a good friend to a chicken bone. It broke on the way down and got stuck in his throat. There was nothing we could do for him. A group of Jain nuns was passing by. They stopped and sat down by his side and began to chant to him. Slowly his pain seemed to pass and he died quietly there, in the middle of all of them. Then the nuns got up and went on their way, quiet, gentle women who would stop for a dog. So you see, there are good people, and there are bad people.

Most of the people who hate dogs—

You're looking surprised. Yes, there are people who hate dogs. You're a puppy now, so you haven't met too many people. But they are out there.

Most of the people who hate dogs actually fear them.

Human beings think they have many different emotions. They think hate and fear are separate things but they are one and the same. Humans want us to frighten them, to evoke fear in them. You're looking like this doesn't make sense. You see, many, many thousands of years ago when men and dogs first became friends, we used to guard their flocks. The wolf and the fox were our brothers, our wild brothers, but we showed our loyalty to our human friends. We would bark in the night to warn them when the wolf and the fox came to steal their sheep and goats, or when other humans came to steal their possessions. We still think it is our duty to warn them but now they shout at us for barking in the night.

We bark this way because our masters wanted us to bark. They wanted us to frighten others away. Human thieves. We bark to strike fear into their hearts. That fear is still in them somewhere. They fear us for our fearlessness. They fear our teeth.

You have only to look into the mouth of a human to see what fire did to their teeth. When they learnt how to cook, they made their food soft. Now thousands of years later, they cook almost everything they eat. They do not need their teeth to rip and tear. They still have teeth that they call canines. But it would make you laugh to think of these as anything close to what we have.

When a human looks into a dog's mouth, there is a moment of fear. Many explain it away, but for some, fear and hate are the twin fruits of the sour soul tree. Or you could say, fear is the bud and the flower; hate is the fruit.

They fear us but they cannot admit it to themselves. And so they hate instead.

A street dog is never going to bite a human 'just because'. There is always a reason. Only, humans never look for reasons. They only look for revenge.

This is what humans are. Most of them.

But there are others too. Like the one who picked me up when I broke my leg and carried me here to the kennel and came to visit me after I was healed. He still comes to take me for walks. He can't take me home because his wife is allergic to dog hair.

And so I learnt that just as all dogs are not one dog, nor are all humans one human. But the dog's way is the way of the sun. It is the way of light. A dog looks for the best in another, in another dog, in another human being, even in a cat.

They've come for you, your new people. Go with them. Be a friend. They don't ask for much more than that and for us, friendship and loyalty are easy.

Keep your tail up, your ears pricked, and make sure your nose is wet. Good luck.

Doggone Gods

TISHANI DOSHI

O n full moon nights my dogs take to thinking they're Celine Dion. There are three of them of varying size, temperament and timbre, and when they sit on the veranda and croon at the moon, they sometimes end up sounding more like an a cappella band presiding over a pig-killing than 'My Heart Will Go On'. When I first moved to this wilderness from the city, I used to worry. Were they being attacked by other dogs? Were they disturbing the neighbours, who might this minute be writhing on their mattresses, reaching for their slingshots? Now that I'm habituated, I know my neighbours are no acousticophobes because they routinely blast Tamil film songs from temple speakers. I've also learnt that dogs must sometimes fight their own battles. So when they start with their howling, I just push my face deeper into my pillow and hope that their moment of Dionspiration will pass soon.

I still worry, though. Not for nothing did I carry bedwetting into early adolescence; I am a worrier for life. I worry about the wind and the trees; about another tsunami; about how often I feel like

Antoinette from *Wide Sargasso Sea*, thinking, 'What am I doing in this place and who am I?' Mostly though, I worry about my dogs, because they've adopted me rather than the other way around. So while I feed and bathe them, vaccinate and deworm them, wipe cruds of infections off their ears—and have immortalized them in several poems and a novel—these canines are intent on doing their own thing. Two of them refuse collars, and all three of them know where the gaps in the brick compound wall are, so they come and go like the women talking of Michelangelo.

When my husband and I moved to this remote stretch of beach on Tamil Nadu's East Coast Road, we had not anticipated having dogs. We were peripatetic writers, so pooches didn't figure in the equation. Our descent into dog mania started innocently, as I suspect it always does. We were befriended on the beach by a biscuit-coloured fleabag, as charming and persuasive as a Neapolitan singer. We named him Salvatore, and our caretaker, a sprightly Tamil lady, rechristened him Selvadorai. He soon brought in a beautiful, haughty black creature, whom we named Bagheera. And between them they spun kingdoms. Our population soon rocketed from two to sixteen. Five adults, and the rest in varying stages of puppyhood. And while I knew in the pit of my worrisome tummy that sixteen was a sweet but unsustainable number, I still felt only hit after hit of rapture every time I walked down the garden path and a splodge of black and white furballs rushed out to attack my toes.

'You know this is getting to be a problem, right?' my husband said one day, when he saw me in a dishevelled state, heading out with the dog poop scooper in one hand and the dog pee mop in the other. Friends from the city would visit, raise their eyebrows and exclaim how charming our rustic, dog-filled beach life was, silently thinking that we were on our way to floating off the deep end.

I should mention here that my dogs are Indian native dogs, considered by some to be the first domesticated dogs in the world. They appear forty-one times in the prehistoric cave paintings of Bhimbetka—depicted in hunting scenes (one of them even led by a leash)—and in the form of five-thousand-year-old Harappan terracotta figures, sporting collars and their most convincing begging poses. The technical term for these majestic animals is 'pariah dog'—something, I imagine, that was coined with the same casual spirit with which we're asked to attest to not being an idiot or lunatic on an Indian marriage certificate. As a gesture of affection I suppose you could call them pi-dogs, which at least has the sheen of cutie pie, but mainly they're known as strays or mongrels. Whatever you want to call them, you'll see them everywhere in India—sunning themselves on road corners, rifling through garbage, getting kicked around, dodging cars; some mangy and thin-ribbed, others miraculously hearty. At last count there were thirty-five million of them.

The problem with my fleet of dogs was its matriarch, Bagheera. She'd come to us full-grown and wary of human contact. So, while she happily accepted food and led the charge on our evening beach walks, she didn't allow us to touch her. The other problem was that we lived in the boondocks—an hour from the nearest supermarket and two hours from a multiplex cinema, which made it inconvenient for a vet to make house calls. Eventually, I managed to persuade the Blue Cross to drive over and pick up the adult dogs for sterilization. We had to lure Bagheera into the house with Milk Bikis and throw a net over her. It was like a scene out of *Old Yeller*. I may as well have reached for my shotgun, I was blubbering so much. These dogs had never been in a car before. They'd known nothing but this stretch of beach and the salt in their nostrils. When I went to visit them a few days later in their morose little kennels, I longed for a score of Hans Zimmer to engulf me, but all I got was a hit of incontinent piss and iodoform. 'I'm going to take you home soon,' I told them. 'Everything's going to be all right.'

Far from it, in fact, as, soon afterwards, things slid into full-on tragedy. While I'd been away, one of the medium pups, Jock, had got into a fight. His face had swollen to the size of a birdhouse and his neck was filled with maggots. Back to the Blue Cross we went, but he didn't survive. Soon after, an epidemic of canine distemper wiped out the littlest of the puppies. And then, there was the poisoning. The neighbouring villagers, fed up with their chickens being killed at night, laid out poisoned rice at the front gate, leaving us with only one dog—Bagheera, the one who, in fact, had been stealing the chickens.

To go from having no dogs to sixteen, and then back to one is a bit like being stuck in the pages of a newspaper where all the bad stories are happening to you. Apparently there are such people as pet bereavement counsellors, but they probably live close to the multiplex cinemas and specialize in pugs who've passed on to doggy heaven, rather than these part-wild, part-domestic creatures. Things were awfully quiet for a long time. When we walked the beach, it was a bit like surveying the lone and level sands of 'Ozymandias'. Life without a pack was a life without play.

My friend at the Blue Cross (now on speed dial) said he'd come to the village and explain that poisoning dogs was a criminal offence. In fact, a few months later, further down the coast, it was discovered that the panchayat of Marakkanam had given cyanide to four hundred dogs and buried them close to the seashore. More recently, in Kerala, there have been protests about the state's position on the culling of strays. Animal welfare civic bodies in India are obviously underequipped and overwhelmed. And still, all these dog dramas would just be part of the general drama of Indian life, if it weren't for the out-of-control and totally upstaging cow drama, which begs the question of relativity. Clearly, this is no country for stray dogs or rationalists or Dalits or women or homosexuals or Muslims—or, for that matter, idiots or lunatics.

Or is it only for idiots and lunatics? I can't decide.

Earlier this year, in an epistolary exchange, poet and dance producer Karthika Nair and I talked about our mutual obsession with dogs. In her poem 'Shunaka: Blood Count', she pays homage to Sarama, the mother of all dogs. Her Sarama, she says, was inspired by her parents' Indie dog and Arun Kolatkar's Ugh from *Kala Ghoda Poems*. We talked about why it was that dogs had lost their footing in Indian mythology—having had a decent standing in the Rig Veda, but getting short shrift in the Mahabharata, which begins with a dog getting beaten up. Elsewhere, Alberto Manguel, in the brilliant essay 'Dante's Dogs', examines the relentless insults hurled at dogs in the *Commedia*. He observes correctly that 'to call a person a "dog" is a common and uninspired insult in almost every language', and asks why, despite being important and loyal fixtures of the thirteenth-century Tuscan household, dogs were so often depicted in stories as 'quarrelsome, envious, gossipy, and greedy'.

What good, after all, has it done a dog to be man's best friend? You schlep around with him, help retrieve divine cows, wait, pine, and in the end, what? You're denied entrance to the gates of heaven. You wait twenty years like poor Argos in the *Odyssey*, and when your master comes home he ignores you, so you die of heartbreak. You're the dispensable friend, expected to give up your life in order to save your master's. Even that word, 'master', which necessitates the counterpoint, 'slave', is offensive, which is why my heart fills arrhythmically, knowing that the only reason our Bagheera has survived so long is precisely because she doesn't trust humans. She comes close to the ring of love, but never submits to it.

We have three dogs now—our lone survivor, Bagheera, and two other Indies, Buggy and Zelda. When we run along the beach, they sometimes point their noses up to the sky and howl. And because my husband and I don't see people for days, because we think they must be trying to talk to us, we howl back at them. We go like this running and howling, and I think we must be the luckiest doggone gods in the world.

But still, I worry.

Pali

GULZAR

Pali was not a dog!

Pali was a Boxer; we would go for our morning walks together. He was very sensible: he wouldn't let anyone come near me. After we returned, when I sat on the balcony with my tea, his bowl would be put there as well—and he would have the same biscuits that I had. If, by any chance, he was served different ones, the displeasure would show clearly in his eyes.

'Who do these servants think I am?'

And he wouldn't eat.

When I went into the office room for the day's work, he would come there as well, like clockwork; he would settle himself on a *durrie* close to me. In the evening, we would shut the office and go back together.

Pali was a friend, a companion, and many more things besides …

But whatever he was, Pali was not a 'dog'.

पाली जो भी हो, कुत्ता नहीं था!

पाली बॉक्सर और मैं सुबह एक साथ ही घूमने निकलते थे—
समझदार था! किसी को मेरे पास नहीं आने देता था! वापस आकर जब मेरी चाय
लगती बालकनी में, तो उसकी प्लेट भी साथ ही लग जाती थी! जो बिस्कुट मैं लेता
उसके लिये भी वही बिस्कुट होते! अलग होते तो नाराजगी उसकी आँखों में दिखाई
देने लगती!
'ये नौकर मुझे क्या समझते हैं?'
नहीं खाता था—
ठीक नियम अनुसार मेरे साथ दफ़्तर में आकर मेरे पास ही दरी पर लेट जाता! शाम
को दफ़्तर बन्द कर के एक साथ घर लौट जाते—
पाली दोस्त था, हमदर्द था, बहुत कुछ था—जो भी था, कुत्ता नहीं था!

A Poem about Pali

There was a problem:
How was I going to call Pali now?
My friend Partipal, Pali and me
The three of us were sitting in the drawing room.
What if I said 'Pali' and Partipal replied?

'When did you get a dog?' Partipal asked.
Pali looked at me sideways.
I never call Pali a dog
(Though when I'm angry with him I might sometimes call him an ass).
I said, 'He was very small when he came—
I mean, when I brought him home.
He would fit in my palm—
I could put him in my pocket.'
I was afraid that Pali might interrupt me with a bark at any time.

Partipal said, 'Dogs are known for their loyalty.
There is no animal that is as loyal as a dog.'
'What about you, aren't you loyal?' I could hear Pali mutter.
'I think there's no more loyal servant than a human ...'
'But why do dogs bark when they see another dog?' Partipal asked.
'That's their language, yaar,' I said.
'What else—are they going to speak Urdu? Leave it.'
But Partipal's needle was still stuck in the same place:
'Why do they say it's a "dog eat dog world"?'
Pali looked like he might answer: 'And men are their own worst enemy.'

बड़ी मुश्किल में था, पाली को 'पाली' कह के अब कैसे बुलाऊं?
पर्तिपाल मेरा दोस्त और पाली...
ड्राइंग रूम में हम तीन ही थे
बुलाऊं 'पाली' और पर्तिपाल बोला तो?

पर्तिपाल ने पूछा, 'ये कुत्ता कब से पाला है?'
कनखी से मुझे पाली ने देखा
मैं पाली को कभी कुत्ता नहीं कहता
गधा कह दूं कभी गुस्से में लेकिन...
मैं बोलाः
'बहुत छोटा था जब आया था... मतलब जब मैं लाया था
हथेली पर उठा लेता था पूरा—जेब में आ जाता था मेरी...'
मुझे डर था कि पाली भौंक न दे...

मगर पर्तिपाल फिर बोला—'वफ़ादारी तो कुत्तों की!?
वफ़ा के मामले में इसके जैसा जानवर कोई नहीं है।'
'क्या तुम नहीं हो?' ज़रा सा बड़बड़ाया पाली
'हमें भी आदमी से अच्छा ख़िदमतगार अब कोई नहीं लगता।'
'मगर कुत्ते को कुत्ता देख कर, क्यूं भौंकता है?' पर्तिपाल बोलाः
'वही उनकी जुबान है यार! छोड़ो!! और क्या वो उर्दू बोलेगा?'
मगर पर्तिपाल की सूई वहीं अटकी हुई थी
'कहावत क्यों है, कुत्ता, कुत्ते का बैरी?'
'वही करते हैं आदम भी!' नज़र पाली की, कुछ यूं कह रही थी।

Partipal went on:
'It's very difficult to take fourteen injections, if a dog bites you.'
Pali muttered under his breath:
'And if you bit me? I would die—probably of shame!'

I was getting a bit agitated by now
—And that is something Pali can always smell out—
He brushed his tail briefly against me, and winked
As if to say, 'Take it easy.'

Finally Partipal got up to go. He laughed and said:
'The dog doesn't say much. Looks like he's taken after you.
What have you named him?'
I took a deep breath and said:
'Partipal. But we lovingly call him Pali.'

मगर पर्तिपाल बोलाः
'बड़ा मुश्किल है चौदह सुइयां लगवाना, कुत्ता काट ले तो!'
ज़रा सा फुसफुसाया फिर से पाली
'हमें तुम काट लो तो मर ही जायें.... (शर्म से शायद?)।'

मैं कुछ कुछ सटपटाने लग गया था
वो पाली सूंघ लेता है...
ज़रा सा दुम से छू के, आंख मारी, 'टेक इट इज़ी...!' (जाने दो जी)

बलाख़िर उठ गया पर्तिपाल जाने के लिये... बोला
'बड़ा कम गो है ये कुत्ता (हंसा पर्तिपाल)
मुझे लगता है कुछ तुम पर गया है!... नाम क्या है?'
मैंने लम्बी सांस ली बोलाः
'पर्तिपाल! लेकिन प्यार से हम पाली कहते हैं!'

Tingmo's Day

TINGMO with
ARUNAVA SINHA

Salmon sushi falls
Tingmo darts to snap it up
The dog writes haikus

It's four-forty-two
What do you mean it's still dark
Wake up now lazybones

Open up those doors
Must go to the balcony
Bark at all those dogs

Fifty-two kilograms
My walker is very slim
When I run he flies

Must. Inspect. Tyres
Hmmm these treads smell really good
Let me like this post

Balding shorty comes
Five biscuits wait in the jar
He gives me water

Brown leaves are falling
The season be changing
Take me for a run

Oh, they've made the bed
Jump up swoop down muss up sheets
I must scratch my chin

Why are you staring?
I woke up grumpy today
We are allowed moods

Look, party tonight!
Guests who love me are coming
Meet greet eat them up

They are sitting down
I think they will eat dinner
Quick, make soulful eyes

I love my breakfast
But I cannot lie can I
I love their food more

Is that a black car?
If it's black it must be mine
Let's go for a drive

This is a small car
I am quite large tbh
But I fit anywhere

Need to smell the fumes
I will sit on you of course
Roll the window down

Food food food food food
Food food food food food food food
Food food food food food

Are those tears I see
She who gives me snacks looks sad
Let me climb on her

Rain. No, sun. Or clouds
Climate change is real, they say
Yeeawn. It's naptime

Oh. Doorbell. Footsteps
Must bark madly at the door
This is my welcome

Give me love, right now
Enough, let me go at once
Can't tie me in chains

Wait is that the leash?
Are we going for a walk now?
Yippee de do daah

I hate this collar
If I make my neck thinner
I can wriggle out

I did it! I'm free
Make a run for it right now
Bald guy will chase me

I know what he thinks
That I might get lost somewhere
I'll let him panic

Look, I'm at the gates
This is where I should slow down
Nonsense! I will run

Grrr! Some guy in green
Has grabbed me and won't let go
Now they'll take me back

It's quiet around here
Balding man just stares at screen
When will mum be back

Must jump on the bench
Mum is coming upstairs now
Ready? 1-2-3

Lick slobber nibble
I have knocked her to the floor
She's fine, she's laughing

Sleep sleep sleep sleep sleep
Twitch snort wail thump turn sniff growl
Sleep sleep sleep sleep sleep

Nemo

RAJDEEP SARDESAI

He came into our family as another winter-born baby: Our son, Ishan, was born in February; our daughter, Tarini, was a January child; and Nemo entered our lives on a cold December day. He instantly spread the warmth and cuddliness of a toddler in our home. He was two months old when we got him, a gift for our daughter who was about to enter her teens.

My first recollection is of this ridiculously small Beagle pup staring at us with the most beautiful hazel-brown eyes and soft, floppy ears, looking a little lost and bewildered in his new surroundings. After years of living in rented accommodations across Delhi where landlords explicitly mentioned 'No pets allowed!' in the lease agreement, we had just moved into a new house, our first 'home'. It had more space than we could have imagined and, at long last, a pet dog who was part of the family.

We called him Nemo because Tarini's favourite film as a child had been the delightful computer-animated adventure film *Finding Nemo*, revolving around the escapades of a friendly clownfish.

Dogs usually have short names: It just seems to make practical sense not to get into a tongue-twister when it comes to naming pets. 'Nemo' sounded like the right name for an affable Beagle. Little did we know then that even the christening of a dog might spark off a political controversy of sorts on Twitter. Once, in a light-hearted tweet, I remarked: 'Am taking Nemo for a walk today even as NaMo is criss-crossing the country!' My attempt at clever wordplay was rewarded with an instant angry response from the multitude of Narendra Modi followers on the social media site. Perhaps it wasn't the wisest thing to have done on my part, but even so the outrage was grossly disproportionate. My daughter was distraught. 'Should we change his name?' 'Of course not,' I shot back. 'Nemo isn't going to become another victim of politics!'

And so it was that our fish-named Beagle began his journey with us, a cheerful and comforting presence through the good times and bad. Beagles are small foxhounds, blessed with an uncanny sense of smell and oodles of playful energy. As a pup, it wasn't unusual for Nemo to simply dash off where his olfactory senses took him, be it to the kitchen to investigate what was cooking or to the garden to see what was being planted (the local gardener became an early ally). He also seemed to be particularly absorbed with wooden furniture; it was a familiar sight to find tables and chairs with rough, chipped edges as a result of his constant gnawing at them. Like most Beagles, he could be stubborn with a fierce streak of independence and house-training him required a fair amount of patience. The line between patience and indulgence is very thin when it comes to pets and Nemo crossed it effortlessly on numerous occasions. 'You're spoiling him rotten,' Sagarika often chided me. But the wife's remonstrations notwithstanding, Nemo was doted upon by one and all.

Food is a crucial aspect of this permissive dog-loving environment. Nemo was a dog of refined taste: not for him just another juicy bone. On Sundays, when we cooked up an eggs-bacon-and-toast breakfast, Nemo would hang around in the kitchen, watching enviously as the smell of freshly cooked bacon wafted through the air. His eyes would implore us to give him a share of the bacon crust. 'You can't feed him bacon, it will ruin his diet!' the vet had warned us. And yet, it wasn't easy to resist the beguiling eyes of a hungry Beagle. More often than not, Nemo would get his share of the Sunday brunch. 'At this rate, he is going to become fat and lazy like you!' the kids cautioned me. 'Like master, like dog!' I laughed. In fact, most guests and visitors would point to Nemo's belly as a sign of his being a rather well-fed dog. 'Yes, well fed and content!' I would retort.

On weekdays, he would wait for me to return home for dinner, his tail wagging furiously when he heard the sound of the car approaching the house gate late at night. We would have dinner together: Well, I'd have soup and snacks and Nemo would get a portion of what was left.

On weekends, we had a familiar ritual: a long walk in the local park, if only to build an appetite for breakfast. It wasn't a walk as much as a stroll in the park, neither of us possessing even a single Usain Bolt-like bone in our bodies. We were particularly blessed in our genteel south Delhi neighbourhood to have a green cover, including the wondrous Siri Fort forest whose lush foliage is home to a variety of birds. Nemo, who was used to relentlessly chasing after squirrels in the garden and occasionally barking at the colony cat, was awestruck when he first encountered a peacock, its spectacularly colourful plume unlike anything he had seen so far. All thoughts of pursuit forgotten, he just stared, fascinated. There was this one

occasion, though, when he broke away from his leash to seek out
the peacocks, his curiosity clearly having got the better of him.
I was chatting with a few friends and didn't even realize that Nemo
had left me for better company. It took us a nerve-racking hour to
find him, during which I almost feared that I had lost him and his
adventurous hound spirit to the enchanting world of the woods.

In that flash of anxiety of missing him, I realized just how close
I had grown to my little friend. I knew that he watched over me.
During bouts of colds and coughs, a furry presence bustled outside
my room, as if keeping vigil until I got better. When friends arrived
for get-togethers at our home, Nemo eagerly rushed towards them
to make them welcome, but padded after me when they left, as if to
say, 'I'm still here.' Occasionally, when broadcasting TV interviews
from home, a pair of watchful brown eyes quietly followed the
camera crew around, and then he would sit with them while I did
my bit. And I knew that no matter what time it was when I returned
from out-of-town trips, even to an empty house, Nemo's reassuring
presence would always be there.

Our mateship meant that he slept in my bed, especially in
the long winter months when he liked to snuggle in a warm bed.
Nemo loved the cold: his smooth brown-and-white coat provided
him enough protection against the harsh drop in temperature. We
even bought a little bed for him, but he seemed to derive greater
comfort in sleeping with the adults. He did sleep a lot—another trait
imbibed from his master!

Nemo turned ten last year, a decade in which he was a constant,
ever-loving companion. Our son is now a doctor and works in a
hospital in south India. Our daughter, who dutifully looked after
her 'best' birthday present, fixing vet appointments and giving the

pup a bath, is on her way to a legal career in Mumbai. Which left just Nemo, Sagarika and me in this big bad world of Delhi.

Three, they say, is company.

Nemo passed away in May 2021, a few weeks after the author finished writing this. He is much missed by the entire Sardesai family and friends.

Chaos in a Coupe

DIVYA DUGAR

We arrive at the Nizamuddin railway station an hour before the departure of our train and make our way to the parcel office to book the dogs—an important step in travelling with dogs on Indian Railways. Ranjeet, the local taxi driver who has been ferrying our odd family of six—three humans, three canines—since the start of our travels with our dogs, once again starts to question why we travel with these desi dogs (mongrels), and ask where we are going, and why we have dogs in the first place: something we must have answered at least fifty times, but Ranjeet keeps asking us the same set of questions every time, clearly not convinced by our answers. I suppose it is better than some of the conversations we have had, for instance the one where we had to explain to an auto driver in Udaipur that Pari was a dog, not a goat.

I hurriedly put together all the documents to book the dogs and make my way to the counter. This process has been repeated some fifty times by us by now, and our trio of dogs clearly knows that this signals the start of an adventure.

After getting that slip of paper which is so very essential to our travel with pets, we make our way to the main entrance of the station. The anticipation among the dogs is palpable, with Pari craning her neck out of the taxi window to announce her arrival, Tigress starting to howl in her deep wolf voice, and Marco Polo licking my face as a gesture of thank you.

Ranjeet knows the drill. The luggage is out first, a porter is called, negotiations begin; we are like any other family that looks battered even before their travels have begun. We dust dog hair from our clothes and make our way to the platform, which means running after the coolie, as Marco Polo cannot let the man out of his sight: he is carrying a precious bag packed to the brim with treats and food for him; meanwhile I, managing Marius (the baby in my arms) and Tigress, jump between families on the platform floor and an assortment of boxes. If it was a usual day, we would have stopped ten times to smell and saunter with the dogs, but today all three have a single focus, which is to get on the train, so no platform dogs, vendors or hurried passengers can stop Marco Polo, Tigress and Pari.

By the time we arrive at our compartment adorned with the blinking red sign that says H1, Olivier and I are almost out of breath. The coolie hurries to our coupe. There is no time to waste as the train is about to leave; we make a dash for the door. Just as we unleash the dogs inside our coupe, the engine hisses, and with a jerk, we are on the move.

Marco Polo makes a run for the window seat, while Tigress sits at the other end of the berth, panting. Pari has climbed the side stairs nimbly to access the upper berth. Marius crawls next to Marco Polo while I try to sandwich myself somewhere between the dogs and the toddler. According to the rules of Indian Railways, a passenger is allowed only one dog in the first class; between the two adults, we have three dogs with us, and risk being fined for the third dog or being asked to deboard. But our 27 kg mix hound Pari knows exactly what to do. She ducks behind the bags on the upper berth, placed there strategically by Olivier, and once she is in her hiding position, Olivier covers her with a thin blanket and sits next to her.

None of us are really relaxed till the visit of the TTE (the travelling ticket examiner). A loud knock on our coupe door alerts all of us; I hurriedly make my way to the door with Marius in one hand and all the documents in the other. Once the little pink slip from the parcel office is assessed thoroughly, the controller peeps into the coupe. I issue a loud warning regarding the unfriendliness of the dogs—'Don't go too close'—but it's too late. Marco Polo starts his hysterical barking, which makes the TTE step back in haste. He walks away saying, 'Two dogs,' to which I nod. I step back into the coupe and the click of the door knob as I lock it is signal enough for Pari to emerge out of her hiding place with a happy grin on her tiny face. She knows we are good to go, and so do we; finally we can all breathe and get ready for the next twenty-eight hours that we will spend in the coupe.

We are on board the Nizamuddin–Madgaon Rajdhani from Delhi to Goa, our journey number fifty-seven with dogs on Indian Railways. We have been up since 5 a.m., packing, checking and rechecking everything, walking the dogs, and all of us are tired. Bags are opened, sheets are stretched on the lower berth, pillows taken out, a dog bed laid out with Tigress's favourite blanket. Olivier shares the upper berth with Pari, and Marius is stuck to me on the lower berth, with Marco Polo curled up at my feet and Tigress making a cocoon of her blanket in her bed placed on the floor. Olivier and I can't move an inch, while the four children are already asleep after all the excitement of the morning. I lie awake, taking in the gentle breathing of Marius, the faint snores of Tigress, the warmth of Marco Polo's tiny body on my feet and the occasional peep of Pari, whom I can see in the mirror on the wall opposite. I feel so peaceful; a rare feeling of contentment and warmth washes over me, and the excitement of the journey truly seeps in. All the tension, work, the running around before the start of the travel and what was to follow seem worth it seeing all my three dogs next to me, trusting me on this adventure and following us blindly.

Muffled voices from the next-door cabin, approaching footsteps and the creak of the train wake all of us from a deep slumber. The ruffling of sheets by Pari, a long stretch of legs from Marco Polo and the crying of Marius is signal enough for us to get some food and treats out. After everyone is fed and the mess cleaned, our coupe still resembles a tsunami site, with books, toys and half-eaten treats visible between pillows and spilt water from dog bowls everywhere.

The day is inching to a close; the one thing still left to do is to use our longest halt of the journey, at Vadodara station, for a night stroll. We stand by the train door, impatiently waiting for the train to come to a stop, so as to not waste a single valuable second of the twenty-minute window we have. The canine expectation clearly is of an empty platform with mounds of sand to do one's business on, but Vadodara station tonight is swarming with sleepy passengers, busy vendors and gangs of territorial dogs. The minute we walk on to the platform, Marco Polo pees on the first light pole he lays his eyes on, and then insists on returning to the coupe to safeguard his precious luggage. The girls decide to take their sweet time finding that perfect spot, oblivious to the stares from the fellow passengers, a crowd of bored people following us, and loud debates about the breeds of the dogs and speculations about whether we are in the dog-selling business.

The signal from the guard makes us rush back to our coupe and tuck everyone back in bed; Olivier and I will now spend the night in every acrobatic position imaginable in an effort to get some sleep, while our troop of furry and human children sleep peacefully without a care in the world.

The Elegant Mr Darcy
and the Brooding Heathcliff
ANITA NAIR

For five years, I resisted loving a dog again. For five years, I had lived with a Sugar-shaped vacuum in my life. For five years, I refused to accept the thought of another dog-child filling that space. It felt like betrayal. So I made friends with strays, hobnobbed with friends' dogs; I even was aunt to my brother's dog. But no dog was going to steal Sugar's place.

Then in early May 2019 I was in Chennai, and one evening as I stood by the ocean, a little stray came to stand at my side. Our eyes met and he gave me a great big smile that pulled at the steel vault I had encased my dog-mother self in. I smiled back and offered him my fingers to sniff at. His little stump of a tail wagged furiously and he moved closer. We stood there in companionable silence—I watched the horizon; he watched a crab scuttling. When I bent down to trail my hands through the approaching wave, he sneaked in a giant lick. The steel vault door flung itself open.

Was it the wave? Was it the little dog's uninhibited move of affection? Was it the moment when the sky and sea blended into a

steely grey in which the only speck of colour was the biscuit brown
of my little companion? Was it the abject sense of loss I knew when
two boys from the fishermen's colony came ambling by and the little
dog left with them? Was it the expression in his eyes as he looked
back at me apologetically? All I knew was that I could no longer
live without a dog in my life.

Later that night, Leela, one of my dearest friends, posted an
album of her sister's dogs: a Chippiparai couple and their litter of
eight puppies. Through the night I kept looking at the photos and
videos. When I returned to Bangalore, I called Leela and told her
I was ready to love again. She decided to gift me one of the dog
children. Two days later, the pup reached Bangalore. We went to
pick him up from Leela's home.

A pup came running towards me and leapt into my arms.
I hugged him tight. Leela looked at me wryly and said, 'That one
isn't yours!'

I continued to hold him tight and just then an elegant pup
trotted in. 'This one is yours,' she said.

I reluctantly put down the pup in my arms. Dear heart, hold
still, he is not yours. Let go. Now.

I took the elegant Mr Darcy in my arms and cuddled him. He
shoved his snout into the crook of my elbow and made himself
comfortable. The other pup's eyes grew big as if to ask: What about
me, Mummy?

'What about the other one?' I asked.

'Well, the people who were supposed to take him in Trichy
didn't show up. So the man brought him along to Bangalore. He's
going back to Mayavaram later today,' Leela sighed.

I looked at the pup. He had a worried expression on his handsome face as if to say—now that we have found each other, are you really going to let me go?

I knew then that our destinies were linked. I may not have recognized the tie but he had. I took a deep breath. Count till ten, I told myself. You will change your mind by then. The pup at my feet whimpered.

That he would have to go on a ten-hour journey by bus was just one part of it. The unassailable truth was that he chose me and even in that first moment, we signed a pact to love each other till death do us part.

'May I take him too?' I said.

Leela laughed. 'Are you sure?' she asked. 'They will grow up to be big dogs!'

I don't think I was ever more sure in my life. 'Yes,' I said, scooping up my brooding Heathcliff into my arms.

When you tell the universe your innermost desire, the universe makes it happen. It may take time to evolve but when it does happen, the soul raises itself on winged feet and nothing is ever the same again. I thought I had only room for one dog in my heart. It seemed that I had room for two.

And no, they are not called Darcy and Heathcliff.

Taking a cue from their heritage, they have names to match their looks and line. Sunderapandi and Nachimuthu.

SUNDERAPANDI:

This thing you call Monday . . .
Does it ride in on a bicycle
Or fall plop like a mango?
Does it scurry in with bandicoot feet?
Does it call like a cuckoo?
Does it lie on its back
Pleco in the pond, suckerfish?
Does it leap in the air
With a frog's full-throated croak?
This Monday thing . . .
Does it growl and bite?
Does it sit and stay?
Does it have a tail with a wag?
Does it leap and bound?

This thing you call Monday
Isn't it just another day?

NACHIMUTHU:

So you think you have a problem?
Let me tell you about mine.
It's called a tail
Not what she writes
But that thing on my back
Slender and splendid
My aerodynamic wind turbine
Curling like a query
Giving away all that I feel.
Coward tail
Hiding between my legs
When I am pretending to be brave.
Stiffening at the sight
Of a cat, a crow, the delivery man
Wagging at friendly faces
And girls with treats
Last one to leave the room
The first one to feel the rain.

So what do you do with your problem?
I place mine on my brow
And hope it will stay.

Siddhi: Queen of the ATM

ATUL SARIN

As the posh English voice over the British Rail speakers announced, 'Train leaving for Heathrow Airport,' my heart skipped a beat. Cold rain pelted down on to the train window as we passed hundreds of suburban houses, all looking the same. As the sun set, the lights came on inside the houses; I was sure the residents were all busy watching TV, discussing the weather, worrying about heating bills and their bus passes for the horrendous commute to work.

Thank god I had finished with all that and left it behind me. I had just sold my business and bought a house in Goa, in a tiny, picturesque town called Siolim.

'But what will you do?' cried my mother. 'You have such a good business in the UK.'

'I want to run a guesthouse and help at a rescue centre,' I replied confidently, even though I had no knowledge about either. It was 2005, before the 'Goa bubble' burst, after which many people, from different parts of India, rushed to Goa to live there.

I had managed to buy a decent-sized villa with a huge garden that boasted mango, jackfruit and banana trees, and was surrounded by magnificent palms.

I arrived in October, a great time to be in Goa, as the paddy fields, palm groves and hills were all emerald-green, covered in thick, lush foliage, following the onslaught of the monsoon. Even the piles of garbage were green! Miniature waterfalls had erupted everywhere. The locals were enjoying the sunshine and taking the time to relax before the tourist season began in mid-October. There was lots of merry Balcao banter (balcony chatter), and small things like the price of mangoes or the opening of a new ATM were so very important.

As the taxi pulled up outside my 'House in the Tropics', despite the beautiful sunlight, I was not exactly beaming with joy. The town looked grottier than I remembered. Stray cows wandering the streets, hungry stray dogs, mounds of garbage and traffic everywhere. A far cry from the sparkling pavements of London! Waking up the next morning to the magical operatic tunes of koels and bulbuls vastly improved my mood. A flock of parakeets zoomed above me, squawking and chattering noisily, with the stragglers calling out, 'Wait for me, wait for me!'

The house was a beautiful, Portuguese-style villa built in the 1930s, with intricate mosaic floors, high ceilings, dark jackfruit-wood doors and mother-of-pearl windows. It was time to start the 'spring cleaning'. I purchased a mop, much to the amazement of Usha, our treasured home help. A stout, military type with a heart of gold, Usha also doubled as the chef, introducing me to culinary delights like poha, upma and my favourite, puran poli, a delicious, layered roti stuffed with powdered lentils and jaggery and laced with cardamom.

'What's that for?' she yelled, looking at the mop. 'My idea of cleaning a floor is to throw a bucket of water over it and shut the door.'

The previous owners had left behind an old dog called Tuffy, and two cats. This was brilliant, I had my instant pets. I had only had one pet before in the UK, a very cuddly and spoilt Labrador, who had passed away peacefully at the age of nineteen.

The condition of the street dogs in Goa saddened me. Why were they there? Did they belong to someone? Why was the government not helping them? I had many questions, and no answers, but I did know one thing: I wanted to do something to better their plight.

The next day, Usha arrived in a huff. 'That Cat's-Eyes Fernandes is here, no doubt to have a good old snoop!' she muttered under her breath as she waddled off, adjusting her beautiful flamingo-pink sari.

My next-door neighbour walked in.

'Pleased to meet you, Mr Atul, please let me know if I can be of any help?'

She was in her sixties, tall and elegant with a large round nose. Her face was framed with a Queen Elizabeth hairstyle. As I greeted her, I realized why they called her Cat's-Eyes. She had the most striking blue-grey eyes. She was quite the vision!

'My name is Perpetua Mavis Fernandes, but all my friends call me Mavis, or Cat's-Eyes. I have some very exciting news!' She beamed as if she was about to make a big announcement. Pressing her hands down on her spotless, pressed cream dress, she slowly said, 'Siolim's first ATM is opening tonight, and we are all invited to the inauguration. You are coming, I hope? Everyone wants to meet you!'

I didn't think I had a choice in the matter!

Fortunately, the ATM was across the road from me. Fragrant marigold and tuberose garlands adorned the door that led to a tiny, dimly lit interior. A small tent had been set up to the side with plastic chairs in every colour imaginable. There were about thirty guests, dressed in their best attire, including the sarpanch. There was the obligatory Mirinda orange drink, some delicious samosas and sticky jalebis. This was where I first met Gopal, who was nearly six feet tall. He must have been in his early forties, with a handsome chiselled face, hair dyed jet black, oiled and slicked back, and of course his moustache, curling up at the ends, which I imagined was his pride and joy. Dressed in his neatly pressed grey uniform, he greeted me.

'Good evening, sirji, I am Gopal, the security guard of the ATM. I am from Odisha, and very pleased to meet you. You see I have a "third eye", which lets me see good people like you ... you know, not like some of the Dilliwallas who don't even look at me, or forget to thank me when I hold the door open for them.' He grinned. 'But you are a good one.'

It was then that I noticed this furry creature looking up at me. She was beautiful, a long-haired chestnut-coloured dog, with matching warm amber eyes.

'Arrey,' said Gopal, 'this is Siddhi! I give her biscoots every evening. A five-rupee packet of Tiger biscoots; she costs me a fortune!'

Siddhi wagged her tail joyfully as if she could sense we were talking about her.

'Sirji, she also has the third eye, she can tell you are a good one. She is very *chalaak* and crafty.'

Siddhi beamed up at me, wiggling her bottom. I could have sworn she understood every word we were saying. Mavis walked in regally, wearing a shiny deep-purple dress, which reminded me of my favourite chocolate in the Quality Street box.

Holding her glass of Mirinda, as though it was champagne, she exclaimed, 'This dog is so clever, Mr Atul, I bring her rice and prawn curry every Friday, and she seems to know when Friday arrives, for I always find her waiting for me!'

As the party wound down, I said goodnight to Gopal and Siddhi. 'I suppose you must be exhausted, Gopal,' I said. 'Time to go to your home and sleep.'

'No, sirji,' he chuckled, 'Siddhi and I sleep here, in the ATM. I have a long cardboard box flattened out and she has a gunny sack bed. I am doing "double shift", as I have to send much money home. The drought has crippled my family.' Siddhi gave my hand a quick goodnight lick, as she curled up on her dirty sack.

I walked home, thinking of how many people and animals in India have to struggle to survive, and still seem happy with the little they have.

The next morning I sat on the veranda sipping my coffee, and watched the street come alive. Although my house was on the main road, there was a huge front garden all the way up to the road, giving me some privacy. A troupe of langurs descended on the huge mango tree, much to Tuffy's disgust. He paced around the tree and growled at them. They totally ignored him. There was something odd, though: The tree was full of baby langurs, squealing in delight as they played catch, swinging perilously from branch to branch.

'Where are the adults?' I asked Usha.

'Arrey, don't you know, sir, this tree is their nursery. You see, one "aunty" in the front and one in the back, acting as guards. The other adults have gone in search of food. Since many flats are being built, their trees have been cut down. They are very brave; they have to cross the main road too, poor things. But be happy, sir, that they use this tree, because it means they trust us and give us blessings of Lord Hanumanji.'

Tuffy was not impressed with this blessing!

As I marvelled at the 'nursery' and watched the ever-increasing traffic, I felt as though I was being observed. Was it the aunty monkeys? No, from across the road, I saw Siddhi looking at me, wagging her tail. The traffic was horrendous by now. It was 9 a.m. Buses, trucks, four-wheelers whizzed past with bikes weaving in and out of them, many with up to three schoolchildren and an adult. And of course, the bread man on his cycle, tooting his horn, as if it was going to make a difference! Oh my god, I thought as my heart missed a beat. She is trying to cross the road. I instantly phoned Gopal.

'Please come quickly and catch Siddhi. She is trying to cross the road; she will get run over.'

'Sirji, no tension,' he assured me with a laugh. 'She crosses that road at least ten times a day.' As if to show me, Siddhi crossed the road with the skill of a world-class footballer. She came running to me, and started dancing on her hind legs. I gave her some food, which she ate with relish before wandering off, as if she had another appointment to keep. Another source of food, I bet, I thought to myself.

What I had forgotten was how hot October can be in Goa. With lots of water everywhere after the monsoon, it was also very humid. However, I was happy to be in the warmth, especially after speaking to my sister in the UK, who told me that she had the central heating on full blast, and it was getting dark by 5 p.m.! My garden was looking great, with bougainvillea of every hue in full bloom. It always amazed me that it was the leaves that were colourful, and not the flowers. A couple of red-crested woodpeckers were busy drilling holes in the coconut trees, landing and taking off in what seemed to be a split second. Having finished major electrical and plumbing work, I was ready to start renting rooms out, and already had some bookings.

Siddhi was a regular visitor now, and her visits were the highlight of my day. If only a human could be so delighted to see me every day, I said to myself. Such unconditional love, followed by a good morning howl, and her happy dance!

But this particular morning, Siddhi was different. She looked sad and kept swiping my hand with her paw.

'Siddhi, please let me drink my coffee in peace,' I said. But she did not stop. I knew she wanted me to follow her. We both crossed the crazy, busy road, with Siddhi in the lead, and went to the ATM. Gopal had a very puzzled look on his face.

'Sirji, I don't know what's wrong with her today. She did not even touch her biscoots.'

Siddhi kept walking. I continued to follow her down a small dirt path, off the main road, until she stopped by a huge banyan tree. With its draping aerial roots and its shiny white bark, it looked like an enormous friendly ghost. A few feet away, some 'development' had started, and the land was being cleared for another block of flats. No doubt illegal, I thought to myself. Even worse, a delivery of laterite stones had been placed inside a huge hollow in the base of the ancient tree.

'For god's sake,' I yelled, 'this tree is going to die!'

Meanwhile, Siddhi had begun whining and was looking into the huge opening.

'There is nothing there, Siddhi,' I said. But then I heard a sound.

'Hello, Uncle, are you the doctor who has bought the villa?' A boy, about twelve years old, sat in the tree base, in his school uniform.

'Hello,' I said, 'I am not a doctor, but how can I help you? What is your name?'

'Swapnil,' he replied in a sad little voice. He brushed away some dead leaves and … I will never forget what I saw.

A dog lay on the ground with wounds all over her skin, dehydrated and panting, unable to get up. There was a huge gash on her neck, with maggots pouring out of it. But that was just the beginning of this nightmarish scene. Next to her lay two dead pups, covered in flies. Swapnil picked up a third pup.

'This one's alive, Uncle, but his leg is broken and swollen.'

The pup was gorgeous, almost like a Golden Labrador puppy, but covered in fleas. Gangrene had set in in his broken leg, and he was in great pain.

'What happened here, Swapnil?' I asked, fighting back tears.

Swapnil started sobbing. 'Uncle, this is Sweety. We love her so much. We used to feed her regularly, and then one day, she just disappeared. Gopal Uncle said he saw her a few weeks ago, being chased by a pack of male dogs. He heard her howling in pain, but could not find her. Siddhi led me to her today …'

'Sterilization' was the first thought that crossed my mind. There was only one rescue centre in north Goa, but we needed so many more. My thoughts were interrupted by a sudden rapid movement. The dead leaves were actually moving.

'Quick, move, Swapnil,' I shouted, 'it could be a Russel Viper.'

'No,' Swapnil smiled, even though tears were streaming down his face. He brushed aside the leaves, and I saw that it was Sweety wagging her tail. Despite being in so much pain, I thought to myself.

'She knows you will save her baby, Uncle.'

As I gazed in awe at this beautiful brave mama, her tail stopped wagging, and her eyes glazed over. She went completely still. She was dead. I went numb. I picked up the pup and took him home. His leg had to be amputated, and once he was fully recovered, I decided to keep him. He would limp around Siddhi and follow her everywhere. He was a beautiful dog and, despite his disability, was strong-willed and could be very fierce when he wanted to be. Eventually, he preferred to stay with Siddhi in her precious ATM. They both became mini-celebrities, and an endless stream of tourists and locals would bring them treats.

'I call him Sadhu,' said Gopal. 'Sirji, I was amazed that Siddhi let him join us at the ATM, but I'm glad it has all worked out. Our little Miss Chalaak is getting old. New male dogs are sniffing out her territory, eager to get the prime ATM space, where food and security are available. But not with Sadhu around, he can fight off even the biggest of dogs.'

One morning, in January 2015, Gopal rang me, sobbing.

'Sirji, please come now,' he wailed, 'I think Siddhi is no more.' I rushed over to find her lifeless body on the gunny sack.

'She was about five years old when I started working at the ATM,' Gopal said through his tears. That meant she would have been at least fifteen years old. To my surprise, I had no tears.

'Don't cry, Gopal, she was a free spirit, and had an amazing life. She is definitely smiling at you now from heaven. I always meant to ask you, Gopal, how did Siddhi end up at the ATM in the first place?'

'I am not sure, Sirji, but Prashant the shopkeeper said a foreigner was looking after her, but had to leave the country. She left ten thousand rupees with a family and lots of food to look after her, but they threw her out. She started sleeping outside the shop, which then became the ATM. I was the one who named her Siddhi,' Gopal said, his eyes beaming with pride in his tear-streaked face. 'It means perfect ... fulfilment, I think.'

How appropriate, I thought.

Mavis arrived with a bunch of white hibiscus flowers so beautiful that they almost looked like silk. She wept as she lay the blooms on Siddhi's lifeless body.

Fifteen years later, Welfare for Animals in Goa (WAG) is one of the largest rescue centres in the state. We have a *gaushala* (cow sanctuary), where we have rescued over five thousand cows. We also run a rescue clinic, where we have sterilized over five thousand cats and dogs, as well as organized countless adoption drives and rescues.

I would like to think that Siddhi inspired me, but in fact, as usual, she was 'one step ahead' and actually showed me the way.

Rest in peace, my dear friend; I will never forget you.

The Dogs of War

AANCHAL MALHOTRA

On 18 January 1915, from Milton Hospital, England, a wounded Sikh wrote a letter to his brother in Punjab about the fine landscapes he had seen during his time in *vilayat*, while fighting for the Empire in World War I. 'My dear brother,' the letter reads, 'this is a very fine country ... they have an excellent way of doing things, and there is such beauty.'

Such letters, originally written in various regional Indian languages, censored and translated into English by the British Censor Mail, are fascinating accounts of Indians in the War. It is estimated that by spring 1915, Indian soldiers on the Western Front (present-day France and Belgium) were writing nearly 10-20,000 letters a week. But in this particular letter from the wounded Sikh, a rather simple line catches my attention. While describing the lifestyle of the people of rural Flanders, he writes, '... [T]hey use dogs to drive their animals [that is, cattle], and extract butter from milk.' In another letter written on 20 February 1916, to Sher Singh in Ferozepore District, Punjab, from Bakhshish Singh of the Sialkot Cavalry Brigade in France, we find yet another mention of dogs: '... [T]he dog plays with the cat and tends to the sheep, churns the butter, and draws the cart and guards it too.'

As I read this, I look to my right, where my two dogs—five-year-old siblings, a male and a female Spaniel–Beagle mix—are curled up lazily. Juno is perched on a throw pillow as if it were her throne and Keats, stretching lazily across to the coolest spot on the floor, rolls on to his back and resumes his nap. Can I imagine these two drawing carts and tending to sheep? Could they ever churn butter? I chuckle as I imagine them eating the butter, but certainly not churning it.

The letters of Indian soldiers are peppered with accounts like these about several animals they encountered during the War. Some, like horses, mules and camels, are more popularly understood to be used for communication, transport of ammunition, medical supplies, food and water. However, other animals too remained crucial to the war effort—messenger pigeons, canaries used to detect poison gas, trench cats for companionship, regimental mascots like monkeys and bears (it is recorded that a Canadian battalion brought a black bear with them to Europe, which was given to London Zoo, where the creature inspired the fictional character of Winnie the Pooh), and of course, the trusty dog. The Imperial War Museums estimate that over sixteen million animals were in service—across various theatres—during the full course of World War I.

During the War, dogs were valued for their acute sense of smell, speed and loyalty. They were in high demand and according to several sources, could often be seen in the trenches. It is no surprise that man's best friend should accompany him through war as through life, selfless and faithful. In a BBC report, newly uncovered records show that in early 1917, the War Office informed the War Dog School of Instruction in Hampshire to officially train dogs for front-line duty. About 7,000 of these were family pets, and others were recruited from dogs' homes and the police forces. Ultimately, up to 20,000 dogs were trained during the War.

The newspapers and records of that time are glowing in their representation of front-line canines. There is a 1917 field photograph of a German war dog fitted with apparatus for laying down telephone wires. He is seen walking across a muddy landscape, the telephone wire clearly visible and stretching out behind him from the container on his back.

There are several dedicated Great War forums that focus on the particular and preferred breeds of dogs used and the duties they were given. The most popular types of canines were medium-sized, agile, intelligent and easily trainable—Border Collies, German Shepherds, Boston Terriers, Doberman Pinschers, English sheepdogs and Airedale Terriers, which was the most common breed used by the British Army. Similarly, the duties were multifold.

Sentry dogs were trained to accompany a specific soldier or officer while on watch. They were also trained to quietly stand on the top of the parapet of the trench, next to their master's gun barrel, in order to let the soldier know whether an enemy was approaching the barbed wire. Dobermans were frequently used for this purpose. In 1916, the *Dundee Evening Telegraph* reported that a watchdog on the front-line never barked, but rather gave a low growl to indicate the presence of a hostile force.

Scout dogs were rigorously disciplined in nature and trained to patrol ahead of soldiers on foot, inspecting the terrain that lay ahead of them. If the enemy were approaching, rather than barking and drawing attention to his troops, the dog would raise its hackles and point its tail.

Casualty dogs or mercy dogs were first trained by the Germanic armies of the nineteenth century and known as *sanitatshunde* (sanitary dogs), and equipped with saddlebags of medical supplies. During World War I, these dogs were trained for months to go out into the battlefield and locate wounded soldiers. They would then either stay with the injured until human aid arrived or bring back something belonging to the wounded soldiers. Often, they carried first-aid kits on their backs for the wounded to use immediately. Photographs show large kennels built near the front in northern France to house sentry and casualty dogs.

One of the most important roles of canines on the front was as messenger dogs. During heavy barrages and gunfire, when all other communication was lost, it was dogs that made their way across terrains with messages of vital importance. Messenger dogs serving in the British Army were specially recruited from Battersea Dogs' Home in London, and then trained at the War Dog Training School in Shoeburyness. Dogs that successfully completed their training received an overseas posting to kennels at Etaples, in France, from where they were further posted to kennels near the front line and joined various combat units.

In the collection of the Imperial War Museums is a photograph taken at the Army Veterinary Corps HQ Kennel in France on 19 May 1918 where a dog handler of the Royal Engineers (Signals) is reading a message brought by the messenger dog. The caption tells us that the dog—still quite wet in the photograph—apparently swam across the canal to deliver the message!

As with many stories from the War, those related to animals can also be quite tragic. Like soldiers, animals too had to bear the brunt of constant shelling, difficult terrains and the fear of unthinkably loud noises. Added to that was the disadvantage that they could not speak when hurt, could not voice where they might have been hurt, and often succumbed to their wounds.

Once again, I turn my attention to my two dogs, recalling how the pair tremble during storms and harsh rain. On Diwali, when the world outside is burning crackers, Juno and Keats burrow their faces into our bodies, huddle next to us in bed or crouch under chairs, hiding from the noise. I wonder how they would fare if trained for war, just as many pet owners may have thought when they relinquished their beloved dogs for front-line duty. But regardless of how difficult the circumstances are, one cannot disagree with the fact that a dog will do his duty and serve his master till the end. They are the most faithful and pure species and will give selflessly and without expectation.

The story of an Airedale called Jack is just that. In 1918, Jack accompanied a British battalion in France as a messenger dog. During an intense barrage four miles behind the front line, every communication line with headquarters was cut off and unless they were informed that reinforcements were immediately needed, the entire battalion was at risk of being killed by the enemy. It was impossible for any man to have dodged the rain of bullets and fire, and here Jack came to the rescue. A message was slipped into a pouch attached to his collar and the courageous animal ran through the barrage of enemy fire until he reached headquarters. He was badly injured when he arrived—a broken jaw, a severely splintered leg—but he did his duty, delivered the message, and then fell dead at the receiver's feet.

The very first time I read this story, I cradled Keats into my lap, tears streaming down my face and into his fur. To think of losing a beloved animal, and particularly in this way, is heartbreaking, and yet I am filled with inspiration and hope due to Jack's deed of bravery. The Dickin Medal, instituted in 1943 to honour the work of animals in World War II, has since been awarded seventy-one times to dogs, pigeons, horses and cats, but if it were available for service in World War I, Jack the Airedale would have certainly earned one.

According to Kathleen Golden, curator of the National Museum of American History's Division of Armed Forces History, 'The phrase War Dog is a technical term ... before World War II, they were considered mascots.' In a brilliant image from the *Illustrated War News*, a battalion of French troops is seen on Gas Mask Parade, a routine observance at the front. Each member can be seen equipped with a gas mask, including their mascot dog who is outfitted with his own custom gas mask. Mascot dogs were incredibly popular with troops in the trenches as they acted as a comfort and a reminder of home and the normalcy of life before the War. They were morale boosters, and several photographs show these dogs being affectionately tended to by the soldiers. In the trenches, there also existed a disturbingly large number of vermin and rats that would feed on rotting food and spread diseases, and small dogs proved invaluable in catching these rodents. A photograph from 1916 shows a little terrier dog in the lap of a standing officer, proudly overseeing his catch of over twenty-three rather sizeable rats from the trenches.

Perhaps the most famous story of a mascot dog is that of Sergeant Stubby—a decorated dog of World War I, serving in France for eighteen months, and the only one to be promoted to the rank of sergeant through combat. The Boston Bull Terrier started out as a mascot of the 102nd Infantry, Yankee Division, and when brought up to the front line, was injured in a gas attack early on, which gave him sensitivity to gas. This later allowed him to warn soldiers of an incoming gas attack. His list of accomplishments includes helping find wounded soldiers and even apprehending a

German spy! Stubby was the first dog ever to be given a rank by the United States Armed Forces. He died in his sleep in 1926 at the age of ten and his remains were gifted to the Smithsonian Institution, where they remain on display.

During the course of World War I, it is estimated that 484,143 animals lost their lives; this included thousands of dogs. The kindness and loyalty of canines, as friends and companions to humans, has filled pages of literature; but it is equally important to acknowledge the incredible courage and grit shown by dogs as soldiers in war. For centuries, they have protected their human companions; and I for one cannot imagine life without or beyond my beloved dogs.

Dogs of a Lifetime

GILLIAN WRIGHT

We were not a doggy family—or for that matter a particularly animal-friendly one. As a child, I had to smuggle my gerbils and George the guinea pig into the house and present them as a fait accompli. Our cat, Benny, was a stray who adopted us, rather than the other way round, and it was only when I was in my early teens that Peter and Thomas Rabbit were welcomed with hand-built, airy rabbit runs.

In my early years I was very wary of dogs. I used to walk back from primary school on my own. I would climb the curving hill of Heatherdale Road in the quiet Surrey suburb where I was brought up, past a house with corner towers that I was convinced was a *bhoot bangla*. Its attics were crowded with shelves piled with antique silver and the sitting room was hung with ground-sweeping velvet curtains, around which whooped and scooted a horde of happy guinea pigs. They had the run of the ground floor. I know all this because the lady who cleaned that house also came to clean ours. I would occasionally accompany her to see the guinea pigs and explore the mysterious attics packed with antiques. Goodness knows if she had permission to do so, but she presented me with an antique silk parasol with a dark wooden handle inlaid with ivory, as well as a double-ended scent bottle.

Just beyond this *bhoot bangla*, every day on my way back from school, I would see a big, black dog. It had a collar but was not chained. It stood motionless, in exactly the same spot, at exactly the same time, every single day. I now realize it was a Labrador. As I wasn't much bigger than it was, I would cross the road to avoid it. Then one day I saw a passer-by pat it. A few days later, I plucked up the courage to do the same. After that my walk home wasn't complete until I had met and patted the dog.

I became much more friendly with dogs thanks to my grandfather. He was a countryman, and had worked with plough horses as a boy before World War I. In England, horses were the natural animals for ploughing, like the bullock was in India. My grandfather and his parents lived in a 'tied' cottage, which meant it belonged to the landowner and they could only live in it as long as my great-grandfather worked his fields.

Sadly, my great-grandfather developed epilepsy, a disease very little understood in those days. He was packed off to an asylum, where he remained until he died. He never saw his family again. My great-grandmother and her two children were thrown out of their tied cottage. By then war had broken out and men were being sent to the front in huge numbers, resulting in unprecedented job opportunities for women. Having little option, my great-grandmother set off for London where she got a job as a 'clippie', a ticket checker on a horse-drawn tram. My grandfather was apprenticed to an ironmonger, and he remained an ironmonger until he retired. Then he went back to his first love, the countryside.

In the lovely county of Somerset, he bought a house and a parcel of land adjoining an expanse of forest. He built a henhouse and filled it with Rhode Island Reds, and an aviary for exotic finches, golden pheasants and diamond doves, acquired a goat that ate any clothes it could reach on the washing line and two dogs: Daffy or Daffodil, a miniature Apricot Poodle, and Buster, a dog who defied description. Daffy was sweet but it was Buster who was the star. He walked with assurance and loved life. Part rough-haired Jack Russell and part god-knows-what, he was like a miniature tank—unstoppable. Being rather short, he relished bounding and leaping over field tussocks, all four legs off the ground simultaneously. His jaws were immensely strong and it amused us children to lift him off the ground by his leash while he held on to the other end with his teeth. Perhaps a geologist in his last birth, he never came back from a walk without a large stone to add to his rock collection. We would marvel at how he loved stones.

But it wasn't until after I came to India over forty years ago that our home also became our dogs' home. The first dog I shared a house with was Rofie, a black Labrador, who looked adorable sitting under a jacaranda tree, surrounded by fallen blue blossoms, but not so adorable when she had an evening out at the local rubbish tip and came back bloated and very smelly. But she was a great character, very loving, and had several litters. One of her puppies came out golden, so we called him Swaran. Mother and son got on immensely well and were great dogs to go on adventures with. Rivers in the early 1980s were cleaner than they are now, and they would swim together. If you threw them a stick, they would swim back to you, side by side, yellow head by black head, each holding one end of the stick. When Mrs Gandhi was assassinated in 1984, they were in Kasauli, waiting for Mark and me to return from a couple of days'

reporting in Mussoorie. We had to rush back to New Delhi, where
the anti-Sikh riots were beginning. It was a month or so before we
were able to go and collect them. Oblivious to the human tragedy
taking place around them, Rofie and Swaran had continued to have
a gala time in the hills, playing with a red desi dog called Jackie, and
generally not missing us at all.

Sadly, neither of them lived to a ripe old age. We were
heartbroken. But then we heard of a litter of Labradors in the home
of General Mayadas. My partner, Mark, immediately set off to see
them. He had lived with dogs, especially Labradors, since he was a
child. Once the litter was seen, it was a foregone conclusion that one
of them would be coming home.

And so it was that Soni came to live with us in 1, Nizamuddin
East, New Delhi. It was a home-cum-office with a small garden.
The home was the ground-floor flat, and the BBC office was on
the first floor—but both were home for Soni. She grew up with us,
very rapidly in fact, and was everybody's friend. Avrille Turner ran
the office and sat behind an L-shaped desk, with a typewriter on
one side, on a comfy swivelling chair. Soni discovered she could fit
behind Avrille on the chair, and so she spent much of the working
day perched there, peering over Avrille's shoulder to see what she
was doing and always ready to greet visitors. Unattended, she would
adopt the role of office shredder and shred any papers she found in
the wastepaper baskets—or in the huge bin underneath the ever-
clattering UNI ticker machine which printed out many metres of
news every day. This could be inconvenient. Those were the days
before the internet and the ticker machine was an important source
of news.

One very quiet day, once the monthly office accounts were ready
to be despatched to London, Avrille and I wondered if anyone would

notice if Soni signed them instead of the assistant chief of bureau. So we pressed her paw down on the ink pad and solemnly marked each page with her paw print. The accounts were despatched, and I certainly don't recall them being rejected.

Avrille occasionally took Soni home for a night out. Soni was a party animal who liked to join in the dancing. Her mastery of hide-and-seek also made her a great hit at our friend Shobita's daughter's birthday parties. Samiha and her friends would hide while we held our hands over Soni's eyes and counted. Then Soni would be told, 'Search and find,' and off she would go, gales of giggles indicating when she had found them. The custom of taking perfectly good cake and smearing it all over the birthday girl's face was deeply fascinating to Soni and she was always eager to lick Samiha clean.

Despite being extremely intelligent, coming when called was not always Soni's strong point. In those days there were many more dog-friendly spaces in Delhi than there are now. Dogs were allowed around Rahim Khan-i-Khanan's tomb, and one evening when she was a big puppy, I spent hours there trying to catch her. She refused to come because she was having such a good game of football with the local boys. In those days there was no ticketing at Purana Qila either. The underground areas and dips and mounds were great places to explore and full of very tall grass. Clouds of red munias, now officially renamed red avadavats, would feed on the grass seeds. Soni would play sit-and-stay and then, on the command 'Come!', run up and down hills for a bit of biscuit. But one afternoon she disappeared into the long grass following a smell. We shouted ourselves hoarse for almost an hour before she deigned to reappear.

Arab ki Sarai, now part of a World Heritage Site, was unticketed too. It was where we took our daily walk and in the monsoon were lucky to be able to see a variety of basking snakes. When we were with Soni, I generally stamped my feet to warn the snakes we were coming and to encourage them to get out of her way. Once though, she had gone ahead by herself. I still remember the sight of her suddenly leaping high in the air, and then the head of a cobra rising briefly in its characteristic pose before turning and slipping away into the grass.

Soni loved to travel, and she sang more than any other dog I've known. When she sensed we were going on a long car journey up to the hills, she would push her nose out of the window and sing for hours. She would then wait patiently by the side of the road at the mechanic's workshop after—as always happened with our Ambassador and, later, our Contessa—the clutch would wear out and the car would start lurching up the hillside like a kangaroo.

Her patience was immense. In the Delhi of those days, which was far less congested than it is now, I would leave her sitting outside shops and she would wait without moving until I reappeared. Once, I even left her for twenty minutes outside the computerized reservation office near Nizamuddin railway station while I booked a ticket. I would never dream of doing that in today's Delhi. This patient quality also made Soni a great birdwatching companion. Together we would walk through the fields to the banks of the Yamuna, where we saw godwits, greater flamingos and short-eared owls among the tamarisk bushes.

Soni's charm won over even people who didn't generally like dogs. One friend was fascinated by her ability to sit up on her haunches and beg—something that our cook Ram Chander had taught her. However, she was not always so charming with fellow canines. Once, she was introduced to a champion golden Lab, in the hope that they might have puppies, but the meeting was far from cordial. After the champion reached home, we received a rather shocked phone call from his owner. 'Your dog,' the man said with some anger, 'has bitten my dog's balls!'

We never succeeded in this aspect of Soni's life. But she loved us still and as she grew older I realized that there is something wonderful in the long-matured love between a dog and its human companions. Senior dogs give a special, gentle kind of affection. When she was old, Soni needed help standing up and climbing the two or three steps into the Arab ki Sarai gardens. When setting out in a car, she no longer tried to jump on our heads and shoulders from the back seat in her excitement but sat placidly. She became deaf and barked rather a lot. But she was still our beloved friend. At night she would put her head on the edge of the bed and make soft noises to ask if she could climb up. We didn't refuse, even though she was a big dog and liked to stretch out.

In medieval churches in England you find, laid out on their tombs, the life-sized carved stone images of the knights and ladies buried below. Very often their feet are resting on their trusted dogs. Perhaps they too realized that there is nothing so comforting as the touch of your dog at your feet when you go to sleep, and perhaps no better reason to hope for the afterlife than the belief that the dogs of your lifetime will be waiting there to greet you.

Part-Time Dogs

JAI ARJUN SINGH

The one with too many names …
(Chameli)

I was marching Chameli to the vet's clinic early this year—to dress the latest in her procession of wounds—when the watchman, opening the small colony gate to let us out, cuffed her affectionately and said she was getting the old spirit back. '*Aaj subah yeh road pe bahut tez bhaag rahi thi,*' he told me. '*Shaayad chhabbis January mein shaamil hona chahti hai* (She was running very fast on the road this morning. Maybe she wants to be in the Republic Day parade).' Later, he mentioned that Chameli knew the gate timings well, and obeyed orders—'If I tell her to go to gate no. 3 instead of this one, she'll promptly head there.'

Many such exchanges take place about Chameli, since most animal-friendly people in my nook of Saket, south Delhi, know her well—and, as often happens with street dogs who are patronized by various sets of humans, she is known by many different names. Depending on who does the calling, she is 'Guinea' and 'Tilly' and

'Noorie'—and even an inaptly masculine 'Jimmy'. Once, after I had returned with her from another vet visit and dropped her off inside the gate, a motley group of people—a guard and his friends, a local electrician, a vegetable vendor's kids—gathered around to make sympathetic sounds and examine the enormous bandage around her midriff. Some of these humans barely knew each other, but they found common ground in discussing her adventures. And Chameli-Tilly-Noorie nearly sprained her neck, she was turning her head so fast from one talker to another.

Smaller, more compact than most 'Indies' or 'desis', Chameli is among the most important non-domesticated dogs in my life. She found her way into my mother's flat (which is also my home office) a few years ago after becoming friends with our Lara (also a desi), and soon began spending time indoors—staying overnight during the chilliest winter weeks, sharing an air-conditioned room with Lara in peak summer afternoons.

A few weeks after we made her acquaintance, I learnt that she did 'belong' to someone, technically speaking. She had been adopted as a pup by a nearby physician and looked after by the twenty-four-hour staff at his clinic—but the living arrangements there didn't suit her, or maybe she had already become accustomed to the lay of the land. Thus began her itinerant life. Today, I take some pride in the fact that though Chameli still often crosses the road to meet her friends at the clinic (the guard and I sometimes WhatsApp each other her photos), she spends the bulk of her time at or around my place. I am the first among her many friends (no, 'owners' doesn't work). But she has never allowed herself to be fully adopted. She treasures her independence too much for that. Which can be very worrisome if you're a responsibility junkie.

In her fitter, sleeker days, another name bestowed on her was 'CID', because of her investigative air and because, despite her modest size, she was good at making sure other dogs stayed in their designated territories (though she herself regularly crossed borders with impunity). She would climb up on large cars and chew on their antennae, or pluck crows out of the air. But recklessness, a short temper and a propensity to run through barbed wires often got the better of her, and the injuries followed apace. An abscess once became so deep and dangerous that I had to take her nearly every day for a month and a half to a far-off vet (someone we trusted more than our local doctor). Weeks of antibiotics caused further complications. She hasn't been as active since then and grumbles a lot; at times she seems listless for days on end.

As I write this now, sitting in a sun-dappled balcony, Chameli is wandering around in the park below. Or she was a few minutes ago, looking up and smiling, wagging her tail but also saying, 'Not now, I have a cosy patch of sand here,' when I beckoned her up. For all I know, she will soon be crossing one of the colony roads overrun by careless or callous drivers. I have to stay prepared that something bad may happen one day, and that I won't be on the spot to deal with it immediately.

... And the one with no name
(Kaali)

(I'll narrate this bit in my own voice, thank you very much, Jai!)

It was one of the biggest shocks of my action-packed life. It was bad enough that this human had duped me and taken me for a long car ride without warning—so what if I love jumping into cars and autorickshaws uninvited and looking at the astonished expressions of the people inside, I don't like being at the receiving end of the surprise—but see what he did when we reached the clinic! '*Sir, isska naam kya hai?*' asked the girl outside the doctor's room, opening her book, and I swelled with pride. I was going to get a name at last! And it would be written down, recorded for all time! 'We've never really given her a name,' Jai said, 'but okay—Kalmuhi. That suits her. Put that down. K-A ...'

Both the girl and I looked outraged. 'Can l write Kaali instead?' she asked. 'Sure,' said my writer friend, and, never one to miss a chance at a potshot, he added, 'she is black all over, skin and soul.'

I didn't know the exact meaning of 'kalmuhi', but it couldn't be anything good—the only times I had heard the word before was when the bad-tempered old women in our colony said it to their ayahs, and it sounded like a curse.

So there I was, scorned and condemned yet again—by the very people who have fed me and let me into their house for years. What did I do to deserve this?

All right, so I run after people in my lane—visitors walking by, courier boys on their noisy motorbikes, newspaper boys on their cycles—and if I catch them, I nip them on the ankle or on the calves if they have nice chunky ones. Sometimes this draws blood, and if that smells nice, I snarl and try to get a grip on some other part of their body to see if that might bleed as well. But so what? It's my essential character, this is my lane, these are my people, and their ankles are mine too; I enjoy the screams and the tears and the smell of the fear—I like it that everyone is scared of me.

Because, deep inside, I'm just a frail old creature who is paranoid because her eyesight is failing and her teeth are no longer strong. The truth is you have to get the first shot in before the world trains its guns on you.

All my paranoia really began with my timid Chotu. For so many years—ever since he was a tiny pup, my last surviving one—it was

just the two of us, together all the time. Having killed my other
babies, those speeding drivers kept targeting him too. He was always
a bit slow and stupid; I've lost count of how often a car or bike tyre
brushed against him while he was sleeping or playing. Many years
later, when Jai and Abhilasha called a doctor home to check why
my obese child was having trouble walking and climbing stairs, the
doc said the joint pains might be an aftereffect of an accident when
Chotu was a puppy. If I could speak Humanese, I would have told
them the whole story right then. It would help them understand why
I run after bikes and vans—and their cruel tyres—whenever I hear
them in the lane. But all they see is that the neighbours constantly
complain about me, and once in a while someone lands up at the
door, wailing loudly, to show them a bleeding foot and demand
money for shots.

Still, they continue to feed me and keep me warm during the
winters, and were very sympathetic and caring when Chotu died—
but secretly they must hate me. Maybe that's why I never got a proper
name. There was one name I liked, but it didn't stick. Abhilasha was
fussing over Chotu one day—she always liked him better—and
cooed, 'You're my Gucci.' Then she gave me a sideways glance and
said, in a more cutting voice, 'And that makes you Prada, I guess.'

Prada would have been good. It is a name with depth and
character, and the harshness of a Delhi summer day—unlike all the
coochie-coo (or Gucci-goo) names these humans usually give us. But
it never came up again.

What they have most often called me in all the years I have been
here is 'Chotu's mother', or just 'the mother'—even after Chotu was
gone. And I suppose I don't mind being called that.

(All right, over to you, Jai.)

Those who aren't very close to animals (and I include here the many people who 'own pets' but mainly regard them as part of the decor, or entertainment for kids, and the servants' responsibility) won't understand the many possible gradients in the relationship between a dog lover and the street animals in his or her vicinity. There are the dogs whom one adopts, and who become housebound. They are full-time children: You fret over them, closely monitor diets, figure out remedies for the smallest things, and finally, when the time comes, you grieve for them. But there are also the dogs who have spent years on the street and are unwilling to be fully tamed.

Chameli is one. Incredibly affectionate as she can be, keeping her leashed inside the flat isn't an option. (I had a hard enough time just getting her to stay for twenty-four hours after a skin-grafting operation once, even though she was dosed and groggy.) One has to let them loose, steel one's heart.

Nameless Kaali is another—still a part-timer who enjoys walking the mean streets, though in her old age she has begun spending much more time (anywhere between sixteen and eighteen hours a day) indoors. She was right about Abhilasha being fonder of slow-witted, over-sized Chotu, but that changed in later years, especially during the 2020 pandemic when Kaali began participating in Abhilasha's singing practice at home. To call her a musical dog would be an understatement—'She is a true Rasika,' a friend remarked after seeing a video. Teachers of classical music, listening to her in the background during Zoom sessions, have, with dead seriousness, advised noting Kaali's control over sur and taal, and emulating it.

However, Kaali's routine creates its own special situations. Having to get up and open the door for her at 3 a.m., for instance, because she simply must rush downstairs to the aid of a friend who is being outnumbered by dogs from a rival lane. Worrying about keeping her comfortable and fed if we have to be away for a few days. With a proper house dog, such as Lara in my other residence, one has live-at-home help. But how to manage with a '75 per cent home dog', as Kaali has now become?

All that said, both Kaali and Chameli are almost-pets; we keep a very close eye on them, and make enquiries if they go missing for even a few hours. There are the many, many other dogs one doesn't track so closely, but feels a strong responsibility towards. The ones I might see from a distance, properly meet only for a minute or two every couple of days—but if a wound has to be attended to, one must act fast. Even if it's infuriatingly difficult to get hold of them.

The one who made it all the way home ...
(Lara's mother)

One of my most heart-warming part-time-dog stories is about an excessively fertile bitch who had for many years been delivering litters of pups, in large numbers, near our back lane. Most of them died, of course, succumbing to starvation or extremes of weather or being run over; a few survived, growing into skinny adults, scavenging for food, very rarely getting lucky enough to invite the attention of the neighbourhood's few animal-friendly houses.

When a new litter was born in 2015, I decided to get proactive. We took two of the surviving pups to Pratima Devi, the '*kutton-waali Amma*' who looked after dogs around the PVR Saket complex in south Delhi, and assumed financial responsibility for their upkeep.

Meanwhile it was imperative to get the mother sterilized, so we got one of our animal helpers, an autorickshaw driver named Ravi, to take her to Friendicoes for the surgery.

It went fine, she spent two days recuperating ... and then, just as Ravi was going to bring her back to our colony, she bolted from a momentarily unlocked cage. The search that followed spanned days—with Ravi and his assistants seeing her and then losing sight of her—and was doomed to failure; even if she was within catchable range, the sound of his vehicle would send her into hiding. It looked like we had separated a dog from her home permanently and condemned her to being hunted by other territorial strays.

People who were trying to help would call up, asking me what her name was, because that might make it easier to approach her, and I didn't know what to say. No one had given her a name. I had never interacted with her at much length myself; it was becoming hard to explain why I felt so responsible for her welfare.

And then, a few mornings later, I got a call from a nearby guard. She was back.

This scrawny, ageing, mangy creature, unsettled by the surgery, bearing a very visible scar, had somehow, over three or four days, found her way back to Saket, a good nine kilometres from where she ran away—through the traffic of two arterial Ring Roads, in a city that is very hostile to strays. And at journey's end she was reunited—if briefly—with her last pup, whom we had been fostering, and who eventually became our Lara (but that's another story).

It's one of those animal tales you sometimes hear about but don't expect to witness first-hand. I looked closely at Google Maps that day, wondering which route she had taken, and marvelling at the many potential hazards that lay along each of them.

… And the one who didn't make it back
(Beautiful Eyes)

It sounds like a cliché, but it's true: he had the most expressive eyes I have seen in a dog, or in anyone really. He was long-haired, black and white, almost certainly part-pedigree, very shy and nervous, always ready to bolt at a moment's notice, but never hesitant about making eye contact. He would even come to me for biscuits and other treats, but move away quickly if he sensed I might be trying to apply medicine on him, or even just pet him.

And on the morning after one of the nicest days of my life, I got the deflating news that he had run away from the shelter where I had had him sent to get a serious ear wound treated. I was in Mumbai for one night for a film-festival ceremony where my book was to be given an award. After an acceptance speech where I mentioned my mother—whose treatment for terminal cancer had recently begun—I headed for the after-party, eager to celebrate after too many weeks in hospital, and hung out with friends till well past midnight. Early the next day, I was waiting in the hotel's coffee shop for my airport cab when I got the call. After three days of treatment, the boy told me, the dog had somehow broken a chain, climbed a high wall and escaped. They hadn't been able to locate him in the forest land beyond the shelter in Delhi's Chhatarpur.

How different the mood had been a few days earlier, on the busy evening when I had succeeded in getting Beautiful Eyes sent to the shelter. It had been painfully difficult to lure him into our house so he could be leashed, but we got him into the van. As they drove away, I looked at his shivering form for what I didn't know would be the last time. In hindsight, given his scaredy-cat personality, I should have found a way for treatment to be administered by a para-vet in the lane itself. Minutes after the van had departed, I received a call about the book award, along with a summons to Mumbai. The news meant everything to my mother, as well as my grandmother who was extremely ill herself—and yet, I can truthfully say that when I went to bed that night, I felt just as content about having facilitated Beautiful Eyes' recovery as about the prize.

And now this.

After returning to Delhi, I drove around with the shelter employees, searching for him, and spent weeks hoping he would make his way back to our lane (like Lara's mother had a year ago)— but no such luck this time.

When I think about him, I try to cling to the possibility that he found another safe space not far from the shelter—he was so good-looking, after all, that many people would have taken to him. But the hope is soon overshadowed by desolation: Was that maggot wound fully healed, were three days of antibiotics enough?

Most of all, I can't forget that on the very same night when I was partying with friends, hundreds of kilometres from home, after a two-hour flight across the skies, doing the things that people do without a second thought, this poor terrified thing was on the run in the dark, trying to find his bearings and get back to the only home—a short and narrow colony lane—that he had ever known.

There have been many other part-timers, of course, straddling and transcending the categories above—far too many to list here. There was gentle Imli, a free spirit who rarely entered people's houses but who graced us by spending the last night of her life in my mother's room. Then there was the regally handsome Paplu who stayed away from our flat after we adopted Lara ... except for a single surprise visit, weeks before mum died. There was my Foxie's mother, a full-time stray who came nervously, very uncharacteristically up our building's covered stairway to check on her pup the day after we had adopted her—and then, reassured that all was well, never came again.

And there were the many dogs we became more familiar with in 2020 when the Covid lockdown began and the responsibilities of animal carers increased exponentially because so many street dogs had been left friendless and hungry with shops and restaurants shutting down. Those stories—the heartaches, the desperate attempts at fundraising when one's own resources were dwindling, the fights and recriminations on animal-welfare WhatsApp groups, the few scattered moments of triumph and usefulness—could easily fill another essay.

Being a carer of part-time dogs is closely linked to spending much of one's time in a passive-aggressive relationship with neighbours who snarl (in person or on the RWA's WhatsApp group): 'If you love these dogs so much, keep them all in your house.' As if that is a realistic option—or as if those are the only terms on which one should be allowed to show compassion to an underprivileged being. Urban 'development' aims to weed out the natural world from our lives; to erase paw prints from cement. It is based on the hubris that we are exalted creatures, capable of living autonomously in our concrete bubbles, after having impinged on the territories of other species; never mind the consequences for the ecology and for our own physical and emotional health.

Even without such hostilities, street-animal care can get very complex and emotionally fraught. For instance, with the best of intentions and an organized plan, getting a lane dog taken away for sterilization—something any conscientious animal lover knows they must do—can be very tough to pull off. Part-adopting some animals while maintaining a distance from others is always tricky too. Succumb to the temptation of putting a few biscuits out for an unfamiliar dog on one of your walks, and the next thing you know, you are being followed every time you pass that way; your responsibilities will grow, and so will your reputation as 'that anti-social resident who encourages strays'. If you adopt a stray pup you have kept an eye on for a few weeks (as I did Foxie and Lara, seven years apart), you will also get to know the pup's mother—and in some cases, the father—and those lives will run parallelly in the background: You might get sentimentally attached to them and feed them once in a while; you might worry about them when you hear a familiar yelp in the distance late at night.

Many years ago, long before I became a 'dog person' myself, I drove my mother to a cramped municipal building packed with little cages to retrieve a street dog she felt protective of; some other residents had had him forcibly removed from our colony. I wasn't personally invested in this mission, I was only doing it for mum—and yet I remember being struck by the look of joy and relief on the dog's face when he saw her and leapt into the car. This memory—and the ways in which it ties into my own first-hand experiences of the past few years—is a reminder of what a big responsibility we have, those few of us who care about these vulnerable creatures. The 'strays', who only know a small patch of terrain as their forever home.

The home that's often marked with their special prints.

Fairy Dog Mother

PARO ANAND

Some people think she is crazy. But that is the only way she can be, to do the things that she does. To chase down errant owners and snatch away the dogs that they choose to mistreat. To rescue those who have been abandoned, harmed, hurt. She is Shreela Debi. And she is a true Fairy Dog Mother.

We were introduced to her by our daughter Aditi—who is another crazy dog mother, by the way. Of course, we'd had dogs before. Dogs who had suffered in all kinds of ways because we had bought them from unscrupulous breeders (something I am never going to do again). Adopting a dog from Shreela wasn't so simple, however. She doesn't just let you have one of her babies. Yes, they are her babies and she's not looking to give them away without checking who they're going to. You fill out a very detailed form that includes questions like: Do both of you go out to work? Who will be with the dog when you are not there? Where will the dog sleep? And then she comes for a home visit. If the dog is going to be kept with the guard and be a watchdog outside at night, you're probably not getting one of Shreela's babies.

By the end of the interview, I was feeling like a potential bride in a game of matrimonial musical chairs—and terrified of being rejected.

And then there was the visit when we actually got to meet the dogs. She had done some pre-selection for us. We had seen some pictures. My heart was thudding as we went to Leela's Place Foundation. It was more a question of whether we were going to be picked rather than us picking a dog. Really different from those breeder purchases where they are eager to palm off any pup to anyone. And if the pup dies soon after, all the better. It means you might be back to pay some more money for the next one.

At Leela's Place Foundation you have to meet some very high standards.

Gia was gorgeous. It was love at first sight. As Shreela says, Gia is the Sophia Loren of German Shepherds, with her dark, kohl-lined eyes and intensity. She was sitting on one side of a low hedge; we were on the path across it. I was looking at Gia, when I saw her eyes focus, laser-like, on my son Uday. She got to her feet and gracefully leapt right over the hedge, not wanting to waste time going the long way around. I think I yelled, telling Uday to watch out. A running German Shepherd is an intimidating sight and this, after all, was the first time I had seen her. I didn't know what her intentions were. But she just stood up on her hind legs and gave him the best dog hug you can imagine. It was as if she had 'recognized' Uday from another life. She wouldn't let go of him from that moment. He just had to keep holding her, petting her. When it was time for us to leave, she tried desperately to leave with him.

But now we were greedy. We wanted two. Nadia was dressed in a yellow T-shirt to protect a wound on her stomach that she'd mostly recovered from. I wanted to get to know her. But she was eager to go back inside. She was obviously nervy, but we were assured that she was ready to go to a new home.

Their backstories were heartbreaking. Nadia had been tied to a lamp post and left to starve. Worse, she had a huge, deep belly wound that was crawling with maggots. Someone had called someone and the networks worked so that Shreela was soon taking Nadia home. She was probably almost a year old.

Gia was found in Panchsheel Park, a small pup, also a year or so old. Running. Running. Running. Trying to run away from her own skin. Her back had been burnt with acid. Shreela took her home too.

She healed them, paying with her own funds and those from whoever cared to contribute, feeding and nursing them, along with the wonderful Robert who has a heart of gold and the patience of mountains. And once she felt they were ready for a forever home, we were taken to see them. We fell in love.

Finally the day arrived when Robert brought Gia and Nadia home along with Shreela. Almost as if she knew she was home, Gia was immediately up and away, trotting about, inspecting the garden and house, bonding with Uday as though he was a long-lost friend. Nadia was nervous; she stuck to Shreela and Robert. No food, no nothing would persuade her to come to us, until suddenly, in one moment, she came to me, as if I had imprinted on to her heart. Shreela quietly slipped away, tearing up, for she was giving up her babies.

For the next few days, Nadia was the proverbial sheep, following me around everywhere, even into the bathroom. Meanwhile, Gia confidently trotted about, getting to know every corner. Nadia went through some difficult days both emotionally and health-wise, but Shreela was by our side throughout: to the extent of bringing over her own Labrador, Poltu, when Nadia needed an emergency blood transfusion. Poltu's blood seemed to do the trick. Nadia gained height and strength—and confidence. She has now bonded very closely with Keshav, my husband. Through the days of the lockdown, she has been in a state of total bliss. She goes to his little office room every morning and stays there, under his desk, all day. She's a gentle soul, mostly. She occasionally prays to Nandi the Bull, sitting statue-like in front of the sculpture, sometimes for a long time. Nothing distracts her then. She is wonderful with the baby and kids on the farm too. The only time she 'attacks' is if there is a man with any sort of head covering, especially if he's carrying a stick. Then, there have been instances of torn pant pockets. She's never bitten anyone, but it can be unnerving.

Gia is a lean and compact hater of crows, cats and squirrels. She chases them down with a mighty bark and her awesome run at full tilt. She sees no point in dashing after a ball. A squirrel, a cat—yes, totally, there is purpose in that. But what's the point of a ball that won't run away? Same with the jumps. She's so good at them, but what's the point? Nadia, though, loves all of it.

Gia could so easily be a therapy dog. Some months after they came, I was feeling quite low. It was the anniversary of my father's death. Wanting to be by myself, I walked to a quiet corner. Gia followed. I sat on a step and she sat beside me. She just leaned against me, literally lending me a shoulder to cry on. How did she know?

Once I had a severe spine problem and was unable to lie down or sit. I could only walk. So I would be walking about all night. Poor Gia would be exhausted, but she'd go round and round the garden with me, head hung low, wondering when she could sleep. But matching me, step for step.

They are such opposites, really. As soon as they hear the sound of their leashes, Gia goes crazy, running to the gate and back. In fact, she doesn't need a leash on her walks. She is the queen of all she surveys, but is very responsive to instruction and will quickly return when called. Nadia, on the other hand, just *hates* walks. Unless they are with her papa. The sound of the leash drives her into corners, behind curtains and under tables. She actually enjoys herself once she's out of the gate; it's the going out that she detests. What was it in her previous owner's home that scared and scarred her so?

We have some rabbits that run around the garden. Whenever Gia sees them, her hunting instincts snap in and she chases them. Not Nadia, though. She is literally in love with Kuttu the rabbit. They sit next to each other for hours. In fact, it's one of the only times that Nadia is willing to leave our company. If you can't find her, you'll see her sitting side by side with Kuttu. The same with our maid's son. Gia can take him or leave him, and if he is being overfriendly, she will simply walk away. Nadia, on the other hand, loves playing with him and will never snap, even if he is pulling her tail.

But the most fun thing is to see them at parties. Once or twice a year, we have these enormous parties for two hundred people or more. Gia and Nadia just love hanging out at these events. They never steal food or terrorize the guests. If someone calls them, they are happy to trot over and be petted. Otherwise they leave people alone. The star power at our get-togethers are our puppies.

Now over three years old, they light up our lives like phuljharis that sparkle every day.

Barking Up the Family Tree
ANUJA CHAUHAN

We're a very doggish family. We've always had dogs—and, of course, doglore. You know how people have all these hoary old kissa-kahanis about their grandparents and various eccentric relatives? We have those in our family about our dogs too. They're a very vital branch of our family tree.

For example, there was Lucy the Kutiya, who was a good mother, but also understood the importance of me-time. She had a litter of seven ravenous, teething puppies—and when they made her life miserable and her teats sore, she would leap on to my nani's lap and snarl crossly at them to leave her alone. I never met Lucy—she passed on much before I was born—but whenever my kids used to drive me up the wall when they were little, I would announce that I was going into 'Lucy the Kutiya mode', shoo them away, and crawl into my mother's lap.

If a couch, a sweater, or a painting—anything really—is luridly multicoloured, we say it looks like Teeka Singh's turds, because around forty-seven years ago, a jet-black Cocker Spaniel-Indie mix belonging to my nani ate a lot of rang-biranga balloons at a birthday party and pooped out some steaming, wondrously vibgyor-hued sausages the next morning.

When somebody bites off more than they can chew, we say he's 'done a Donny'. An explanation for this is provided in the poem below, written by my sister Nandini Bajpai many years ago to pass on this particular piece of doglore about a dog who belonged to our parents, to her children.

The Dog in the Rickshaw

What is most recalled about Donny
is that he was Stubborn.
So Stubborn that when Nani
took him for his walk
he always refused, refused
to turn back.

Luckily, he wasn't the
Brightest bulb.
So Nani found a circuitous route
which brought them home
eventually.
And that worked fine.

Until the day Nana ji walked him.
Nana, as you know, is very Bright
but just as Stubborn as Donny.
And sometimes (he's your Nana)
his Stubborn overcomes
his Bright.

They left. Two hours passed.
And Nani knowing
two Stubborn beings
can get into a
Standoff
began to worry.

At first Nana ji didn't
remember Donny's ways.
He just kept walking
and after a reasonable amount
of time turned back.
Or tried to.

No matter what Nana ji did
Donny would only go Forward.
He could have tricked Donny
quite easily
but remember what I said
about Nana ji?

'You want to keep walking?'
Nana ji said.
'Let's go then.
We'll walk, and walk, and walk.
Until you are so tired that
You will turn back.'

No one knows how far they walked
before they sat down
panting
exhausted
by the side of the road
and had to hail a rickshaw.

Nani laughed when
she saw them coming
up the street.
Thirsty, hot, Stubborn mad
Dog tired
in a rickshaw.

More recently, in our nuclear family that comprises of our bossy housekeeper, my husband, our three children and me, we have three dogs, and we all more or less agree that each one of these dogs has a corresponding soul-buddy in one of the children.

Django Doodle Alva, the oldest, is a surly Lhasa Apso whose cute, fluffy looks are very misleading. Django is an extremely fussy eater, is very picky about whom he befriends, has bad eyesight and needs frequent haircuts. Everybody agrees that this corresponds exactly to our eldest, Niharika, with her bantamweight feistiness, contact lenses and aversion to early-morning Bournvita-and-badams. Winsomely curly and (on occasion) extremely surly too, Nika herself feels a certain kinship with surly Django because 'he had the most disciplining while growing up, wasn't allowed on the good carpets, or given scraps from the dining table, unlike rowdy Goldie or bloody Chhabbis who have been basically permitted to get away with murder'.

Moving on to rowdy Goldie, who is essentially my mother-in-law's dog but came to live with us when he was nine because Mamma retired from active politics and could no longer provide him with a massive sarkari lawn in which to run amok. Air-lifted to Bangalore, Goldie philosophically accepted that he was no longer the First Dog of Rajasthan and slowly came to terms with his new station in life, which included not only a much smaller patch of grass, but also playing second fiddle to the aforementioned surly Django.

Goldie (we all agree) is like my middle child, Nayantara. Large, very affectionate and extremely courageous, Goldie is also slightly unpredictable, and was famous in Lutyens' Delhi for bounding about and biting several Very Important Politicians (who I personally feel had it coming). The most famous Goldie-katha is about how, every Diwali, while other dogs cowered beneath beds and inside cupboards, he would come charging out of the house like a furious golden streak to 'scold' the fireworks and 'save' the children from the anars and chakris and ladi bombs that were 'attacking them'. He would pick them up in his mouth and run around with them even as they continued to spin and sparkle and hiss between his clamped jaws.

Nayantara tends to rush to her family's defence in a similar fashion (even when we ... er ... don't really need it), hence the comparison. Like Goldie, she's also tall, cuddly and mostly amiable—until she is roused, and then she can be just as fierce.

And so we come to bloody Chhabbis, our youngest dog, who corresponds exactly (according to my daughters) to my son, Daivik. Chhabbis is an Indie whom I heard yelping like his heart would break on 26 January last year, when the rest of the family had gone to church. (See, sniffs my ma-in-law, nothing good ever comes out of being godless and bunking Mass!) I walked down the road and found a pup in a deep manhole, trying desperately to scramble out. He was about the size and heft of a bunch of dusty black grapes. When I knelt in and plucked him up, he stopped yowling at once and cuddled into my palm. Back in the house, he let me wash him in the bathroom sink and the water ran off bright orange. (That's Bangalore mud for you.) He drank bowlfuls and bowlfuls of milk but it took him almost a day to pee—he was that dehydrated. He is supposedly like Daivik because 'he is cossetted and spoilt and a nudist'—meaning that he loves to wriggle out of his collar and promenade naked down the street. Also 'because he eats out of a plastic bowl, hates to bathe, has one brain cell, and an inordinately high opinion of himself'.

Brand-new legends are being written about Chhabbis every day. The latest are all inspired by his skills as an escape artist. He rips through hedges, wriggles through fences or leaps over gates to go trysting with his lady friends in the night.

My father—who is eighty-six and the current joy of whose life is to break quarantine, escape the gates of his township and go for long nocturnal jaunts on paths unpatrolled by well-meaning, corona-fearing security guards—calls me up and gleefully reports that he is 'indulging in Chhabbis-like behaviour'.

And so the doglore continues ...

My Fearless Gaddies
BULBUL SHARMA

When they arrived as tiny, furry pups I never thought my two Gaddies (Himalayan sheepdogs) Rocky and Rolly would become such fearless warriors. In six months, they had grown into tough, alert guard dogs with a sharp nose for trouble. They roamed the five-acre orchard all day, looking for action.

My home, in a remote mountain village of Himachal Pradesh, is surrounded by a dense deodar forest and many wild animals often steal into the orchard. Langurs come for the peaches, porcupines for the vegetables, civet cats for the kiwi fruit and rhesus monkeys for everything that is growing on the trees. Then, of course, there is the sly leopard lurking in the shadows, interested not in fruit or vegetables but in my brave guard dogs.

Gaddies are essentially working dogs and roam with shepherds all over the Himalayan region. They follow the shepherds as they trek up to the green meadows on the higher mountains during summer and then come back with them to the warm areas of the plains during winter. They keep a sharp eye on the flocks of sheep and goats, making sure the herd never strays away from the path taken by the shepherds, and never let any strange animal come near them. I have noticed the Gaddies that belong to shepherds often wear collars with metal spikes to protect them from any leopards they might encounter along the way.

Rocky, one of my pair of Gaddies, was a leader but a bit lazy. He would sniff out a gang of monkeys much before Rolly and send a signal to her in their canine language. Rolly would charge like an arrow, leaping over ditches, scrambling through thorny shrubs, and then race up the hillside at top speed. Rocky would follow but at a leisurely pace. He always reminded me of the generals of the World War I who drew the front lines but preferred to send their men into battle to face the enemy fire.

Rolly did not seem to mind, though. She actually loved a good fight. Brown eyes blazing with fury, the hairs on her back raised in an arc of black fur, she would bark fiercely at the monkeys, the sound echoing all over the hillside. People in the village knew at once that Rolly had sighted the monkeys. They began their own fight by noisily banging on tin drums and making those special war cries that all hill people are experts at. Rolly always chased the thieving monkeys well beyond the orchard boundaries. For some reason, it was Rocky who usually got the credit! Everyone in the village called him 'Bahadur sipahi', even though Rolly had fought most of the battle.

During the summer months, when my grandchildren came to visit me at the orchard, Rocky would change into a playful pet dog, much to Rolly's horror. He learnt to shake hands, fetch a ball and even beg for biscuits—something no self-respecting Gaddi would ever dream of doing. Rocky, I think, in his heart of hearts, would have loved to be a cuddly pet instead of a working guard dog. Rolly, on the other hand, was a true Gaddi—stubborn, independent and forever alert.

Gaddi dogs get their name from the Gaddi tribe, their original masters. They are also known as Indian Panther Hounds and Bhutias, and are fiercely territorial. The most handsome and regal creature in their clan is the Kinnaur Sheepdog, which looks like a young lion and moves with amazing grace. I had the good fortune to have a Kinnaur Sheepdog many years ago. He was called Kaiser and was famous in the village as the 'Chota Babbar Sher'.

Our Rolly was faster and more alert than the noble Kaiser was. I think it is because the rhesus monkeys and langurs have now become smarter and the Gaddies need to work harder to protect their territories.

Sometimes my Gaddi pair would take a day off from work and wander into the forest. I would worry about their safety but they always returned before sunset for their evening dal and roti. They often caught wild fowl and hares and ate them with relish, probably to make their vegetarian diet more interesting.

One day last summer Rocky went into the forest and didn't come back. We never found out what happened. I was told later by my neighbour that once a Gaddi dog slows down, he is no longer safe from his main enemy in the forest—the leopard. Rolly, not happy to be left alone, went to a happier hunting ground soon after. We have their daughter, Irie, who is now guarding the orchard all alone and doing a great job. I will get a partner for her soon; Gaddies need to work in pairs.

Gaddies are all heart—and they take a piece of our heart with them too.

Pumba and I

KESHAVA GUHA

I am descended, on one side, from dog owners rather than dog lovers, and on the other from—much more common in India—people with no relationship with dogs. I grew up with dogs, but for a long time they meant little to me. That is not, I am sure, something I would have admitted at the time: nobody who has a dog or dogs in the family does. But it is something that became obvious, eventually undeniable, in retrospect.

I did just say that I came from a line of dog owners rather than lovers, but I want to qualify that statement. I was thinking of my mother, whose fondness for the dogs that she keeps is pragmatic, bounded and notably unphysical. Her father, who always kept dogs, must have been similar. But her mother, my Nani, was close to dogs in a way that I never really saw for myself—she died when I was eight—but have gleaned from stories.

The most told of these tales concerns a Cocker Spaniel called Shikari, whom my grandparents kept when newly married, in Madras (now Chennai) in the 1950s. Nani, prevented from pursuing

her career as a college lecturer by the patriarchal mores of the time,
had taken up painting. She started attending classes: a source of
acute distress to Shikari.

One day Shikari followed her out of the house and trotted
inconspicuously behind her to the bus stop. It was only on the bus
that she discovered him. Embarrassment came easily to Nani; to
arrive at her art class in 1950s' Madras accompanied by a Spaniel
must have been mortifying.

The next time, she made sure that Shikari did not leave with
her. But once she was away, whoever was watching the dog had a
moment of laxness. Nani was in the middle of her class when Shikari
arrived. He had known, of course, where to get on and off the bus.

This story was always told to me, when I was a child, as a legend
of canine intellect. That aspect is undeniable, even if, like all family
legends, it has grown in the telling and cannot be taken as perfect
truth. But I'm more struck, now, by the strength of the attachment
it implies, on Nani's part as well as Shikari's. As a child I longed to
meet this Birbal in Spaniel form. Now I feel a different longing: for
conversations I never had with Nani about her dogs, about their
attachments.

I was eighteen, and home for the summer from university, when
Aldo arrived, shortly to be renamed Pumba by my sister. We hadn't
planned to get another dog. But an Italian family we knew in
Bangalore had recently had a litter of yellow Labs and had decided
that one of those they had planned to keep was too much of a
handful. And so he came to us at three months, initially as naughty
as warned; but, as with so many creatures of different species,

his personality at that age was a poor predictor of the future. It was clear, in any case—and this too is far from uncommon—that what we might have called naughtiness was really just the evidence of an active mind.

I was diverted by Pumba's arrival without suspecting that he and I would ever have a significant role to play in each other's lives. But during my second year at university I had a breakdown, and eventually was compelled to return home for a year. It was in this space of illness and recovery that Pumba and I grew close; there was illness on both sides. Our attachment was first forged through trips to the vet.

We can be even less objective and reliable in assessing our dogs than people are with their children, but I think every vet who has attended to Pumba over the years would attest to him being the Platonic ideal of a patient. So too the many people who, enviously watching his calmness and cooperative stoicism, have asked me how we trained him, and don't believe the entirely honest answer that we didn't.

Vet-Pumba and home-Pumba aren't the same; the latter can be anxious, neurotic and a Goldilocks when it comes to weather (this in Bangalore!): he hates summer, and winter, and monsoon most of all. But both vet-Pumba and home-Pumba have always shared a perfect gentleness, and a hunger for company—ideally human rather than canine.

It may be that an alienating illness that diminished my capacity for human sociability was what drove me to embrace a different kind of attachment over that year of recuperation. But whatever its origins, in healthier circumstances the attachment only grew. After college I returned to Bangalore to try to become a novelist. When, three years later, I decided that I had to leave Bangalore, there was only one cause for doubt or conflict; one reminder of the essential selfishness of my departure, as well as what I too was giving up.

The Covid-19 pandemic brought me home to Bangalore again, for my first extended spell in four years. Over many brief visits during those years, I had come to accept the consequences of my betrayal in leaving. Affection remained, but trust, less so; put differently, I was less important to Pumba than before. My sister was as close to him now as I had ever been, if not closer. During each visit some of the old intimacy built up again—and then I would leave.

During the lockdown we spent several months together, on different terms than previously. Pumba had grown old. He had lost his confidence; the old eagerness for company was now neediness. He could be irritable, which we had never seen before. Like so many dogs his age, he was constantly in pain, and with every week there were new infirmities, new indignities. I felt, more acutely than I could always bear, his total dependence on me and the limits of my capacity to offer relief.

Those who make facile distinctions between human and animal natures are ignorant of how humans and dogs alike are transformed by intimate attachment. Jane Goodall has described the Spaniel she grew up with, Rusty, as the most important teacher she ever had: it was through Rusty that, in defiance of the scientific orthodoxy of the time, she understood that chimpanzees had emotional lives and individual personalities.

Pumba in old age, living with chronic pain, has often made me think of the oft-anthologized D.H. Lawrence poem, 'Self-Pity':

I never saw a wild thing
sorry for itself.
A small bird will drop frozen dead from a bough
without ever having felt sorry for itself.

Anyone who has cared for an ill or elderly dog knows that they feel, and express, self-pity. Yes, this has to do with them not being exactly 'wild'. But what is called self-pity is in fact a social quality. It is a desire for the recognition by another of one's own pain. It may be that wild animals whose lives are social feel sorry for themselves, and show it to each other—but humans are not around to see that show of dependence. People and dogs share their self-pity with each other constantly; what we're really expressing is emotional interdependence.

Why Do We Go Looking for Children of the Heart?

MANEKA GANDHI

A mother's heart is a strange thing. It nestles in a bed of pain, its beats are full of fear and come irregularly. It has scratches on it, healed and unhealed wounds, dark blood. If you want to experience the most extreme pain, then get yourself a mother's heart.

Any love has its share of pain, but the love of a mother for her child and the agony and terror she experiences constantly—even when her child is thriving, happy and doing well—cannot be described.

Being in love is also an exhilarating feeling. It's how I feel when it rains in my forest house during the monsoon, or when I hear the coo-ee of the koel, or when I look out of my office in Sultanpur and hear the distant voices of children playing cricket. I care for thousands of beings and I fall in love easily: with ants and crows and monkeys and even leaves. (I start the day by talking to a pipal tree that seems to have adopted me.) But every few years I find a being whom I love intensely.

Taklu was a bald mynah who appeared suddenly in my garden. I watched him for a few days through my window. He was completely alone, shunned by the other birds. He stood outside my window, waiting for me patiently, and when I went into the garden, he came to walk with me. I like to think that we discussed matters of the universe, but the truth is that we walked in the silence that exists between a mother and a son. We sat together in peaceful silence. He never came near me, but for three years he never left my side. I rushed home from Parliament every day, breathless with anticipation and longing. And then, one day, he was gone. I have always had a special bond with mynahs and I look for Taklu even now, many homes and many years later.

Then there was Bruno: a violently insane dog that was born to be mean. He came to me as a pup and refused to sleep anywhere except on my neck. He would bring rotten meat from outside and put it under my pillow, bite anyone I liked, chase every other dog in the house and stand over them as they cowered, nudge open the fridge and throw out as much as he could. He refused to be collared or led anywhere. I was fascinated by a creature so determined, so perverse. Mothers often fall prey to Stockholm Syndrome; I was no exception. Bruno developed a huge wart on his leg. I had it removed and he died. It took me years to recover.

I have always had dozens of rescued animals in my house. I like them all, but I see them simply as passing through on their way to a better rebirth. I avoid strong bonds because my body and mind cannot bear much more hurt.

But every now and then a Gudiya comes along. She was a blind and deaf Dalmatian with an infected uterus. Thrown into the gutter by a breeder who could not get any more children out of her. We brought her home, had her operated on. She bonded with me immediately. She was so happy, so clever, so elegant. She smelt me out and came bounding to me whenever I came home. Despite her blindness, she hardly bumped into anything. She slept on my bed, jumping up with her long, beautiful legs. She responded with affection to everyone and had such a good sense of humour that we all laughed with her. But as time wore on, she developed arthritis, the pain of which made her irritable and distressed. She struggled to climb on to my bed so we set up a mattress for her next to it. There were days when we even had to help her stand. Yet with each passing day, I loved her more and more and spent hours stroking her down. When she stopped eating and started moaning softly, I knew I would have to help her out, and so we put her to sleep. She struggled terribly and now I can't remember anything of her life except the last moments when she refused to die gently. I cried for months.

Years went by. Animals came and went. When the Covid lockdown came, on the night of 24 March, I knew I would have to be there for all the thousands of people who needed help with the local administration, travel and feeding passes and food for the animals they were caring for. So I gave my phone number out into the public domain. I received close to six-hundred emails and almost three-hundred phone calls every day from people who need help with an animal-related situation. I tried to solve each of their problems, even when it brought me into hateful conflict.

In this avalanche of cries for help, I received several emails from a girl in Patna about a Chow Chow who had been abandoned on the road, and whom she had picked up after he was bitten by some street dogs. She had tried to find a home for him, but he attacked everyone there and was so furious that no one would keep him. On a whim I told her that I would pay for her to fly him to Delhi.

Thus arrived Goofy, who was anything but. His eyes were crusted over so he couldn't see, his black hair was matted and full of ticks and fleas. But he stepped out of the dog box like a king, made straight for the sofa cushions in the office and fought a long and hard battle with them till they died. No one would go near him.

I loved him from the minute I saw him, dishevelled, smelly and blind. I sat and talked to him for hours until, one day, he allowed me to touch him. He had been beaten, chained and starved, and had spent months defending himself on the road. Yet he was a calm, mature dog who accepted the horrors of life stoically. He simply wanted to be friends with the alpha dogs in the house. He followed them around, imitated their antics, gave them respect, and yet they ignored him and played tricks on him, often taking a nip at him. He never fought back, just stood still and called for me. And wherever I was in the house, I would come running and soothe him so that he could develop some courage again.

We had his eyes operated on so that he could see a little bit. When we shaved him, his curly black hair came back white! He wore an Elizabethan collar for months and he loved it—it was like his crown (and I think he felt protected from bites). Cushions, though, were another matter. He simply hated them. I think he had been beaten with them or perhaps beaten when he tried to sit on them. Every time he felt low, he would argue with them and give them a large hard bite with a mouth that was otherwise so gentle that when I put food into it, it felt like cotton wool.

Slowly, the fun part of him emerged. He would wait till I went for a bath and then run away with my clothes just so that I would follow him. When I went for a walk, he would trot behind me for a bit and then round on me and lie flat on his back, demanding a belly rub. He loved sitting with his hind legs sticking out, his belly on the cold tiles. Many months later, when he and I lay on the cold floor together and I told him he had beautiful feet, he reached out and gave me a small lick for the first time. I thought my heart would burst as I hugged him. I remembered a wise woman who had said to me many years ago that a son is like the bee in a hive above you; if you are still you might get a few drops of honey every now and then, but if you disturb him or attempt to counsel him you will get stung.

And so my son was never counselled. He was embraced gently when he allowed it and adored all the time, even when he was busy exploring, and ignoring me completely.

I had Goofy for less than a year. He developed a haematoma on his shoulder and I went to a vet to have it drained. He developed tick fever again and at the vet's he picked up the most dreadful of all canine diseases: distemper.

I drove for hours every day to a vet in a neighbouring district. I stood while he was being injected and I felt the pain of each needle. Goofy was calm but I was not. We tried every form of medicine, including all the quack anti-distemper *nuska*s in the market. But Goofy's condition continued to worsen, his skin started bleeding, his eyes gave way and finally the distemper reached his brain. I sat with him while he slipped away; I could not stop apologizing to him. At that point I would have gladly given my life for his.

I see his sturdy little black-and-white body even now, passing by the dining table, turning the corner ...

Tears have pooled in my eyes for the last forty years, waiting for a reason to be released from their prisons. And now they have one.

Why do we go looking for children of the heart? Why did I love Goofy? Perhaps because he accepted everything that life threw at him, and still looked for joy in the cracks.

My heart is in the ICU of the universe. I have not had the fruits of the monsoon; the pink clouds have passed me by; the koel is silent.

Death, Dignity, Dogs
NAOMI BARTON

'Don't love her too much. You can't love her so much that she needs you.'

—My mother, on dogs

This is a story of two dogs, Melo and Angel (and Baby makes three).

It is a story about the question, 'What is Love?'

It is a story of the only correct answer, which is, 'Baby don't hurt me, don't hurt me, no more.'

It is a story about the things that live in the dark.

It is a story of dogs that bark at them.

In October of Frankly, the Worst Year in the History of All Time, that is 2020, I came back home after staying away for seven years.

The circumstances were profoundly funny, the way very sad things tend to be.

It started when I wrote a will. I thought, as a newly minted adult, it was The Right Thing to Do while looking down the barrel of our collective impending mortality. This is something that happens when you work in news during a global pandemic.

I have since been informed that this is not how wills work. You appoint an executor. You distribute assets. You do this in your fifties. And you do not, in fact, send an email to your mother, with no conversation leading up to it.

In such cases, a very reasonable reaction is for said mother to presume that her daughter has exited this earthly realm via a staircase of her own devising.

This becomes much more likely if, like me, you have been on anti-depression medication for two years, and in therapy for four.

My mother woke up and read that email first thing. Then she tried to call me.

She tried again. And again. And again.

I didn't pick up.

So, she thought. The child is dead.

She did the sensible thing, which was to call my workplace.

My workplace did the sensible thing, which was to believe her.

That is how I woke up that morning to a copy editor at my doorstep, asking me politely if I was alive, and whether I'd tried to kill myself the night before.

I had not, I said.

Are you quite sure, he asked, confirming the detail, as copy editors are wont to.

What are you doing here, I asked.

He explained.

I offered him tea. It seemed the thing to do.

This meant he had a front-row seat when I closed my eyes and called my mother, to inform her that I was, against all expectations, alive, and probably going to die of embarrassment.

She didn't laugh.

'Ma,' I said weakly. 'I'm fine. I was sleeping. It was just—for fun.'

She was crying too hard to yell at me. I started to sweat. This had never happened before. Things were Very Bad.

I weakly floated the idea that perhaps she should not have leapt to conclusions. The copy editor raised his eyebrows disapprovingly. My mother hung up.

As it turned out, it was to step on to her flight, which she had booked five minutes after reading my will. Apparently, the usually unflappable staff at Bombay airport will hold the flight for you when you turn up late, with crazed eyes, and tell them your daughter has tried to kill herself. Evidently, a lot of the regular rules of the world change to accommodate that, which, as a concept, is very good of the world, but was terrible for me.

Two hours later, my mother stepped into my house, hugged me, and didn't let go.

Orpheus begged and pleaded and lost, but with Demeter, Hades took orders quietly.

'It's time to come home,' she said. It was no longer a question, and my moral high ground was slippery.

This is how we found ourselves at a railway station a week later, with Melo refusing to get on the train.

Melo is eight years old. She was a rescue who came into my life a year ago. She is a brown dog who turns a gorgeous autumn Irish Setter russet in the sun.

She has the long, deep coat of a Golden Retriever, with fluffy paws, feathered legs and the elegant, tufted ears of a Collie. Her tail is a long-fringed plume of a question mark that says, 'Underneath the fancy fur, my friend, I belong to desi streets.'

I didn't see any of this when I chose her, though. She was hiding underneath a bench surrounded by hyperactive, loud puppies at the shelter's adoption day. Well-meaning potential pup parents tried to pet her as she cringed beneath the bench.

Melo did not perform. She was not a big fan of people and hated loud noises, and that day was a combination of too many people, all making loud noises. They wanted her attention, and she refused to give it.

Fundamentally, Melo knew that people were not nice. She had learnt that the hard way. She had been in the shelter for seven years.

I was watching her sitting there, when she looked at me with big caramel eyes, and then turned away. She did not gaze at me and say, 'It's me.' She did not put her soft head in my lap trustingly. She did not walk straight up to me and say, 'Take me away from all this.'

She looked away and panted, stressed, and I sat next to her for a while and didn't say anything at all.

I got up.

'What about—her?' I said, pointing to the bench.

'Oh, that's Melody. She's sweet. But she's not social,' the shelter lady told me.

'Huh,' I said.

'She has a lot of anxiety,' she said.

'Ah,' I said.

'She doesn't trust men, doesn't like children—'

'I'll take her,' I said.

We already had more in common than anybody else I had ever met. She was perfect.

Delhi is not a city people come to stay in, unless it is already their home; it doesn't know what to do with new blood. Unexpectedly, betraying my Bombay roots, it fit me. I stayed, rooted, as friends and lovers swam into my life and away in a relentless, annual tide. Perhaps this is what happens when you're in your late twenties. Perhaps it is easier to love people with a built-in expiration date. Perhaps I am easy to leave.

But I wanted someone to stay.

I wanted someone who wouldn't just love me while they were waiting for their life to really begin, and I didn't want to be someone's beginning. I couldn't stand belonging to someone, and I wanted someone who was all mine. I wanted to wake up by myself every morning for the rest of my life. I did not want to be alone. I wanted a friend, not a lover—but more. How much more? All of it. I haven't found a word for that yet.

So Melo came home.

I gave her a bed, and she gave me a reason to come home at night. She took me on walks where I had been too scared to go alone, and made me go out into the world, every day. She made friends with my neighbours who had dogs, and scoffed at the ones who didn't. She made me feed her properly, every day. Even if I survived on coffee, cigarettes and cheap kathi rolls, she had fresh meat and veg. Every day.

After four years of living on that corner, watching people come and go from high up on my fourth-floor window, I became the Didi with the Dog. Melo was the Dog Who Did Not Play. The children, holding hands, would shout Melo-Dy when we stepped out, and I would shout back Hello-Dy, and they would fall over laughing.

Melo was friends with the downstairs dogs, the brindle hounds Rodney and Gazelle. She loved Rodney with her whole heart, and he bounded up to play with her when I whistled. She thought Gazelle needed to learn her place, and Gazelle, in full agreement, lay belly up and weed herself in terror and joy.

With the dogs on the corner, she had an ongoing feud, and they shouted insults at each other when we went to the grocery store. She fell injudiciously in love with young Sultan, the gorgeous, shining-black part-German Shepherd part-Lab, acting like a pup half her age, as they ran across the park, nipping gently at each other's hocks. She would stand in the sun, laughing up at me with her tongue lolling, flinging herself into freshly cut grass.

Days I had to stay in bed and watch the ceiling, shivering, she was there.

I could reach my arm down and find her, and she would lick my fingers.

Whenever someone famous kills themselves, the internet bursts with reminders to check in on your depressed friends, and to be there for them. What they do not know is that the most efficient way to be there for someone is to live under their bed.

Melo did not scare away the monsters, because the only thing a monster is scared of is another one.

But she was there.

Every morning, she woke me up at 5 a.m., singing with the azan outside our window. She was a cold nose in my ear, a leaping, jumping delight, ready for her walkies. We went out, and we came home.

I brushed her beautiful soft coat every morning and sleepily, she let me, turning her head inquiringly if I stopped.

She did look at me trustingly then. She did put her small soft face in my lap. Only I would be the one looking her in the eye and saying, 'Take me away from all this.' And every time when my fingers sank into her soft fur, she did.

She still did not like people. I didn't either, so this worked out superbly.

Home was my matchbox flat with a bright yellow wall with blue plates hung by long bookshelves. Home was a ratty, ancient armchair that was second-hand two hands ago, and a couch Melo would mutinously pee on if I left her alone too long. It was piles of books, in corners, within reach from every seat. Our bedroom was white— walls, linens, curtains. For eyes to be quiet after the outside. We fell asleep with the shadow of the cotton-silk tree dancing across the wall, every night.

So Melo did not want to get on the train. She wanted to go home. But I hauled her in anyway.

A train ride later, and all at once, we were home—new home, old home, ancient and fresh. I hadn't come back in seven years. I wanted to call it something else—the house—the old house— mum's house?

But with a definite, menacing certainty, it insisted that I was back, and this was home.

It was dark.

The brooding, chaotic violence that accompanied my father was not here. He had been politely asked to move in with a friend so that I could stay. I had not spoken to him for years, and this was the first time my mother had picked me.

But it was still—unmistakably—his turf.

The walls were covered in senseless colour, leftovers of concept art which had tired of itself midway. Baffling kitsch littered every surface. An earthen fish. A box of the packets in which rolling tobacco comes—all empty. A resin statue of Jesus with a broken arm.

There were cables—charging cables and USB cords and LAN cables and plugs, taking root and reproducing in drawers in every room, crawling over spaces where sense might have lived. There were cables for technology that hadn't existed since 2007.

There were twenty-seven drawers—I counted. Inside the dark caves of their frames, they were covered in fine, creeping white mould.

Then there were the hobbies. A wall full of earthen pots with holes drilled into them, through which tiny lights would be pierced. A black board, through which fairy lights were stuck like pixels to make a tacky, tired Christmas tree, flashing blue and yellow. It was never taken down, but it forbade a real Christmas tree in its place. It insisted on being art.

Huge, dark furniture loomed, grabbing shins and biting toes when you walked across the room, eating the sunlight that fought its way in.

Heavy curtains covered in a year's worth of dust shrouded the windows. The books were behind them. It was from this house that I had inherited the instinct to hoard books, like a librarian who happened also to be a dragon. Books were treasure. And like in my home, they were in every room, but twisted, like the reflection in a circus mirror. Here, they lived carefully slotted into shelves built into the windows, and they kept out the light.

Books are not meant to block out the light.

I remembered why I left.

This was where light came to die, and a broken, blinking facsimile demanded to take its place.

Then suddenly, a brand-new, tiny dog bounded up to me, and let out a volley of barks.

Angel was two years old. They had adopted her just two weeks before I arrived. She was a small black-and-white Spaniel, the white flecked with black as if sooty fingers had stroked through her fur.

Her original family had loved her very much, and had trained her to go to the toilet for her business. She did not have her own basket, because she lived on their laps, in their arms, and had done so since she had come to them a week old.

She was meant to be their retirement plan—they had bought her for forty thousand rupees, and were told each of her pups would fetch the same price when she was bred. But by the time she was old enough to breed, she had caught a skin infection that caused her fur to fall out in patches, and she had been shaved so often that the hair grew back sharp to the touch. Suddenly, she was too ugly to breed. When the lockdown came, her family, who lived one day at a time, jostled into a house inside a single room, all having lost their jobs.

They could no longer afford to love her.

They cried when they gave her away.

There was already one dog at home—Baby, whom Mum had adopted nine years ago. She was seventeen now, and half-blind. She was a rescue too, and had barked exactly twice in her life.

She was soft in the way that the absence of hardness is. Baby was independent; she only needed to be fed, and appreciated a pet, but didn't really need one. She slept a lot. She liked two meals a day.

She went on her own walks. She was a good dog; she was good at being invisible.

Still holding my suitcase, I looked at Angel doubtfully. She suffered from the curse of small dogs, which is that they have to prove themselves to big dogs, and they seem to want to do that by saying, 'COME ON THEN, IF YOU THINK YOU'RE HARD ENOUGH,' with absolutely no provocation required. The world is made up of big dogs, if you are a small dog.

Melo growled.

Mum started.

'She growled? Melo's aggressive?'

'No, she's just got good boundaries,' I said.

'Yes, but will she fight with my dogs? I mean, of course she's my dog too, she's my grand-dogter, hehe, but with Angel? And Baby?'

'Of course not,' I said. 'She's my dog.'

Three days later, Melo bit Baby.

For a week, Melo cowered. Nobody had yelled at her. Nobody had said anything, really. But she hid under the bed, anguished, knowing I was upset, that she had Done Something Wrong.

She didn't come out to be cuddled. I didn't want to cuddle her. She gnawed at her paw till it bled, which made me feel guilty and upset. Every time she emerged I would bandage it, and she would flee under the bed as soon as I finished, away from me. Every time. I hated myself.

I had to keep her locked in my room, and in a fit of furious, defensive rage, I locked myself in with her. We only went out for walks, and ate our meals silently, alone. Mum couldn't leave the house, quarantined for two weeks with me. She bustled outside, every hour of every day. She was loving. She made food. She came in and chatted about nothing.

She flinched every time Melo walked outside.

I was not going to stay in a place where my dog wasn't welcome. I knew Melo was a good dog. She was a good dog. I knew she hadn't meant to bite; her teeth had nicked Baby in the scuffle, just barely. Head wounds always bleed, and when we had wiped away the blood from the scratch near Baby's eye, we couldn't even find the scratch again.

But there had been blood. And so there was fear.

I knew it was my fault. There had been a plate of food, and I had forgot to separate them.

I was furious at myself, for not knowing my dog. I was furious with Melo, for not being beyond reproach. I was furious with my mother, for being afraid of my dog, who was a good dog. I hated myself for being angry with Melo, who hadn't done anything wrong. I was angry with Melo, for not doing everything right.

But most of all, I was furious at this house, this dark house with its sharp corners, where lifeless things ate up the light, this house that dragged me back every time I ran away. This house, where rage had lived for so long, it had seeped into the walls, and made you vicious to survive. It took joy between the teeth and spat it out, turning it into fear and sorrow. I hated how it leeched blackness into the one pure thing I had.

It had made Melo sad, it made me make Melo sad. I wanted it to be alive so I could choke it to death with my bare hands.

It laughed at me.

'So, ah,' the dog therapist said, looking at me, 'have you had any stress recently?'

'I mean, not particularly,' I said. 'I just moved home.'

She looked at me steadily. 'Been a while?'

'No, no,' my mother interjected, smoothing happiness around her like jam. 'She has her own room. She works all day.'

'And your husband?' the therapist asked.

'He's—not there now,' my mother said.

The doggie therapist sat on the ground with all three dogs. She played with them. She walked away—she came close. She gave them bones. They ignored the bones. She took us out for a cigarette, and Melo went and sniffed her, tentatively, and asked for pets.

She petted Melo.

Then she turned to me and said, 'You're over-bonded.'

'I am what?' I said flatly.

'Melo thinks the world starts and ends with you. You put the sun in the sky, and you make the grass grow. Everything she needs comes from you, and she knows that.'

Melo padded over to me, and I sank my fingers into her fur, clutching. So I needed her as much as she needed me. Wasn't that—right?

'It's not a bad thing,' the therapist said gently. 'But it means that if you're stressed, she is stressed. And then you stress out because she's stressed, and you're both in this cycle.'

'She also gets annoyed if I feed Melo,' my mum piped in helpfully.

'You feed your dogs twice a day and I feed her once, Mum,' I snapped. 'And you act like I'm starving her but I'm not; she's happy and she's healthy, and if she gets fat her bones will bow, and you act like I can't look after my own dog—'

My mother turned to the dog therapist. 'Like that,' she said dryly.

'Your daughter is under the bed,' the dog therapist said.

'What?' my mother said.

'When dogs are afraid and unhappy, they will go to a place where they feel safe. Quite often, that's under the bed. Like how Melo goes under the bed. If they are under the bed, you should never, ever pull them out. You should never feed them there, or they start associating fear with food. You should let them be till they come out.'

'Okay—' my mother said, uncertainly.

'Don't feed Melo if your daughter doesn't want you to,' she said briskly. 'If she wants help, she'll ask. Don't try to go under the bed.'

'But—' my mother tried.

'No,' the dog therapist said.

It was a No that went to the bones. She had honed it to a fine point, with dogs, and now it worked on humans.

'Move upstairs,' she said to me. 'Set your distance. Mark your territory, and Melo's. Keep the other dogs away from her if she growls, and don't punish her for growling. She's communicating. She's talking to them, to you. She's saying, "I don't want this." And we reward her for using her words. She's doing a fantastic job of telling you what she needs, and we will encourage that. And if the other dogs bother her, take them away.'

Mum looked unhappy.

'Why do they have to watch their p's and q's just because she can't?' she asked. 'Mine are the compassionate ones, and just because she's—rude—she can just walk all over them?'

The doggie therapist turned to her.

'They are all good dogs,' she said. It did not brook argument.

Soon, Mum started leaving for work every day. She looked after elderly people, and the pandemic made it more important for her to be there.

'Will you manage with all three of them?' she said fretfully, standing at my door. 'Will you love them all? You won't ignore them for Melo?'

'Yes, Ma,' I said, looking at my phone. 'They'll be fed and healthy and happy when you get back.'

She looked at me.

'Okay,' she said.

I don't want to love them all the same, I thought savagely. I wasn't going to. I was going to love Melo, and just keep these two alive. It was going to be fine.

Angel did not get this memo.

Fifteen minutes after Mum left, she scratched at my door.

Melo growled quietly.

'Good girl, Melo,' I said, looking into my laptop and ignoring the door.

The scratching grew louder. I ignored it. Scratch scratch scratch, Angel went, diligently pawing the door to open. It had always opened for her before. It did not open now. Scratch scratch scratch. I concentrated harder.

It stopped.

It was done.

I sighed.

They would learn, and it would be fine. They didn't need to be loved to be okay. Besides, I wasn't going to be mean to them, I just wasn't going to be ... devoted. I already had a dog. Sorry, no vacancies.

Suddenly, a piercing howl broke through my reasoning.

I ran out.

Angel was sitting by the door, looking outside, and howling. She was howling her heart out. She howled and howled and howled.

She was howling because she was miserable. She was so small, her sadness was so big, and she howled to let it out. She was two years old, she had lost her mummy a month ago. Now her new mummy had left her. Angel was crying because she was all alone. She was so small, and being alone was too big.

'Well,' I said under my breath. 'Fuck.'

I walked up to her and ran my hand down her back.

She stopped howling and turned and looked at me. Her eyes were huge. They were what puppy-dog eyes were named after. Pools took notes on how to be limpid.

She nosed my hand, and tentatively wiggled her bum. She didn't have a tail—they'd docked it when she was a week old. All that was left was a black patch in the shape of a Beatle's haircut, which she wiggled now.

'Fine,' I said. 'But you have to be quiet, and let me work.' I bent down, scooped her up, and took her to my room.

Melo growled.

I said, 'Good girl, Melo,' and set the puppy down.

The puppy jumped back up and planted her paws on my knees. She had her eyes on, adoring. She beamed at me, panting, tiny pink tongue in her soft grey face.

'No,' I said weakly. 'Down, Angel.'

Within about two weeks, Angel had colonized my life.

For the first week, she missed her mummy, and would chase middle-aged women she saw on walks, yanking at her leash, while I was left mumbling apologies in her wake. She was a nuisance. She wanted my mother, or her old mother, basically some kind of mother, who was not currently available. She did not understand anything. She never came when I called; she wanted to fight dogs six times her size; and she barked at everything.

If it rained, she barked at the sky. She jumped up to the window and barked at the neighbour lady cooking dinner. She barked at butterflies for flying, she barked at the grass for growing. She barked to tell the world that she was here, and she was watching, so it had better get its act together.

At night, she would put her little paws on the bed, and beg to be allowed up. I declined. She was persistent and determined. She figured out that she could take a running leap and climb up herself. As I lay myself to sleep, there she sat next to me, staring at me like a tiny furry stalker.

'Why are you looking at me like that?' I asked her, cross.

She walked up to me, curled up in the crook of my arm and laid her small head upon my shoulder.

'Oh,' I said stupidly.

My arm curled around her without waiting for permission. I told it to go back. It had a job and was not to waste its time cuddling dogs. The arm refused to listen. It went on strike. The revolution crept through my body and unionized my bones. My spine turned traitor and curled around her. It was blatant, brazen insubordination … Her head was the softest thing in the world.

Angel sighed happily, and I fell asleep.

In the morning, she licked my nose till I woke up, bleary. She wanted walkies.

Melo never tells me what to do, I thought. Melo fits herself around me. With Melo, I was the one driving the car. Angel simply crashed the car, then looked up at me from the conflagration with her big eyes and wagged her bum.

What a horrible device a car is, her happy face said. How much better for you to walk. With me. Now. Because I have to pee. Now. Walkies.

The days I refused to wake up on Angel's clock, she peed in the hallway, despotically.

She was a tiny, horrible tyrant. She deployed her bladder like a fascist deploying troops. If she ever found democracy, she would pee on it.

I wanted to be a bitch. She just wouldn't let me.

Moving upstairs didn't work. When Mum left, if I went up, even if it was just to hang my clothes to dry, a small parade walked with me, with Angel in the lead, scoping out the territory. I followed with faithful Melo, and Baby, who didn't like to be left out. Melo growled. Baby ignored her. Angel ran everywhere and peed on the washing machine.

I loved it. I loved my little caravan. They didn't like each other, but they all loved me. I couldn't get a glass of water without having a dog underfoot. I complained about it with transparent delight.

Angel looked at me with an addictive adoration. She stopped yanking on her leash. She climbed into my lap when we watched TV. I would find myself watching for her to follow when I left a room, same as Melo, and they both came together. When Melo growled now, it was a grumble, and Angel would automatically turn away. I crowed. She was a Good Dog! Good dog, Angel!

One day, she bounced into my lap, and I held her tight—tight tight tight—and she looked up at me. I was gone. I was hers now as much as I was Melo's. I grinned at her and cooed.

'Who's my little banana? Is it you? Are you the most beautiful girl in the world—'

'You shouldn't love her so much,' my mother observed, snapping me out of it.

I looked up guiltily from the small dog in my arms.

'Make up your mind,' I said. 'First I loved her too little. Now I love her too much.'

'I don't want a dog that wants to be held all the time, and you're encouraging her. You keep letting her up on the bed.'

'You let her up on the bed first,' I said.

'No, I didn't,' she said, lying.

'How am I not supposed to love her?' I asked, aggrieved. 'She didn't let me not love her. She made me love her. I didn't want to love her; she made me. It's her fault. Yell at her.'

'She's a dog,' my mother pointed out, unfairly.

'Why don't you learn to love her more?' I asked mutinously.

'Because everything goes away,' my mother said, now upset. 'You can't hold on to anything. Nothing's yours. You have to be— enough—by yourself. You can't love anything so much. You can't let her love you so much that she needs you.'

I looked at her.

'You can't love her too much,' she repeated, helplessly.

That week, we cleaned.

My mother called the carpenter, who dismantled the big, heavy bed, and set it again in a corner, away from the windows.

'I didn't know it fit there,' she said absently.

We pulled out the drawers, all twenty-seven of them. I hunted down every cable like a madwoman, with Melo and Angel following me, putting them in a clear box I bought for the purpose, tying them all up with red tape. Angel decided she wanted to live in the box, so I put some red tape on her head. Melo huffed at the fuss.

We turned the house inside out and laid everything across the floor. Use Pile. Throw Pile. Give Away Pile.

'This is from 2012, Ma,' I said, waving a tube of rancid moisturizer.

'Yes, but you can still use it,' she said. 'Or we can give it away. It all cost hard-earned money.'

She stared at it for a few seconds, torn, then looked away.

'You do it. When I'm not here. So I don't have to see.'

She turned to cabinets, and with single-minded focus, started pulling things out. Tools. Drill bits. A set of paint brushes. Carrom coins. A wooden magazine rack. An air fryer. Paper plates. Jigsaw puzzle bits.

'You're right,' she said, turning over a shoehorn and tossing it.

'It's all fucking rubbish,' she said, wonderingly, holding a handful of ravel plugs.

'I want to throw it out, but they won't let me. I can't find this house under all this rubbish. I can't do it alone, so I just—'

She flung a set of visiting cards venomously across the floor.

'Ma,' I said. 'Do you want to take the books off the windows? We can put them in the drawers. They're empty now.'

We looked at each other, and started to laugh.

Postscript

About a year after I wrote this, Angel lived up to her name and made her way across the rainbow bridge. In her three years on this undeserving earth, she had grown to be a therapy dog to housebound elders, who looked forward to her visits every week. She packed more joy into her brief time with us than any of us could have ever conceived, and while I would like to say that this was a consolation when she was taken from us, I would be lying if I said that. It was unfair, and unnecessary. In her honour, I hope you make sure your dogs are given their tick treatments with the regularity they require to avoid the galloping tragedy that is tick fever. It's my firm belief that Angel understands exactly how unfair this is, and is distraught by how much her passing has left us wounded. As such, I'm sure she is waking up every morning and peeing on God. She will always be a Good Dog.

The Dogs Someone Drew

MAHESH RAO

Pollen, strawberries, dust mites, chlorine. These were some of the triggers that various members of my family had to list on allergy questionnaires in hospitals and doctors' waiting rooms.

There was one more, which to me seemed especially sad: dogs.

Although I wasn't the one with that particular allergy, I knew I had to be careful not to trail dog hair and dander into the house. Petting other people's dogs was a rare treat; adopting one an impossibility. There was a certain pleasure to be had in simply watching a fuzzy head hang out of a car window, ears streaming behind, or a glistening nose push through the bars of a gate as you walked by. But it was never quite enough. As a consequence, I resorted to the solution that presented itself for anything that was beyond my grasp: the certainty of make-believe.

The first fictional dog with whom I enjoyed an intense engagement was Scooby-Doo, the bumbling Great Dane created by Hanna-Barbera in 1969. The most striking thing about

Scooby-Doo, at least initially, was his size and unwieldiness. He looked like he might be distantly related to a horse—and it seemed perfectly natural that he would have trouble coming to a sudden halt or preventing himself from tumbling down a flight of stairs. For a child, he also had what we might today call 'relatability': always hungry, accidentally ingenuous, frightened of lots of things. There was a certain comfort to be had in the predictability of Scooby-Doo's world. No matter how abominable the ghosts and ghouls that tormented Scooby and his gang, you were secure in the knowledge that in fifteen minutes they would be unmasked to reveal an ordinary, if unpleasant, mortal. I was so attuned to Scooby and his antics that the first time I saw a Great Dane in real life, it was as though an inexplicable collapse had occurred in the division between reality and fantasy. All I could see was that Scooby-Doo for some reason was leashed to a bollard outside our local supermarket, a fact that was in equal parts thrilling and disquieting.

A couple of years later I found my way to another dog, part of a very different gang. To a bookish child the obvious appeal of Charles Schulz's Snoopy was his great ambition to be a novelist. 'It was a dark and stormy night'—it was not the most auspicious of opening lines but Snoopy could be forgiven because he showed discipline, commitment and drive. So much of writing is simply showing up, and how many other dogs would perch on their kennels and bang away at a typewriter with the devotion displayed by Snoopy? And even if what we saw of his writing failed to captivate us, we knew that he had it in him. Here was a creature who could see right through the delusions humans created for themselves, and then summon up greater delusions of his own. Like all the best authors, he could veer between patient observation and shocking narcissism. Above all, he had an acute sense of how to navigate the many indignities of being viewed as just a dog. How could Snoopy not end up writing a masterpiece? I certainly was convinced that it would one day appear on the shelves of my local bookshop.

From American suburbia, I moved on to the many worlds occupied by Hergé's Belgian investigative reporter and the Wire Fox Terrier who was constantly by his side. There was a purity about Tintin's sidekick, Snowy, not because of his name, but because of the simplicity of the ligne claire drawing in which he was rendered. You could imagine that he would appear on the page in just a few deft strokes but with all the elaboration that the moment required. Snowy was doughty, loyal and wise, but not in a way that grated. He was the kind of dog who would warn and admonish Tintin who was just about to walk into a lamp post, only to walk into a different lamp post himself. He was endearing because his occasional superiority was shot through with fallibility. There would almost always be an open pit waiting somewhere for Snowy. At his core was a deep engagement with morality: He was often troubled by angelic and devilish versions of himself, each of which tried to convince him that their chosen path was the right one. He did not always make the best choices—he could rarely resist lapping up alcohol that had leaked out of bottles or casks—but he was fully aware of the consequences of his transgressions and seemed to wish always to do better next time.

The presence of these fictional dogs in my life might seem like a poor substitute for the real thing now and yet, I did not feel deprived. When they leapt from the page or the screen into my imagination, they seemed to activate all the joy, empathy and warmth that might come from having a real furry muzzle thrust into your hand.

They slowly revealed their nature, and in doing so, they enabled me to inhabit their world.

Yes, someone else drew these dogs, but in some strange way not quite comprehensible to me, I gave them life.

A Dog Called Crazy

RUSKIN BOND

After Grandfather died, Granny's sole companion was a dog called Crazy.

Crazy was a small dog, a black-and-tan of mixed ancestry—part Terrier, part Spaniel, part street dog. He had, in fact, been found on the street by Granny while he was still a puppy. He was lost, wandering in the middle of a busy road, in danger of being run over by a car or a tonga. Granny brought him home, and he grew up to be a lively little fellow, friendly to all, but devoted to Granny, who shared her meals with him.

I saw them only when I came down from boarding school in Shimla for my winter holidays. Granny's home was in Dehradun. My mother and stepfather lived in another part of Dehra, but I enjoyed staying with Granny because she had a good cook who made the sort of curries and cutlets that I liked. Schoolboys have their priorities!

So do small dogs.

Crazy's priority was keeping the cats away from our house. Our neighbour, Mrs Ghosh, kept cats—several of them—and they were apt to come over the wall and sneak into our kitchen. Crazy spent a lot of his time chasing them away. He was a good runner, but he took care not to catch any of them—not since he'd been scratched across the nose by a cornered tabby.

Crazy's greatest pleasure was running round and round the house. It was a small bungalow with plenty of open space in front and at the back, and whenever Crazy felt that life was getting a little dull, he would go for one of his sprints. Usain Bolt wouldn't have been able to keep up with him. Crazy would dash around the house three or four times, chasing an invisible quarry, and then subside on the veranda steps, panting but very pleased with himself.

Although he was never tied up, Crazy seldom wandered beyond the gate or the garden walls. He did not trust that road outside, where, as a pup, he had had to dodge the traffic. On warm sunny afternoons, he would rest in the shade of the old jackfruit tree— waiting for a cat to appear!

Winter holidays came and went. Granny grew older. So did Crazy. So did I.

Crazy was about eight and I was thirteen when Granny died. She passed away in her rocking chair, rocking gently on the veranda.

For days, weeks, Crazy was inconsolable. He stopped chasing cats. He stopped running around the house. He barely touched his food. Where had Granny gone, the only person in his life? The cook and I fussed over him, and so did others, but there was no response.

Then one day, when I was sitting on the veranda, and Crazy was curled up in a corner, he suddenly woke up, sat up, got to his feet, and began whimpering. The cries turned to a moan of something like joy, and I was amazed to see him running about and leaping into the air and barking apparently at nothing.

Something—someone—was there.

For a second, just a fleeting second, I thought I could see Granny standing on the veranda steps, her hand stroking the uplifted head of the little dog now frantic with happiness. She had come back for him.

The vision passed, the only time it happened to me. But for Crazy the vision was still there, and for days he followed her about the house, the garden, the little orchard—the happiest dog in the world.

And one day they walked away together and were seen no more.

Dogs Never Die

ABHISHEK JOSHI

Five years ago, on the eve of Ruskin Bond's birthday in May, Kaalicharan breathed her last.

Fourteen winters young, she exhaled for the very last time. She didn't push up the daisies or 'kick the bucket', but just died. No euphemism could conjure away, conceal or cure this pain—neither then, nor now.

Revisiting that cold grey evening after all these years still leaves a lump in my throat. There's so much to unpack, my guilt and my grief. I wish I could have been a better boy to the wonderful friend that she was. Pulled apart in the grist mill called life, I saw her way less than I should have. Over the years, college, a job and life happened, and somewhere along the way my visits home shrank to that odd Diwali break. I feel sorry for all the vacations when I didn't come home. For all those lost chances where I could have met my best friend who would lift the weight off my shoulders and make me feel light at heart.

Fourteen years is a remarkable life span for a large mountain dog like Kaali, but I still wonder why it wasn't thirty, remembering I had heard of a dog who lived that long. I don't have pictures from Kaali's puppy days, but I vividly remember her proud dark face with a snow-white 'French cut' looking around at everything cautiously. How I hid her in my denim jacket as we came downhill. How she looked at the sun unflinchingly.

When you lose your dog, the outside world moves on as if nothing has happened. But for me a semblance of my childhood had gone silent forever.

Rescued from a garage, Kaali saw me through my school days on to corporate life; she was the closest friend I ever had. Over the seasons, her eyes turned from their honey shade to a cloudy vacuum, and I could no longer see myself in them. No, she wasn't blind, but the signs were there to see. Age and all the ailments it brings. Yet, she remained happy.

With her passing, an entire childhood melted away like a scoop of ice cream in the May sun.

When you lose your dog, one who has seen you mature (or not!) from your childhood fancies, you lose the scale that pins you to reality and relevance. You lose the glue that bound everything together for you.

Why do we always learn a little too late?

Sometimes when I am rearranging my bookshelf, I still come across a stray coal-black strand of dog hair hidden in the pages, as if a bookmark to the past.

Cherish what you have—for finite are our moments, and limitless the traps of life to fall into. Dogs have figured the Zen way, though. Unlike the world and worldly common sense, a dog's happiness isn't defined by square feet. Not measured in spoons or bowls. Even a tennis ball is happiness. I remember how, so often, Kaali would come running and throw herself on the freshly mowed grass—and if you happened to be sprawled on the lawn flicking through a comic book or Ruskin Bond's stories, you'd feel her bear weight on your limbs or your back. Memories come in waves, not to haunt but to caress.

Love at the end of all things should be like this: like how a dog loves you. You may be lost in the world's design, the little goals, planning that blueprint for life, while standing patiently, the dog waits for nothing but only you.

As another stray gust of wind brings her fur, coiled like cotton candy, to me, I know no vacuum cleaner can wipe her memory away. Ever.

Dogs never die.

Borrowed Dogs

NILANJANA S. ROY

The cats know. They always know.

The oldest is nineteen, a gentle ginger tom of forgiving disposition who burrows into my lap, letting me know it doesn't matter, he's just glad we're back from the mountains. The next two—a gorgeous white with a tendency to high drama and a cheerful but possessive black-and-gold torty—take a long sniff at our clothes and stalk away, outraged. The youngest, another ginger, looks up at my husband and me with accusing green eyes. The message is clear: It is bad enough that we abandoned them, but how could we abandon them for the company of *dogs?*

For over four decades, I assumed I wasn't a dog person. My sister has asthma, so I grew up in a dogless *duniya*, never knowing what was missing from my life. I liked dogs, but I didn't know them the way I knew and loved cats. In my twenty years in Delhi, I chatted with stray dogs across different neighbourhoods, ferried the ones who required rescuing to assorted vets, steered clear of the poor fellows who'd received such unkindness from humans that they were prone to attack strangers—but we were, socially speaking, only nodding acquaintances.

Until Piku.

An old friend was in a bind; she had to travel urgently, and her usual dog-sitter had dropped out at the last moment. Would we know anyone who could stay in her cottage, up in the Himalayas, for a few days, and keep an eye on her three dogs? Something got through in her message, some of her anxiety and love for her pack. My husband and I had planned a quick trip to the hills anyway (this was in the pre-pandemic days, when travel was an ordinary affair), and already made arrangements with a friendly cat-sitter who knew our brood well. So we said yes, we'd be there. She emailed us a remarkable document, a miraculous Manual for the Dog Neophyte, which allayed some of my concerns.

Two of the dogs, an elderly fellow we dubbed The Digger and a brisk, alert, queenly creature we named The Commander, formed a meet-and-greet party at the gate of the cottage when we arrived. And there, under the dining table, suffering paroxysms of shyness, in full mourning for her owners who had left the previous day, her tail lying morosely on the floor, eyes watching nervously as we took possession of her home, was Piku.

On that first day, I worried about her. She sidled away when my husband approached, apparently terrified by his beard. The housekeeper, the neighbours, a random driver walking past, all informed us in hushed tones that the other two dogs didn't mind being left on their own, but Piku was special. Could we please tell them if we had to go out without the dogs? It seemed that Piku, who'd been discovered by my writer friend as a brave, forlorn pup trotting along on an empty hill road, had abandonment issues.

I crawled under the dining table and tried to make friends with her, hoping the same tone that worked on cats would also be appropriate for canines. Piku just buried her head deeper in her fur and sighed heavily, shrinking away from me.

It could not be helped. The other two seemed comfortable with us but, as I told my husband that night, we would have to accept that Piku was a shy creature, and hope that feeding her and taking her on walks was sufficient. The owls hooted outside, the shadows of the mountains guarded us, the air smelt of tree bark and moss.

I woke up at three in the morning, cold because someone had stolen the razai. Two liquid brown eyes gazed at me from the pillow, and a fat tail thumped the mattress tentatively. The Miraculous Manual clearly stated that the Digger was not allowed on the bed— he, as we would discover, sniffed out the smelliest dead creatures, the slimiest of mud puddles, and rolled in all of it if you didn't catch him in time—but was silent on the subject of Piku's sleeping habits. 'Piku, are you sure this is allowed—' I began. In response she laid her beautiful head against mine, her nose pressed into my cheek, and placed her paw in my hand. I melted. Besides, she was warmer than a hot-water bottle, give or take the odd flea.

A few hours later, we were woken up by the Piku Dance, a hip-waggling, tail-thumping samba of pure joyousness. In my memory, that week stretches long and golden, punctuated by rousing walks up and down the hills, deep into the still forests; the dogs disappearing to chase monkeys they never actually managed to catch, hurling good-natured insults at other packs of dogs and quietening down at twilight, the 'leopard hour', when everyone hurries home and all animals go inside, and the hills become the realm of the hunter.

My first impression of Piku changed rapidly. She was no shy, quivering creature after all. She had friends among the local dogs, was an accomplished stealer of roast chicken legs, an indefatigable explorer, a loyal friend when I went for longer walks on my own, a bold growler at leopards who passed by on the opposite hill at night—and a terrible flirt, winning my husband over with vulgar coquetry and sighs that said no one could possibly be a better scratcher of bellies or ears than he. At night, she grew winsome and tender. She jumped in a mud puddle and when I told her off, she pretended to be deeply hurt, shocked at my sternness. When I tried to make up with soft words, she gave me a look of bright cunning and jumped in the puddle a second time, soaking herself and us with oceans of mud. By the end of the week, I was desperately in love.

We parted sadly. I crept out of the cottage and drove away, feeling like a criminal. Piku could not believe that, having got on so well, I would leave her. She watched us from the window, the reproach and accusation in her eyes so acute that the first thing I did when I reached Delhi was to call, anxious, guilty, hoping she was all right. 'Piku?' my friend said. 'She's fine, she went for a long walk today.' I chalked up acting to the long list of Piku's skills as my friend said, 'You know, she's quite the heart-stealer.'

The cats lie around in soft heaps in the Delhi heat. Our oldest is now so frail that we are unlikely to take long trips to the mountains for a while, even after the pandemic dies down and the lockdowns end. But from time to time, I think back to that summer week, the forests, the hills, the dogs—and it brings back such joy.

The only dog I've ever had was a borrowed dog, but the place she's made for herself in my heart is solid and permanent. And the cats, curled up at my feet, grow quiet when I tell them the

Thousand and One Tales of Piku. They are still a little jealous, but even they love listening to these stories a lot.

After Piku, every stray dog on the streets, hounded by the inevitable dog haters who complain about their barking and their smells, seems different, seems like an individual. Perhaps they too would do a Piku Samba every morning if they found homes, if they knew they were loved and had a permanent place to call their own.

Sir Simba

ASHWIN SANGHI

G roucho Marx famously quipped, 'Outside of a dog, a book is man's best friend. Inside of a dog it's too dark to read.'

Most of my writing happens in the early-morning hours, between five and nine. The house is absolutely quiet and the only two awake are Simba and me. I prepare my morning coffee and settle down in my study to write. Simba lies down by my feet, almost providing a blanket of sorts. So, my take on Groucho: Outside of a book, a dog is indeed man's best friend.

Simba is now three years old, but I still remember the frightened puppy who arrived in a crate after a long flight from Guwahati to Mumbai via Delhi. Simba had been in the oxygenated cargo hold for around seven hours. When I gently lifted him out of his crate in the cargo section of the airport, he was trembling. I held him close to my chest so that my heartbeat would comfort him; he fell asleep during the car ride home. I looked at his adorable face and knew that I was in love.

No one awaits my return home the way Simba does. He's a one-member reception committee who makes me feel I'm the most important person to have ever walked this earth. I often joke with my family that my entry into and exit from the house would be utterly inconsequential without Simba. The most incredible quality about him is that he finds every quality about me incredible. He does wonders for my self-esteem! I wish I could actually live up to the image that Simba has of me.

Simba is wise beyond his years. Mostly he just knows what is going through my mind. When I'm writing, there are times when I'm stuck on a particular word or sentence and he'll put his head on my lap. That brief diversion is enough to get the words flowing once again. Of course, that passing moment of adoration results in dog hair all over my navy-blue sleepwear. But it's a small price to pay.

Every Friday evening I pour myself a generous single malt and light a cigar. Simba has now become part of that ritual—he chews on a bone while I smoke my cigar. Just in front of my easy chair there is a coffee table. Sir Simba, as I often call him, will climb on to it and sit there, on his 'throne', so that ordinary humans like us may admire him.

No words are spoken between us; Simba rarely ever barks (except during his weekly bath). But it is this absence of words that makes our communication that much stronger. I wish I could replicate this strategy with some of the human relationships in my life! Simba speaks to me and I listen; I speak to him and he listens. As someone famously said, he is not my whole life but his presence makes my life whole.

There are days when there is a lot of activity. I'm constantly switching between phone calls, webinars, workouts and writing. My location within the house also frequently changes from the bedroom to the living room, the study, the terrace. The only creature who is actually curious and wishes to be included in everything is Simba. I usually drop in for a cup of tea with my parents in the morning, once I'm done with my writing for the day. Simba follows me into their living room as though he's my tail. Often, my mother will greet him first with a 'good morning' before even acknowledging my presence. Serves me right for thinking that Simba's adoration of me is a sign of my importance!

Sometimes I look at him, lying on the floor, lost in some doggy dream that is making him twitch or yelp—it's almost as though he is entirely in that moment. Why can't we humans ever enjoy the simple things so completely? Why can't we simply be? We always seem to be caught in the past or the future, but never in the present. That's the greatest lesson I've learnt from Simba. To my mind, Simba is the most fantastic Zen master ever. Always in the moment. And you know what? When I cuddle, pet and scratch him, I'm in the moment too.

The Canine Commandments

CYRUS BROACHA

Dogs. From the Latin *dogustus*. The Greek *dogander*. The Gujarati *kuttro*. What a group! As far as I'm concerned, dogs are in the Top Three. Alongside wolves and the Beatles.

My name is Cyrus, named after the great king of Anshan, himself a huge lover of dogs. But rather than the word 'lover', which has too many connotations—some natural, some unnatural, but very few allowed by law—I prefer the word 'admirer'. I'm what dogs like to call a 'dog fan', an admirer of dogs.

My earliest recollection of one of these canine wonders is a three-month-old German Shepherd named Caesar. Yes, the Eighties was a time when all middle-class Indians named their dogs Caesar. My dad's friend Srichand had to travel outside the country for a few days, and left Caesar with us for that time.

Folks, I wasn't a deprived child. At 91 kilos and just short of five feet eight inches today, I think the proof is in the pudding. (Literally. I never looked a pudding in the eye and walked away.) As a kid, I had everything. Bows and arrows, an air rifle, a cricket bat, a tennis racquet, a frisbee, Pamela Anderson videos … but nothing came close to hanging out day and night with a puppy. Although, I must say, Pamela Anderson ran Caesar close. When Srichand took him back after four days, I cried for seven days straight. Bear in mind, as a five-year-old, when my parents left me for a weekend with my grandmom, I cried for twenty minutes. And honestly, three of those minutes were more about wiping the nose.

Anyway, to cut to the chase, or in doggie lingo, to the ball, I'm a dog fan for life. And, for the dog people of the world, I have put together my 'Four Commandments'. Of things you must not do. Would have gone with ten, but in today's world, that would be taking up too much of your time, and seven times more of your doggie's time.

Dog people, this is for you:

1. *Thou shalt not love only thine own dog.*
No selective dog-loving. Or only dogs that are 'famous breeds'. Don't make me go all civil rights on your glutes. And don't you dare wag your tail and look at me like I'm a giant biscuit, filled with cream. I've been called worse. To like one dog and not another, based on breed, economic conditions, housing, height, weight or hygiene is simply dog racism. For god's sake, treat dogs better than you treat people. In fact, think of the famous tennis term—it best explains the relation with dogs: Love All. Having said that, it's not completely beyond the pale to casually mention that your Saluki is faster than Rajesh's Pomeranian. I mean that's just a fact, not actual racism.

2. *Walk thine own dog.*
This is my pet peeve. Middle-class India is rife with dogs who aren't looked after by the owners. Amongst the notable crimes against

the canine fraternity, not walking your dog yourself ranks above manslaughter, and just below genocide. During the lockdown of 2020, I saw enough neighbours still not walking their dogs. So, you won't walk him even if you have nothing to do? That's the value you place on (apply suitable French accent here) Monsieur Doggie? I once had a neighbour—let's call him Mohan—who'd give his old Cocker Spaniel to an even older, infirm man to walk. Both looked like they were on their last legs. Which, of course, is still better in the dog's case, 'cause he has four. Dog people, I cannot stress this enough: Walk the doggie, feed the doggie, groom the doggie yourself! Or will away your house, property and money to your domestic worker, and stay in your room (which I'm assuming has Wi-Fi).

3. *Thou shalt not give thine doggy exotic names.*
Especially if they are going to be looked after by and kept with the paid workers of the house. Which is an extension of the previous malady. (Just to be clear, grandparents and spouses are unpaid workers; children are neither paid, nor do they work.) I once knew a paid worker who walked a jolly Labrador, who for some reason he called GS, at the Oval Maidan. One day the lazy owner actually showed up. Turned out GS was christened Zeus. God of gods. Alexander becomes Ogander; Steel turns out to be Estelle. If the doggie is to be cared for by the worker, the worker must be allowed to choose the name. And we all know that India needs some more names other than 'Kalu', 'Julie', 'Tommy', 'Moti' and 'Biscuit'.

4. *Thou shalt not hate a dog.*
Dog haters! They walk amongst us. The embodiment of evil. In my mature view, two things stand out: (a) they are horrible, (b) they suck. Their list of hateful behaviour includes:

(i) Pulling their children away from dogs in a theatrical manner.

(ii) Saying, 'Eh, hold your dog.' Which means they think you are the local sociopath who purposely leaves his over-aggressive Dachshund in the lane to kill all the overweight people around.

(iii) Inviting you over, but not your dog(s). That's just plain poor etiquette.

Of course, people who are actually scared of dogs are not to be put in this category; only the soulless, disconnected, unempathetic, intellectually and aesthetically challenged empty shells of human beings that we dog people encounter from time to time.

So, the obvious question is: Should we kill them? My answer is, 'Yes.' But apparently that is a stand not supported by the government.

So, fellow dog fans, I leave you with my Four Canine Commandments. These have, believe you me, come straight from the dog's mouth. If we come close to realizing this Utopian ideal, then maybe one day, in our lifetime, 'Every dog will have his day.'

Dog people, we who shall ferociously attack the dog haters salute you. Woof woof!

Soul Dogs

MANJULA NARAYAN

Every morning I take three rounds of the fields-fast-transforming-into-buildings sites behind my house. The first round is with Kondhi, the eight-month-old black satin pupper, who has inherited her mother's white chest tuft; the second is with Biskut, her blond sibling, who has decided that he is the man-dog of the family and must protect all of us from the depredations of every sad neighbourhood mutt; the third is with ten-year-old mummy, Kuro, part Spitz, part desi, part Bhutia, part Labrador and full beloved bitch.

Until two months ago, we all set out on our morning walk together. However, that ended the day Biskut and Kondhi leapt over a wall to attack Brown Soxy, the gully dog who had been hurling invectives at them since the day they first stepped out of the house. I lay sprawled on the ground with Kuro wailing beside me after attempting unsuccessfully to haul her fat body over the wall to join in battle. No more walks en doggy famille after that.

Which is a bit sad because we've had some great walks. Like the time right at the start of the lockdown, when we wandered through the silent fields following a magnificent peacock and his harem until they slipped into a marigold plantation. Or the time we gaped at the family of nilgai that had wandered down from whatever is left of the Aravallis, the huge grey bull fixing us with a stern eye while the calves nibbled on the leaves of the thorny kikar with their mother. Even the normally rambunctious Biskut knew not to bark at that giant father beast; we just stood there in silence, staring at those 'blue cows' in wonder.

These days our walks are more sedate. Kondhi stops to chat with Bogo, the neighbour's four-month-old pup named after our overgrown bougainvillea patch where she was found. Biskut gives Spike, the area's dominant desi, the evil eye when he attempts to get too close, which he does every day. Kuro greets her friend Spotty by peeing copiously next to her; Spotty is always honoured. Occasionally, we meet Sol, the white Pitbull rescued from a breeder, and sweet Emma, a cheerful girl Pitbull who's had a happier life. There's also stray Striata, who bows low as soon as Kuro appears, and the two elderly Golden Retriever brothers who would doff their caps at Kondhi, if they wore them, as they walk past.

As you can see, I'm very clued in to the social lives of the dogs who share my home. In fact, I'm more clued in to their social lives than my own, which is now practically non-existent, unless you include the girl at the store where I stock up on dogfood, and the vet.

Even the late great Bejan Daruwalla couldn't have predicted this canine turn in my life. I only adopted Kuro because my kids were pestering me for a dog. I liked dogs but had never had one before; my childhood was spent with cats. So I didn't know what to expect. Or maybe I expected a cat who barked. Kuro certainly leapt right into my arms like a cat the first time we met. And that decided the matter. She was four months old, hyperactive and traumatized from having been abandoned. But she settled in pretty quickly and we soon learnt to live with her eccentricities, like barking at dogs twice her size (and scaring them too!) and squiggling her eyebrows to send telepathic messages so we knew exactly what she wanted from us. She taught me that dogs have memories and deep feelings and a sense of humour; and an unerring talent to pick out the one rotten bastard in a crowd who wished me ill. You know that Bill Murray quote? 'I'm suspicious of people who don't like dogs, but I trust a dog when it doesn't like a person.' It is true.

Living with Kuro also made me think about religion, about the place of animals in the Scheme of Things, and about the souls of dogs. On a 2014 trip to Ladakh, I was struck by something the twelfth Gyalwang Drukpa said about the violent dogs rounded up from Leh and rehomed in an animal shelter in the mountains: 'There's something about the karma of these dogs that they behave the way they do.' And indeed the huge curs that snarled at us were nothing like the sweet, friendly giants you see ambling around the city.

Until Kuro's arrival, I had considered myself a run-of-the-mill rationalist–agnostic. Ideas like predestination and karma are apt to irritate rationalists, and dog karma(!) has a particularly cutesy vibe that sets it firmly in the 'not to be taken seriously' box. But some things are just meant to be. As I got to know my crazy dog—she even attempted to speak, yelling (I kid you not) 'Mamma' when she wanted my attention—I began to think more deeply about interspecies friendship, about humankind's capacity for cruelty, and about animal rights.

Kuro also taught me to strive to live without filters. You'll never meet a dog who says one thing when she actually means another. Dogs are totally WYSIWYG creatures. It's a quality that I, a scheming, duplicitous human, attempt to emulate. And while I rarely succeed, it is nice to know that there are other, more honest ways of being. Kuro also made me think of how companion animals profoundly affect our sense of well-being, and how our dogs can literally save our lives—taking care of a beloved dependent fellow creature can save an individual from the hopelessness and inward focus that is only steps away from deep depression and grievous self-harm.

I mean, imagine this scenario:

X wakes up, stares at the ceiling and wonders about the point of it all. 'Maybe I should kill myself, end this purposelessness,' he murmurs, as he fashions his bedsheet into a rope to string himself up.

Now imagine this one:

X wakes up. Before he can collect his thoughts, Pluto sticks his wet nose in his face. 'Six in the morning, time for walkies,' he says, tugging at X's pyjamas.

It's really difficult to kill yourself with such an insistent goofball around.

I have three of these. Biskut sleeps next to my bed—on the floor right now because he joyfully destroyed the dream mattress on which he once sprawled—and is in charge of waking me up at daylight. Kondhi is the family love sponge. And Kuro has helped me arrive at a version of the karma theory that has me wishing to be reborn as a pet dog in a kind family that adores me.

I've never understood those who say animals have no souls. My dogs do have souls and it's been my good karma—not so much theirs—that they've come into my life to make me a happier, more honest person.

The Dogs of Marine Drive

SOONI TARAPOREVALA

Post-lockdown, I've been accompanying my father on his daily evening walks. I completely fell in love with the Indies of Marine Drive. They own the place. They're either snoozing, sometimes right in the middle of the pavement; or sitting up surveying it all—their legs regally crossed; or snuggling up to strangers.

I used to wonder how they looked so well fed. One evening I discovered that a group of women arrange to feed some thirty to forty dogs on Marine Drive every day; in addition, they have also got them spayed.

I think Tiger, Sweety, Chumpy, June, Hopscotch, Speedy, Scotch and April must be the happiest strays in the city.

My Life as a Plebeian
Mother to an Aristocrat
MEENAKSHI
ALIMCHANDANI

E ver since I can remember, dogs have been part of my emotional
landscape. I am completely and totally besotted with them.
Their love is steadfast, unreserved and genuine; it's wholehearted, it's
uncritical and so accommodating. Even if I look like a witch on a bad
hair day it doesn't matter to them. Those eyes brimming with love,
that long tail swishing away, those clickety-clack nails are so adorable.

I grew up with dogs who were of all breeds, sizes and
temperaments. These canine buddies of mine included Pixie, a
very small but tenacious Dachshund who was rather discerning in
perceiving the difference between a member of the armed forces and
a civilian; he was known to snarl rather menacingly at non-defence
personnel. We had a succession of dogs. Everyone knew that they
could palm off any puppy or grown dog to me. I was a mistress of the
sneak-a-dog-in strategy. My dog-loving yet long-suffering mother was
resigned to this. We always had an inside dog who was pedigreed,

who I called the 'boarder', and a mutt of dubious origins who was in the compound and was the 'day scholar'. I named one of these 'mixed' varieties Jijaji after he managed to impregnate our lovely delicate Honey.

After I got married and was travelling the world with my marine engineer husband, our peripatetic life didn't allow me to keep a dog, as it would have been unfair to the dog. But my heart didn't stop yearning for a canine companion. This wish was fulfilled when we settled in Pune. Ace, a yellow Lab, became a much-loved member of our family. He chewed through everything, including my husband's credit card. Then the joys of the great white north beckoned, and we immigrated to Canada. My elder daughter found Ace a very loving home where he was treated like a maharaja.

It was rather challenging to move to a new country and a new way of life, with two girls. There was no way we could also include a pet in our rather chaotic home. However, we were more than willing to dog-sit for friends or family who were travelling.

Many moons later, when we were well settled in our new lives as Canadians, we gave in to our yearning to be dog owners again.

My younger daughter, Hashmita, after doing a tremendous amount of research, decided that the best breed that would be an ideal fit for our lifestyle would be a retired racing Greyhound. I kept confusing the Greyhound with the Great Dane and kept saying that it was too large a breed to walk in the icy winter. Actually, the only Greyhound I had ever seen was painted on the side of a bus. Greyhounds have never been part of the popular culture or film and media stars like say Dalmatians or St Bernards.

In spite of our misgivings and doubts we decided to adopt a Greyhound. Hashmita's research was spot on about how very laid-back and low-maintenance this breed is. Greyhounds are great housemates. They require minimal grooming, and their exercise needs are low to moderate for a dog their size. They are compliant and have a personality that helps them adapt quickly to a new lifestyle. Most Greyhounds are naturally well mannered and sensitive. Plus, they are intelligent and respond well to the right training methods.

One of the misconceptions about Greyhounds is that they are aggressive dogs, because most people have only seen photos of Greyhounds racing, with muzzles covering their faces. Outside of the racetrack, however, Greyhounds are usually quiet, gentle, docile and compliant. If you're looking for a watchdog, definitely choose another breed. Greyhounds blend well into families, and most love the company of other dogs.

Another myth about Greyhounds is that they need lots of room to run, and constant exercise. But Greyhounds aren't marathon runners; they're sprinters. At the track, they only race once or twice a week. In homes, they romp for short bursts and then turn back into couch potatoes. While a fenced yard is best, a daily walk or two and a chance to run in a field from time to time is sufficient for them.

Greyhounds are very clean. Their coat is so light and short that grooming is a breeze. They shed only slightly. Many Greyhounds groom and clean themselves, much like cats do. Their coats aren't oily, so they aren't as prone to doggy odour as some breeds are. They're also healthy and are free of many of the inherited ailments that plague other breeds. For example, hip dysplasia is virtually unheard of among Greyhounds. Their average life expectancy is longer than that of most large breeds: twelve years or more.

And Greyhounds are fun.

So it was decided: We were going to be the human family to an aristocratic creature with DNA going back centuries! We were going to be in exalted company!

The modern Greyhound is strikingly similar in appearance to an ancient breed of sighthounds that goes back thousands of years; dogs very similar to Greyhounds appear in temple drawings from 6,000 BCE in the city of Catalhoyuk in present-day Turkey. In ancient Egypt, the ancestors of modern Greyhounds were used in hunting and kept as companions. In Greece, Odysseus's faithful dog Argos is described as a sighthound. The Greyhound is also the only dog breed mentioned by name in the Bible (the King James version).

The unique and highly prized abilities of Greyhounds help explain why they have changed very little in thousands of years. But Greyhounds nearly became extinct during times of famine in the Middle Ages in England. They were saved by clergymen who protected them and bred them for their nobility. From this point on, they came to be considered the dogs of the aristocracy. Only an aristocrat could own Greyhounds; any commoner caught owning a Greyhound would be severely punished. It became common to say, 'You can tell a gentleman by his horses and his Greyhounds.' They remained a familiar sight among the nobility of England in the nineteenth century. Greyhounds were imported into America in large numbers from Ireland and England in the mid-1800s to rid Midwest farms of an epidemic of jackrabbits; they were also used to hunt down coyotes who were killing livestock. They became familiar sights on farms and ranches. Then, the Americans discovered that Greyhounds could also be a source of sport. Sadly, Greyhound racing has since become one of the most popular spectator sports in America.

For Greyhound puppies bound for the racetrack, training starts in earnest when they are six months old; training with a drag lure begins at about ten months. By the time the pups are eighteen months old, they are sent to the track. Only the winners survive. The pups are given six chances to finish in the top four in their maiden race. If they do not, they are retired—put up for adoption, or euthanized.

There are a number of not-for-profit adoption groups all over Canada who liaise with racetracks in the US to save the lives of these beautiful dogs and transport them to Canada by road. These volunteer organizations work tirelessly to find foster homes and then forever homes for these new Canadians.

Hashmita applied to one such agency and had to prove her commitment to adoption by filling in a detailed questionnaire and paying a deposit. We were all so excited when she received a message saying she had fulfilled all the criteria and had been approved to be a 'fur mummy'. So off we all went to choose the dog, in a town that was located in rural Ontario. Soon we reached Ingersoll and located the barn where the beautiful creatures were living.

When Hashmita saw Manny, it was love at first sight. There were two other dogs that had been shortlisted for her. However, it was Manny who won her heart and ours too! He was this gorgeous two-year-old brown brindle with the most adorable brown eyes. As soon as the paperwork was completed and the nominal fee paid, we were on our way home, having coaxed Manny into the car.

When he first met Hashmita, Manny was wary of her. Racing Greyhounds are like children who have been in a boarding house all their lives. It's a very regimented and institutionalized life. They are treated with a lot of love by their trainers but have no family contact. They are also used to living in a crate in a kennel with their fellow athletes. When we reached home Manny was very scared and didn't want to enter the house. He didn't know about homes. Or these strange humans who had come into his orbit.

He didn't know that he was about to start a new life.

With infinite patience and compassion, Hashmita started training him to live in a home. Manny was petrified of everything, as he had never encountered things like a noisy vacuum cleaner before. Or large glass doors. Or stairs. She taught him to climb the stairs. We had crated him in the first few days for his own safety. But soon he was fine and became rather bold. He did, however, have a lot of separation anxiety in the first few weeks. He would bark relentlessly at night, till I moved myself downstairs to sleep on the couch. It took Hashmita and me three months to fully settle him down. And after those initial hiccups he was the most darling dog with the most endearing personality. He started to like going for walks. At first, walks were scary as well, since he had never been on one before. He had never seen parks. Or playgrounds, or bridges, or other people walking their dogs, which for him were the scariest of all.

Manny turned out to be rather social and would stand and stare at other walkers till they came and patted him. He loved the car and would wait impatiently to join whoever was going out. He became a seasoned traveller and enjoyed the car journey between Montreal and Toronto with his mummy. Even my husband who claimed not to like dogs was caught on many occasions stealthily stroking him. Our elder daughter, Priyanka, claimed that he was the best dog ever. Me, I was smitten! Our entire home felt complete now.

Manny was adorable and so sweet-natured. Of course, he did crazy things sometimes like jump on my bed and rip the comforter, but it didn't matter. Even when he drooled all over my light biscuit-coloured formal couch in his deep Greyhound slumber, all was forgiven.

Despite our being extremely cautious about securing the front door and the back gates because of Manny wanting to run out and explore the world, he ran out one morning after our neighbours' son, who had come into our backyard and left the gate open. We went crazy and combed the entire neighbourhood, but couldn't find him. Both Hashmita and I were hysterical with fear and panicking. Luckily Manny was microchipped and was eventually found by Mississauga animal services, flopped on someone's front lawn ten kilometres away from our home. He had followed his Greyhound instincts and decided he was born to run. We were so grateful that he was unhurt.

Manny's presence saw Hashmita through a very challenging time in her life. He was her comfort and her lodestar, her best friend.

We changed Manny's food a couple of times as he was unable to digest it and kept having stomach issues. Following the vet's advice, Manny was put on a grain-free kibble diet; little did we know that this grain-free diet was going to be the cause of a tragedy. Manny kept losing his appetite and then his weight. He just would not eat now regardless of whatever we got him, including McDonald's burgers; it was of no avail. He finally reached the stage where we were hand-feeding him. Multiple visits to the vet too did not help. It was a cold February morning when we took Manny to the vet because he was running a temperature and drinking a lot of water. We had no idea that this was to be his final visit. We were told that he had a heart murmur and that we should take him to the hospital in Oakville, which we did. The diagnosis of the preliminary investigation was that Manny was suffering from an infection in his heart valve and they would try and see what they could do.

After a whole day of sitting there in uncertainty on my own, I was advised that they just could not treat the infection, which had now spread through his body: It was in his kidneys and everywhere. Manny was in a lot of pain and there was no point trying to keep him alive for our selfish reasons. I reached out to Hashmita at work and asked her and Priyanka to come so we could decide what we needed to do. It was the hardest decision we ever made as a family— to put this beloved family member down. Our hearts were breaking and we had tears streaming down our cheeks. My husband was in Copenhagen on work and we reached out to him to ask what we should do, hoping he would have an answer for us. He too was devastated and said to ask the vets to try and save our beloved, sweet boy. Unfortunately the vets said that even if we kept him on antibiotics it was just going to prolong his agony. As I write this my eyes are brimming with tears.

The three of us hugged each other and said a silent prayer, and let the vets enable our boy to frolic across the rainbow bridge. We were plunged into an abyss of mourning and despair. I was deeply concerned about how Hashmita would handle this tragedy. It took her a long time to process the grief. I too was completely broken as I used to work from home and Manny was my constant companion. I kept talking to him, only to realize that he wasn't jumping around me any more. I just didn't want to sit at home. Even with time the hurt didn't go away and I had to really focus on thinking that we had made a decision that was in Manny's best interests. My friends and family rallied around me and gave a lot of support.

After Manny passed, I reached a stage where I was hesitant about getting another dog. It was a kind of mental self-defence to protect myself and my heart from the grief of losing another friend.

But as time went on and I was getting better, my desperation to be around Greyhounds returned. I would go to Greyhound meetups, see a Greyhound on the street or in the park and go chasing after them just to pat them and talk to them. I started going to dog fests and pet expos. Finally my heart decided it was time to love again. Then came the next step of persuading my reluctant husband, who gave in to my entreaties in a weak moment.

One Sunday afternoon I took off to yet another pet expo and met up with a Greyhound-adoption group that I hadn't heard of before as they were rather low-profile. I came home and filled up their application. That very afternoon I got an email from the lady in charge, who asked if I was ready to adopt a Houndie in the very near future. My answer was: but of course! The reason that she had approved me for this fast-track adoption was that we fulfilled all the criteria that this particular girl required: a house with a fenced-in yard located in a quiet street with no cats and other dogs, and empty-nester parents with no young children. A few days later, I was on a commuter train to the very east end of Toronto to see this beauty. She was being fostered by a loving family.

EeVee had come with a few other Greyhounds from the racetrack in Alabama to Ohio, from where the Canadian adoption agency had brought her across the border to Toronto. She had been adopted by two young women who were living in a rent-controlled apartment on a very noisy street; they had issues with her peeing in the elevator and were also unable to cope with her growing anxiety issues.

They were sensible enough to return her to the adoption group. The lady in charge had found her another foster home that already had a Greyhound, to settle her in.

It was love at first sight for me and there was no way I could resist those melting chocolate-coloured eyes. She was so beautiful. Her foster mummy drove her from one end of the city to the other, to our house, to drop her off and settle her in.

Due to all the changes of homes EeVee had faced a lot of trauma, and she was a quivering bundle of nerves. Her tail was perpetually between her legs. She wouldn't get out of her crate. She couldn't handle noise and even a car backfiring would have her shaking. For some reason being around kids used to really upset her. She hated being out for a walk. Everything would spook her.

I had to be really patient with her because of these challenges. A lot of gentle persuasion and a lot of treats truly helped. It took two and a half years to get my little girl to be where she is now. She's still shy but not a Nervous Nellie like she used to be. In fact she's a different dog now. Of course we have to look after her and try to accommodate the issues she does have.

EeVee has become an integral part of our lives now and has taken over an entire couch in our family room.

Believe me, I would not have mentally survived the extended lockdown that Canada had implemented without EeVee. She's my biggest stress buster! Especially in the long and cold winters, she's my motivation to get out and go for a walk even if it's minus 20 degrees. We both bundle up, and off we go.

I feel sometimes like I am a mother to a celebrity. People stop us on the street and want to interact with the aristocratic resident of our neighbourhood.

EeVee truly is my heart dog. Her karma is really bound to mine. I can't even express how deep my love for her is.

You too might want to open your hearts and homes to a rescue dog; there are so many loving hearts with waggy tails who need your love and will reciprocate it tenfold.

A Conversation with Doginder

PRERNA SINGH BINDRA

I am often asked, mainly by 'non-dog' people, if I talk to dogs. But of course. In fact, it comes so naturally that I wasn't aware that I do it, or that it is anything out of the ordinary. It is just the way things are (and should be).

I talked to Doginder all the time. What's more, he listened and understood, which is more than I can say for most people. Doginder was multilingual. My brother and I spoke to him in Hinglish, with a healthy dose of Punjabi thrown in. The help preferred to pour out her troubles in her native tongue, Bengali. When our friend Geeta came over, she introduced him to both Tamil and Gujarati, while a wise septuagenarian he had befriended in Uttarakhand talked to him with deep respect in chaste Kumaoni.

Doginder responded. He did not speak 'people', but if you were attuned, and had the senses, and the sensitivity, to observe and listen, you understood his language. You could communicate, as you can with most animals who we live with (and some that we don't), if only we open our minds and hearts, and listen.

Dogs, of course, are usually silent (unless you count barks) through conversations. They do not 'talk' like humans do, but they nonetheless understand, and communicate. MRI studies reveal that dogs distinguish familiar words, they catch intonations, read body language, and process the emotional content of words. They are in tune with our emotions and respond accordingly. Science establishes that non-human animals—from dogs and elephants to bats and whales—possess agency and emotions, and live deeply communicative lives.

But this piece is not about that; it is about my discussions with Doginder.

So what did we talk about? Anything and everything. Some were casual no-answer-expected questions, like if I had been out for the day I would go: 'So, what did my good boy do today?' If I were home, I might just share resolves and confidences with him: 'Okay, Doginder, I must get off Twitter now,' or, 'I really need to do something about this guy. He is pissing me off.' Or silly rhymes only appreciated by the dog: 'Time to eat, be ready for a treeeatt.' Sometimes I would refer to earlier reprimands: 'Now look, Doginder, I have told you before: Eating stuff off the street is a big NO!'

I would tell him I love him, and if he knew how very much I love him.

My dialogues with Doginder were casual, deep, profound, petulant, fun and most of all brimming with love and caring, just like they would be with anyone you share a deep bond with.

To understand our conversations, it is important to know where Doginder came from, and what he came to be—the heartbeat of our family, and its most beloved member.

Doginder came to us in October 2008, a scrawny, sickly creature. Maggots oozed out of his festering wound and there were days he couldn't get up as he suffered from acute hip dysplasia. But it was the emotional scars that cut deep. His tail was perennially tucked between his legs, his eyes listless and petrified. He stayed curled up in some dark corner as though wanting to be invisible, and when I lifted my hand to pet him, he cowered. Not having known love, he probably expected a beating. Doginder had been dumped, thrown from a car, by a piece of !@%*. I will not write (it's unprintable) what I wish upon that disgusting excuse of a human being—and thousands of others who think of dogs not as family but as disposable items, dumped if found inconvenient.

Doginder had been abandoned.

I could not imagine the horrors of his earlier life, all I knew was they must be erased.

Dealt with patience and showered with love, Doginder healed. His confidence grew: He shed his abject slouch and walked straight. The dull, hopeless look in his eyes disappeared; they now shone. His tail beat constantly in a joyful rhythm, reaching dizzy heights that involved the posterior in case of a reunion—any separation beyond five minutes qualified—with loved ones. He would be beside himself with joy and break into his patented 'chappal' dance—grabbing the nearest slipper or shoe, and gyrating with abandon. A performance infused with little grace, but much gusto.

Doginder hated to be left alone. While he was not benevolent towards his fellow beings—all four-legged creatures were perceived as competition—he loved the human race, even though he had been betrayed by one specimen. He always positioned himself in a way so that we were in his line of vision. It was as though he feared that we would slip away, go away from him. That we would go, and not come back. His life had a single focus, and—despite being a Labrador—it was not food; it was to be with us, wherever we were. In the bedroom, the garden, the car, the loo, even the vet's—it didn't matter. As long as we were there, he would have stood with us, tail thrumming and flying, at peace with the world.

The following is an extract of a discussion we had many times over. Me trying—and failing—to convince him that he did not need to follow me everywhere, all the time. Like most of our conversations, this too went astray ...

ME: Doginder, we need to talk.

DOGINDER (*immediately up and dancing, grabbing nearest chappal in his mouth, tail in a spin, rump twirling, jumping up-down-up as much as his impaired hipbones, backbones, etc., allow*) ...

ME: Doginder, my dearest, relax, relax. All I said is I want to talk.

DOGINDER: Yes. YES! (*wag, wag, WAG*) Isn't that awesome? Finally, I am getting some attention. FINALLY.

ME: Now, my friend. Sit. Take a deep breath. I have some news for you: You don't qualify as a neglected child. Far from it. We have just come back from a stroll, before which I fed you, before which I brushed you, before which ...

DOGINDER (*hastily interrupting*): Can we agree to disagree? That was very long back. TEN minutes ago. Maybe even longer. Since then you have been staring at the stupid screen on your desk. Not that I mind, of course, you won't hear me complaining, no sir. Thing is, I worry, it's not healthy—this preoccupation with the computer.

ME: I am sure. I guess rubbing your tummy 24x7 is advised for my good health.

DOGINDER: I always knew you were intelligent. So, you must know that having a dog—and paying attention to him ALL the time—is associated with a decreased risk of cardiovascular disease. In other words, dogs have a calming effect on you.

ME: Yes ... Doctor Dog.

DOGINDER: Why are you mocking? It's not a ploy to get attention (have I ever asked for it?). This is science—there is even a report from Harvard Medical School. Why are you disbelieving? Don't you have faith in science, like some politicians I will not mention. Huh? Huh? Tell me, this is important and could decide the future of our relationship.

ME: Okay, okay. Don't be a drama king. Don't get agitated. Don't change the subject.

DOGINDER: That's your problem. Always telling me what to do. But at least we are talking, and that's the important thing. Communication is great for bonding, you know.

ME: ... Which brings me to back to the fact that we need to talk.

DOGINDER (up on his feet, chappal in mouth, hind spinning giddily): We ALWAYS need to talk. But, hey, if this is going to be a long conversation, gimme a minute to position myself in front of the AC.

ME: ...

DOGINDER: Why you rolling your eyes? I have not become less tolerant of the heat; the planet is getting hotter. Global warming, you know.

ME: I didn't know, but thanks to you, now I do. Doginder, now that you have your butt in the AC, which is causing the global warming, can we move on ... and talk—no, no, don't you get up ...

DOGINDER: Not get-upping. If you know me at all, you should know that I prefer not to unseat myself when in a position of such cool comfort.

ME (*muttering*): Unless I get up. NOOOO. I am NOT getting up.

DOGINDER (*having heaved himself up, flops down again*): Then why you saying it? You know I have a weak heart, and all this talk of 'getting up' is scary. You wanted to talk, right? How can we talk when you get-upping, and going? Huh?

ME: Look at me. Read my lips. I. Am. Not. Getting. Up. I. Am. NOT. Going. Anywhere. I. Am. Only. Two. Inches. From. You.

DOGINDER: Nine inches, but that's okay. Wait: NOT going anywhere? Forever, and ever? This is important. AWESOME. I must dance (*grabbing chappal, and making a move to rise*).

Me: Noooo, please. Actually, that's the entire point of this conversation, if we are ever going to get to it.

DOGINDER: Point? What point? Explain. You tend to meander …

ME: *I* meander?

DOGINDER: I don't see anyone else in the room. It gets difficult for a guy to follow.

ME: Hold it right there. This is what I wanted to speak about.

DOGINDER: What is THIS?

ME: The fact that you follow me everywhere. Even if I pop into the next room to get a book.

DOGINDER: I am not following you. What are you trying to say?

ME: That you don't have to follow me each time I step out of your sight.

DOGINDER: Let's get this straight: You don't want me to come with you?

ME: Not every time I step out to get a book, chotta, or my specs, or to turn off the gas. You don't need to.

DOGINDER: I might not need to, but I want to. I don't see a problem here.

ME: But Dogguu beta, it's just for a few minutes. Why must you get up each time, especially since you have a back problem and hip dysplasia? It must be painful ...

DOGINDER: This is getting complicated. And yes, it is bloody painful, but I STILL like to go with you. What puzzles me is you see it as a problem. Wait, is it that you don't WANT me to come?

ME: Listen, I just pop out, and back in again ... Why do you have to be with me when I step out for a minute for a book, my specs or to go to the loo?

DOGINDER (*eyes doleful, dejected, tearful*): If I am reading this right, you don't want me around. For the record, that hurts. Like hell. You donnn't wannnt me. Also, how do I know you are going to be back in 'two-minutes'? Popping in and out? Huh. You go for a lot of minutes, 10-20-30. Hours also. Even DAYS. Keeping you within my sight is important. What if you go away? What if you don't come back? Is this part of some diabolical plan to escape? TELL ME.

ME: Relax.

DOGINDER (muttering): She drops a bombshell, then asks me to relax. Typical. Now, I have to be on alert always. NO letting up. WAIT, you are getting UP. OHMYDOG.

ME: Since this conversation was going nowhere. And I am only going to the loo.

Doginder: Loo. LOO. Wait, I am coming too, this is something we need to talk about …

Doginder is no longer with us, and I would give my right arm and leg for him to follow me everywhere, even to the loo, even if I step out for half a minute. I still hear his footsteps padding behind me, and wake up at night imagining his eyes seeking mine for reassurance of my presence, of my love. I feel his breath waking me up each morning, his eyes on mine waiting for yet another exciting day of togetherness to begin—and my conversations with him to continue. Doginder has died—and tears well, and flow, as I write this. He will live forever in our hearts. Always cherished, never forgotten.

These are a few pages from Doginder's forthcoming book. We have co-authored it, but since communicating across heaven and earth is problematic, the book will take its own sweet time to hit the shelves. Though Doginder will say it is because I am bone-lazy.

If you want to know more about Doginder, visit here: http://dogindersingh.org/ and help other abandoned dogs like him find their families and lead safer, happier lives.

Shehzada Ozu:
The Postcolonial Pekingese
SARNATH BANERJEE

My name is Ozu. Amma calls me Shehzada.
By now you know the theme of this book, so there's no point in hiding the fact that I am a dog. But I am a dog who speaks grammatically correct English.

I am named Ozu because of my point of view. The older daughter, Pilpil, went to film school for a couple of years (before moving to apparel design). She was inspired by *Tokyo Story*'s cinematography. Where, typical to the director Yasujiro Ozu's style, the entire film was shot from the POV of a small dog.

Plus I am a Pekingese and this household cannot differentiate between Chinese and Japanese.

Initially, I was Pilpil's dog. Now she only needs me for the occasional Instagram post. These days her mood swings are like the English weather. How do I know that? I'll tell you. I binge-watched all the episodes of *Downton Abbey* with Amma and now I know a lot about English weather and grammar.

Amma is a typical south Delhi sethani. On the one hand, she and the ladies of the colony force the guards to swat away any outsiders entering the local park; on the other hand, Pam and I are allowed to deposit our turds anywhere we wish.

Among her friends is Komal aunty, whose Pam is my girlfriend.

Komal aunty is wicked. In the morning the colony fills up with dog walkers. One time, Komal aunty had a slight brush with one. Anger festered inside her for weeks. A month later she went to Cosimo's owner and told him that their dog walker feeds Cosimo GJs and allows him to sniff Rano's bottom. The fellow lost his job.

Amma is casteist and class-conscious. Well, the entire colony is. But Amma has a good heart—plus she is going through some extenuating circumstances.

The household staff is arranged in ranks according to caste. The cook and the SUV driver are Brahmins. The guards, the gardener

and the cleaners are all Kayasths. The jamadarni and the driver of
the Alto are low castes.

Even the dogs of the colony understand class. On the off-
chance, if a door-to-door salesman of hygiene products did manage

to get through the colony gates, the dogs would make a meal out of him.

Every now and then a pizza-delivery guy gets his ass chewed by Rano. We watch from the balconies.

The colony has some of the most beautiful houses in the city—curved gates, oak staircases, bougainvillea-covered facades, gulmohar trees on the driveways, breezy balconies.

But according to Pam the more beautiful the kothi, the nastier the owner. '*Je schöner das hause desto bosër die Bewohner.*'

You guessed it—Pam's a German Shepherd.

Agreed, Amma and I can be slightly right-of-the-centre but let me tell you, we are not hypocritical.

The younger generation goes to America and gets into the Occupy movements and Black Lives Matter, but back home they don't much question the status quo. To friends back in America, they desisplain, 'We provide the staff with social security—after all, no saying what will happen to them if we didn't.' When they're back home they fold back to the values of their parents.

Bloody double standards.

Anyway, I am familiar with the introduction to *The Wretched of the Earth*. It was in Pilpil's luggage that she brought back after her two years at Tisch. So not only am I grammatically correct but I am also a postcolonial dog.

Amma and I are worried about Pilpil's future—she always gets inappropriate boyfriends. Ideally, Amma and I would go for Arora auntie's Arhaan, the steadfast homo-architectus, family-run business and house in C block. He would fit well with Pilpil's artistic persona.

The slightly adipose-rich young man lying on the sofa is Revant, also known as Chengdo. Chengdo is a Snack-o-saurus. Nuts, chips, peanut-butter sandwiches, doughnuts, burgers, KFC, Mars bars. Only Eminem's mouth can move faster than Chengdo's.

Because schools have been closed for months, Chengdo mostly lies on the sofa with his remote control. His only movements are his rapidly moving fingers and an occasional shift of weight as he goes from one laddoo to another.

Chengdo used to like basketball once, but the school coach, 'builder-of-champions' Rajkumar, made him lose his love for the game. Nowadays, he watches his block friends play at the local park while he resignedly awaits the early arrival of type-2 diabetes.

I have frequent play dates with Pam. We get it off in the backyard next to the pump room. True, I am a mere Pekingese and Pam's a German Shepherd. But even Rano knows about my endurance and skill. Amma says I don't pose any risk of knocking anyone up. They took care of that when I was one.

Pilpil has occasionally caught us in mid-act from her window. But I think she was distracted by her own faraway thoughts.

Hey, it is nine already. Time for the big man to come. (Big but no spine.)

Within seconds of him showering and powdering his body and wolfing down his asafoetida-rich fried dinner, he will climb up to the terrace and have an hour-long conversation with some floozy or the other. If validation was fuel, this guy would be a gas-guzzling Contessa.

Amma still does twenty Surya namaskars every morning and she has a hot bod, but this guy has no time to notice.

I think I'm giving away too many family secrets.

'Locker Schwimmend,' says Pam in her low voice. Although it sounds like a feat in civil engineering, what she actually means is that Rano is a loose woman.

Unlike Pam, I was brought to this house soon after I was born. The kids loved me and all. I was after all Pilpil's dog. But in the end, it was Amma, the one who had the most reservations at the start, who took care of me. Although Amma is aspirational and judgemental and can sometimes be nasty to others, she is still my Amma and I love her—and when the time comes, actually not so far from now, I want her to hold my paw.

Alex: His Search for Inclusion

SIAN MORTON

This is the story of Alex, our wonderful dog, and his search for freedom in a world that denies him, and others, the right to live a normal life, and sometimes, the right to live at all.

First, I should get the legal information out of the way. In the UK there is a part of the Dangerous Dogs Act relating to Breed Specific Legislation (BSL)—which bans four breeds: Dogo Argentino, Filo Brasileiro, Japanese Tosa and Pitbull Terrier, plus types thereof. Type is based on appearance and measurements. Alex is a cross-breed and conforms to enough of the characteristics and measurements of a Pitbull, so is considered to be a Pitbull type. Under the Dangerous Dogs Act (DDA) in the UK, you are not allowed to keep any of the dog breeds listed under BSL; if one does, the dog is liable to be seized and potentially destroyed. However, the law allows for these dogs to be exempted and kept if they are certified as 'safe', the potential owner/keeper is considered to be a fit and proper person and the potential home and garden are fully secure, amongst other things. The dog has to be kept under strict regulations and can potentially be re-seized and destroyed if the regulations are not adhered to. At the time of Alex coming to live with us the rules were very slightly different as a legal change came in shortly after his arrival. However, just a few of the rules currently are as follows: exempted dogs have to be muzzled and on a lead at all times in a public place; they have to be neutered, walked by somebody over the age of sixteen, have specific third-party insurance and cannot be away from the registered address for more than thirty days in any one calendar year. They also cannot be rehomed to someone else unless certain stringent circumstances are in place. All of these things make the life of an exempted dog and their owner a true challenge but we love them so we do whatever it takes to keep them safe.

Alex was under a year old and living happily in a home with his young owner. Somebody reported to the police that he was a Pitbull, and so the authorities arrived and seized him from his family.

He was taken to an undisclosed location and the fight for his life began.

At the time I was mourning the loss of two of my beautiful and beloved dogs, Custard and Wonky. Both had died peacefully at a very advanced age. I had been volunteering with an organization called DDA Watch that assists people, and campaigns against the unfairness of the Dangerous Dogs Act. Due to my bereavements I had not been taking calls as these can be upsetting at the best of times. My colleagues dealt with little Alex and the fight his family had to face to get him home. After some time, and after a large amount of money had been spent, Alex was finally exempted and returned home. He was in a pitiful state and the most important thing was for him to become healthy again.

Unfortunately Alex ended up in a difficult situation; he was unable to stay with his owners, and so he needed someone to step in.

I will be honest here, I didn't want him, I really wanted my own dogs back. So I said no. Then I started having dreams about him, where his face interchanged with my darling Custard. And so, however silly it may sound, I thought maybe this was a sign, and I said yes. It was only ever meant to be temporary and we were going to find him a home better suited to him but, like many things in life, that wasn't how it worked out. Let me tell you what happened.

It was the day we were driving halfway up the country to collect Alex from the kennels he was in. We planned the journey meticulously, with stop-offs for toilet breaks, short walks, food and drinks. We had a large crate in the back of the car filled with lovely soft, warm bedding and I packed treats, water, bowls, a collar, a lead and a muzzle. Again and again, I went over the copious lists I had written out—mustn't forget anything, mustn't make a mistake. This was a taster of how our life would become, though little did I know it then.

We arrived at the kennels and my plan to sit outside Alex's kennel so he could get to know us was totally scuppered. The kennel manager wanted me to sign a form and for us to just take him away. Alex was brought out by a lovely kennel girl, who obviously loved him, and released in a secure area. He was bigger than I thought he would be—although not as big as he is now, after all the treats he's been given! He was also jumping up and down. We didn't get any real time to get to know him and, to be honest, I was a bit scared. I had lived a life with two relaxed dogs and this was new to me.

It took some time for Gavin, my husband, to get Alex's muzzle on, but finally we did, and once he was in the car and secure, we headed home. He was not happy, he was quite scared in fact—and he cried at the top of his voice for a long time. We had already abandoned the idea of any stops on the way and headed straight for home. I tried music, talking, no music, humming, whistling—but nothing deterred Alex from singing the song of his people literally for hours. I was quite worried about him and so I thought maybe it would help if I sang too. So I did, and he stopped; I sang again, but this time he didn't stop, so I sang along with him for a while. Then I heard him sigh and lie down in the crate, totally worn out. By now we were stopped in traffic and I saw Gavin glance in the mirror at him. My singing is, quite frankly, dire, and so, even now, it is a standing joke that both Gavin and Alex grimace when I open my mouth to join in with a CD on a long journey. The desire to get me to sleep quickly on a long journey is something they both share!

Finally we got home. We had a cat then, twenty-seven years old and very feisty. We had made the decision to keep Alex downstairs and the cat in our spare room upstairs so that we could introduce them slowly. Sadly we didn't need to do that as Morrison passed of old age before Alex had been home two weeks. On reflection having a grumpy old cat putting him in his place may not have been a good start for Alex either!

I feel very strongly that any animal you are the caregiver for deserves everything you can possibly do to keep them safe and happy, so we did everything that we could for Alex. Gavin put his crate and cosy bed in the kitchen so he would feel safe. I put some water down and we let him find his way around. I just couldn't help myself and so, contrary to what I had been advised, I made a massive fuss of him. He seemed to like it; he wanted to cuddle in to me and I let him. At night I felt terrible as I shut the kitchen door on him; he didn't seem to understand and I thought he would be scared. We soon learnt that he wasn't scared: he just liked to get his own way and be with us!

It took Alex and me some time to bond. It was instant with Gavin: Alex adored him from day one! I admit to having been a teensy bit jealous—after all I am the doggy one in our household. On reflection I think it was because Alex knew exactly who was in charge, but like Gavin, he often likes to let me think I am! I struggled to understand him because he was so very different from Custard, my heart dog. My initial lack of any rules and 'do what you want' attitude came back to haunt me. Alex became hard to be around when I was on my own with him, so we looked for a trainer to help us. The lovely Robert Alleyne made an arrangement to call round.

Rob arrived at the front door and Gavin let him in. While I fussed around Alex, Rob and Gavin studiously ignored him and got on with the business of discussing the situation. We sat down and Rob asked us some questions. Alex was most bemused but clearly interested. Rob took him to the back of the room and settled him down. I was told to sit down at the entrance to the lounge, which I did. I was ever so slightly scared of Rob's ability to control the situation without raising his voice. We chatted for a short while and then Rob said to call Alex to me, which I did, and he came straight over. I asked if I could praise him and Rob said yes. This proved to be a huge mistake, as I went into dog-mum overdrive and became loud and overexcited with my over-the-top praise of what was his, quite frankly, basic response! Rob sounded slightly exasperated when he said, 'Good grief, Sian, anyone would think he rescued Timmy from down a well!' It was a big lesson: Calm it down, Sian, calm it down!

To start with, either Gavin or I walked Alex every day. But my health was getting worse so we decided to employ a dog walker, and this was where Alex's Angels became a huge part of his life. Sam and Lisa ran Bright Skies and we decided to ask them to come and meet him. Alex was smitten from day one, he adored them and we always referred to them as the Angels. If I said the word 'Angels' Alex's tail would give a little wag and he would head towards the door doing the famous head tilt, a sign that he was ready for whatever exciting thing was going to happen next.

I, in my infinite wisdom, went into full instructor mode and delivered my not insubstantial verbal manual on the exemption restrictions for dogs like Alex to the Angels. Gates were placed at every entrance to the hall, including the top of the stairs. Muzzle training was given: how Alex must always wear a collar and harness, how they must never let go of the lead and never take the muzzle off outside, etc. etc. It was never-ending. Sam and Lisa smiled and nodded and stroked Alex and let him lick their faces but they never once looked bored or showed just how tedious it must have been for them. After all these were professionals who knew exactly what they were doing, and Alex obviously loved them. I gave the go-ahead and his wonderful relationship with his Angels began.

The first time I knew for sure, quite early on, that I had made the right choice was when Alex had a fall. He spotted a squirrel and ran around his Angel's legs, pulling her to the ground. Now the natural instinct of anyone would be to drop the lead, but she hung on to it for dear life as they tumbled together in a heap on the ground. Way to go Angel Lisa, not even a thought to let go, though she was hurting herself in the process. Alex was given immediate checks all over and then brought home straightaway for further assessment. Numerous calls all evening to check on him, and then we went to bed.

At this time Alex slept in his bed in the kitchen. The morning after the fall, I came down to be greeted by a small, furry version of the elephant man. His face was swollen up so much that I knew I needed to get him to the vet. And now came the dilemma: he had to be muzzled to go in the car and to the vet. I knew I had to take him and I knew I had to put that muzzle on. I tried to do it as loosely and as gently as possible, but it truly broke me. As I did it up he flinched and I thought if ever there was a reason for my so-called dangerous dog to bite now was the time; but he didn't. He just stood there and as I cried he tried to lick away a tear from my face. Maybe this was the point when I saw the real Alex. He was an absolute angel at the vet's; initially people stood back from us but he could not have been better behaved. In fact, in a way, he made them feel at ease with his behaviour. The vet dealt with everything, completely at ease, and Alex was sorted out and we came home. A lesson learnt for me, to be proud of my amazing dog and his ability to put people at ease.

Eventually I had to start using a motorized wheelchair and the Angels came along to help me train Alex to join me on walks. Again he surprised me with his innate ability to work something out and adapt to it. Don't get me wrong: Alex can be very naughty when he wants to be, but when the situation demands it he can rise to the challenge and get on with it. I noticed on my 'pre-approved' walks, tried and tested to be wheelchair-friendly, that people avoided us, and I was guessing that it was because of the muzzle. Alex has the most gorgeous face, white with a beautiful ginger patch over one eye, but the muzzle was black and harsh against it. He had never tried to get it off, so I removed the top strap and covered the rest of it in coloured tape. Then I watched—and now people reacted differently. They smiled and asked if they could stroke him. They brought their dogs over to meet him and asked questions, which I was more than happy to answer! I started bringing treats with me and sharing them with other people's dogs and I noticed a wonderful change—those dogs started running over and sitting in a circle around my chair. Alex always stood patiently and calmly, waiting his turn. People were amazed and delighted. I felt like we had crossed a bridge and others were seeing Alex as a dog—and not a 'dangerous' dog. Children seemed the most intrigued and so I brought with me some long treats so that children could, under supervision, feed Alex through the muzzle. They loved it! I wished I had done it earlier, to be honest.

Alex also won over our wonderful postman Steve; he even came in to have his photo taken without Alex wearing the dreaded muzzle, and he calls out to him when he sees him round and about. Alex wags his tail, a sure sign he loves you, as due to his spinal injury wagging is not something he does on a regular basis—he needs to be really happy to do that! Air brakes were something Alex was scared of, so we bribed the rubbish bin collectors to give him treats that I would sneak out to them. Turned out they needed little persuasion: They loved him and brought their own treats when my supply ran out. When we see them out and about they shout out his name as a hello and then they wave. Alex bristles with pride and raises his head so they can see him clearly. He is becoming more vain by the day!

It took us time to learn how to make Alex's life fulfilling. For dogs like Alex life is not normal: Everything is restricted once he leaves his safe place, our house and garden. He loves to go for a walk and so when you say the word he becomes excited and does the obligatory head tilt, the lead collar and harness go on and he is really bright and happy. Then we get the muzzle out and he is conflicted, he doesn't like the muzzle and doesn't want to wear it, but he does want to go for a walk. He comes slowly to you with his head and his whole body drooping. It is one of the saddest things to watch. What must life be like being so confused? I wanted to make it better, but I didn't know how. So we started researching and found out that it was up to us to make the changes. We adhere strictly to the law in every sense, not just because it is the right thing to do, but because one mistake from us could potentially end in Alex being taken away and losing his life!

We found alternatives that would allow Alex more freedom without breaking the law. One of the first things we did was to find a fully secure field that we could rent for an hour or so, and took him there. I had done my research but I still asked hundreds of questions of the owner when we arrived. She was patient and understanding. Once safely inside the field, Gavin took Alex's lead and muzzle off. I don't know what I had expected but Alex just stood there, like he didn't know what to do. I didn't understand at all: Surely this was the time when he could just run and be like a normal dog, but no. Then I realized that his life had been so constricted for so long that he didn't know he could move freely. So Gavin started to run and Alex looked at me and I said, 'Yes, go,' and he did. Tentatively at first but then he started to run, gathering speed as he went. The grass was long in some places and at some points all I could see was a head appearing and disappearing, just like a spring lamb. I am loath to admit that I cried, big heaving sobs, because he was free and that is how his life should be. He shouldn't spend a life of watching others have the freedom he should be able to enjoy but can't, purely based on his looks.

We looked at what he seemed to be interested in and one was water, he just loved water. We used to go to the seaside with our old dog a lot and whenever we had taken Alex he would pull towards the splashing of the waves. So Gavin bought himself some chest waders and we packed the car and set off. I sang, the males in my life grimaced and howled in equal measure; I ignored them and carried on caterwauling to my heart's content. When we got to the beach, I sat in my chair on the harbour wall and Gavin donned the waders.

Alex looked bemusedly at his Dad but was infinitely more interested in the crashing waves. I watched with a sense of pride as they strolled down the beach together. Gavin had the lead held tightly in his hand. As they reached the water line, I saw Alex gaze out and imagined a big sigh. By now I felt excited for him. Gavin waded in past where the water was knee-deep and to the point where Alex could swim. He swam beside Gavin for some time while Gavin stayed beside him, always hanging on to the lead and with Alex securely muzzled. No breaking of laws, but some freedom.

From that moment on we found lots of things Alex could do: mental agility games, training, snuffle mats, puzzle feeders; Gavin made things for the garden and we discovered so much about Alex that we hadn't known. He was super smart. Alex loves his food and we discovered that he could open doors in the house. I kept blaming Gavin for leaving the larder door open until we realized one day that Alex was opening it. So we put a slide-along bolt on it—and yet it still happened! I was convinced it was Gavin until I peered through the edge of the door one day to see Alex standing up with his front paws balanced on the draining board while he moved the bolt across with his teeth! I was cross, proud and impressed with his ingenuity all at once. So we had to instal child locks too. Alex doesn't really bother too much with doors any more. He has trained me so well that he only has to give me the command and I give him whatever he wants; see what I told you—he is a very smart dog indeed!

We met particular people that Alex loved who we named the Aunties Who Adore—and they do, so very much. To save us from travelling miles to the field we were going to, a very kind lady offered her secure field which was quite close to us, so Gavin is now able to take Alex there as often as possible. She wanted to remain anonymous so we call her the Fairy Dogmother, and Alex adores her.

Nobody was going to stop us from going on holiday and we meticulously planned trips away that would include Alex. We don't travel light because of my wheelchair, and Alex's crate, toys, bedding and clothes for every single occasion! The car was full and I stayed in the back seat with Alex—we slept curled up together a lot of the way, all the time with me holding the lead in my hand and with the muzzle on his face. Hours upon hours with breaks for resting, toileting, eating and drinking. Alex revelled in it most of the time, he would sometimes look to us for reassurance but a quick thumbs up and he knew not to worry. We first went to Scotland and had a wonderful time: We popped into local pubs with Alex and people asked to have their photograph taken with him. Sometimes I feel like a minder to a little furry superstar! He took really well to every new experience; I often think how far he has come from the confused dog we had initially met.

The second holiday was a risk, mainly because it included a ferry. We obviously could not leave Alex in the car alone on the ferry, that would be breaking the rules; but we couldn't take him inside either. So we sat with him on the deck. He looked to Gavin for comfort because it was a bit choppy, but dealt with it so well with his Dad on the floor with him, giving him much-needed cuddles so that he felt safe and secure. If truth be told I was more scared than he was and would have joined in that comforting cuddle if I could have got on the floor! This journey included nine hours in the car one day, a stay overnight in a hotel and a further nine hours travelling the following day, but it was so worth it and we had the best time in Orkney. We had one night in the hotel to break up the journey and while Gavin got the luggage out of the car, a full-time job in itself, I went to the toilet in the room. Alex meanwhile was by himself in the room—and when I came out I saw that he had made himself nice and comfy in the freshly made bed! It makes me laugh now because from that day onwards, even after our return home, he has pretty much slept in between us every night. Even if he starts off in his bed, we wake up to him curled up somewhere on ours. He likes the comfort of us all being together and feeling the warmth of each other. So much for the dog I didn't bond with; now I have become so bonded I can barely move without him being there!

But I digress; let's get back to that wonderful holiday. We had been invited by a lovely lady who ran a dog rescue and had an annexe attached to her house. It was fabulous; we spent days exploring, visiting points of interest, and Alex ran and played in the secure fields with a wonderful bull breed belonging to Chris. We had so much fun and he was greeted with joy wherever he went. My favourite scene from that whole trip was seeing Alex standing near an excavated site with his head held high and with the wind blowing so hard that his ears were standing up.

Last year we took him down to Wales to stay at the beautiful Rose Hill Cottage. Again, we had acres of fields and woodland all secure and safe for him to play in. Sadly during that time we had to return home for a day for a funeral. Our plan had been to take Alex home, leave him there, go to the funeral and then return and pick him up to take him back to Wales. It would be a long trip but we felt we had no choice. Then the wonderful owners of the cottage, who lived on site, offered to look after him while we were away. I was so grateful and not worried as they had bonded so well with him and I knew they understood the rules. There was a door from the cottage into their kitchen so after walks and snacks they left Alex in the room next to their kitchen with the door closed. Oops, I had forgotten to mention he could open internal doors! So Philippa turned round and Alex was standing there, in her kitchen, where her four dogs were. In he went and just stretched out in front of the warm oven, happy as they come. I sometimes wonder how he feels when he can run about at times and at other times he can't, it must be a bit confusing; but then again those times of true freedom must feel so good and be worth it.

Alex had a long course of hydrotherapy, which seemed to help with his movement a bit, so we decided to take him to a swimming pool for dogs and humans. I have no sense of direction and my geography is barely existent, so I booked a session and told Gavin it would take about forty-five minutes to drive there; turned out it was nearer to three hours, oh dear! We had the place to ourselves and Alex was given a life jacket to wear. Gavin got in down the steps, and Alex ignored him. I did the same, and Alex ignored me too. I was convinced he was scared of the steps, so we went into the middle and splashed about a bit to try and make it exciting; still nothing. So now I was getting out and Gavin started to swim. Alex was so intrigued by this that he dashed down to the other end and just took a flying leap in! They had a swimming race and I watched as they were neck and neck before I saw Alex glance beside him as Gavin reached for the end—and that was when he spun round and swam in the opposite direction to beat his Dad hands, or should I say paws, down!

Alex looks after us by barking at everything outside the house and visible through the window: paper bags, wind, trees, anything really. We put privacy covering on the bottom of the windows—genius! Apparently not, because there is a large windowsill: so he just stands on it and barks.

Alex is nine years old now and slowing down a teensy bit, but every day I am grateful that we have him in our lives. He has proved that it is possible to live a full life within the restrictions of the law, but of course he shouldn't have to. Some time ago there was a government discussion regarding the Dangerous Dogs Act and specifically the area of Breed Specific Legislation. When asked about the innocent dogs that didn't make it through the process and were killed, an attendee referred to them as 'collateral damage'!

I would like to say that dogs are not, and should never be, considered 'collateral damage'; they are innocent, living, breathing creatures who deserve the chance of life, and an unrestricted one at that. I am not foolish: Alex is a big, powerful dog, but he is also sweet-natured, well trained, friendly, funny, kind, clumsy and soppy. I am a responsible owner and his needs come before anything else. If he says hello to you one day and wants a cuddle and then backs away the next day, I would respect that and will insist that others do too. The law needs changing, for everyone. The current one does not protect anybody. All I ask is that changes are made to make it fair. Don't kill and restrict dogs because of how they look.

I have learnt many things since Alex came into our lives but I think the most important is this ...

Whatever restrictions life puts on you, make the most of what you can do. Find ways around the things that are stopping you and do the very best you can to live life to the full. When I can't do something or see a way forward, I think to myself, 'What would we do if this were happening to Alex?' And then I find a way. Thank you, Alex, for helping me see a more positive way to live.

The Call of the Heart
TANDRALI KULI

If you have a dream you follow it, if you have a goal you work towards it, if you have ambitions you do everything to achieve them—but most of my early years, and to some extent even now, I was confused and adrift. I am the kind to go with the flow. I have always known what I do not want to do in life, but I could never answer what it is I do wish to do; except that I'd like to do something for animals.

The first kindergarten art competition subject I chose was 'Your Pet' (my ever uncertain and indecisive mind knew that was the subject to choose even in those early years). And memory throws up a pretty banal picture of a girl on a chair with her pet sitting near her feet that my very proud mother hung up on my bedroom wall for years afterwards. The sight of a hungry stray digging up a half-buried coconut shell with fierce determination broke my four-year-old heart and made me naively declare that I would feed all the dogs in the world when I grew up (and to think that feeding just forty-seven mouths is burning a huge hole in my pocket now!).

As a six-year-old, I cried uncontrollably for a dog I saw hit by a car in Kolkata, knowing it was too late for any help. Sitting in the back garden with the clichéd 'Tommy', a brown-coloured mongrel who was my constant companion for many years, and whom my dad had dognapped off the streets at my demand—every snippet from my childhood memory album is rife with animals, especially dogs. So it wasn't really an exaggeration when my mother voiced her biggest fear: that her daughter would 'go to the dogs'. But I started on that path pretty late, only after I joined college; I see today's kids follow their hearts when they are still in their pre-teens.

Delhi and college brought new friends into my life, but most importantly it brought dogs—many, many dogs. Dogs that took over my life, sidelining the friends of many years; but they also gave me purpose and in hindsight a lot of exposure and knowledge to the world of animal welfare. For a long time after I stopped going out with friends, stopped my weekly jaunts to the Sarojini Nagar market, refused invitations from friends to hang out till those friends gave in to the obvious and stopped calling, all my free time (that is, the time outside of college and sleeping hours) was spent at the shelter. It all started during one college autumn break when I decided to put my first foot forward to follow my passion, stepping into the sanctity of Delhi's oldest animal shelter. It was a revelation, the kind that no amount of books, media or preaching can impart. And it was definitely not for the weak-hearted. Animal welfare toughens you up like nothing I know. It is like boarding a ship in stormy seas, oscillating between heights of great happiness and intense satisfaction to the pits of acute depression and tremendous frustration, with severe emotional fatigue thrown in as well. You never get to sail in still waters. But it's no less an addiction for people like us, who live for the next successful rescue and rehoming high. Without that high we would be lost.

Seventeen years and over three hundred fosters and five hundred rehomings later, I am still here. At Friendicoes SECA: deeply entrenched in animal welfare activities, married to a veterinarian (little surprise there!) and with my own household of fourteen rescue dogs (that's the number presently, though it keeps changing). I still continue to foster, which I have realized is actually my biggest strength and something I am immensely proud of. Since consistent fostering isn't easy, most times you end up getting attached and cave in to adopting. Which in itself isn't a bad thing, I have done it myself a few times, but it often seals your fate and you can no longer continue fostering because of limits on both resources and space.

Fostering, I have found, gives a dog the best chance of finding a suitable home. Overcrowded shelters do not make for a relaxing atmosphere and cannot provide detailed attention. And a dog or a cat or any animal for that matter loses his or her individuality in the shelter, amongst the sea of other animals. One can never see their actual persona in the shelter. Their survival instincts demand that they adapt to the environment around them; so many adoptions end up unsuccessful when the dog or the cat fails to behave in a perceived way that is expected after a short meeting at the shelter. This is where fostering helps. Apart from reducing the burden on shelters and providing better medical as well as general care for the dog or the cat, it also means a hygienic, comfortable and soothing home environment where the animal can destress and be his or her own self. It also presents an opportunity to socialize the animal and condition him or her to home living with particular boundaries and lots of individual attention, something they crave over everything else. And when the time comes this helps make the right match while rehoming, leading to a successful adoption. Because, believe me, the right match is the key to a happy adoption.

Over the years I have experienced some fosters that are easy to let go of, mostly when they are overenergetic and need loads of extra stimulation that I find hard to give in my chaotic life and multi-dog home—or if maybe that personal click just didn't happen. But there have been some heart-wrenching ones that needed a lot of self-reflection and self-preaching before I could let go (with a sadistic hope somewhere at the back of my mind that the adoption would fail and the dog would return to me). The ones that come to mind the most are Candle, a beautiful Pitbull girl I fostered for six long months; Valentine, a blind St Bernard boy; Kenzie, a gorgeous young male German Shepherd; Rembrandt, an Indie puppy with a broken leg that I had nursed; and Twinkle, a very recent foster who was an Apso girl. If I had a say they would all be around me as I write these words but they are all fortunately lovingly ensconced in the beds and bosoms of their doting humans, each one in a fabulous home. For I have learnt that passion without practicality cannot last long. In my selfish desire to hold on to them I cannot afford to forget that my resources are limited and that there are more dogs out there who need my help.

The years in rescue have also taught me that successful rehabilitation needs to be logical and sensible and not just emotional. At the beginning I would take every rescue dog home (every one of them who caught my eye) only to find that most are left with me for life because no one else wanted them. For example, however much I may be in love with that Rottweiler sitting at the shelter who is breaking my heart with his soulful eyes, I have to sadly remember that his chances at a home are next to nothing compared to that of the Labrador next to him—because most people prefer a Labrador, which has the reputation of being a family dog and good around kids. Therefore, much as it pains me, I am forced to settle on the Labrador—because I can only foster the one, and obviously it's smarter to foster the Labrador. If you have a thousand dogs to choose from and homes for only ten of them, the wise thing to do is to choose the most easy-going, social and friendly ones of the lot. It may sound cold and even callous to some and it is in no way an easy decision for me—it was something I struggled with a lot in my initial years because I have a tendency to always fall for the one that no one usually wants. But time, experience and my small reserve of wisdom have taught me to sieve through my muddled thoughts and play for the best outcome, which is to rehome as many dogs as possible without personal choices interfering with it. That's not to say I don't have my fair share of indulging in my impulsive, emotional decisions—which is how I came to have fourteen dogs sharing my home and hearth.

In much the same way, a successful adoption means making the practical and balanced call and taking home the dog that suits your lifestyle and family—and not the one that is aesthetically more appealing to you. Sadly, I have found it works the other way round for most people looking to buy or adopt a puppy. The decision is entirely driven by what appeals to the eye and the breed that is the latest trend. This alone is the reason shelters are bursting with abandoned pedigreed dogs discarded by families ill-equipped to deal with their needs. People like us go hoarse shouting on social media and everywhere else we can be heard about the perils of impulsive pet shopping and adopting, but there's little you can do in the face of new money and intense commercialization of the pet industry, especially in a country with lukewarm legislations for animal abuse and cruelty.

When it comes to rescuing a puppy or a dog from the streets, the ever-necessary but unpopular practicality rears its annoying head once again, dictating what the prudent course of action is. A 'rescue' is not just calling the animal helpline or getting the animal off the streets. It also means seeing it through till the end. What's the end? That would be a proper, lifelong rehabilitation for the animal in question. Sadly, there simply aren't as many homes as there are animals out there. So it might be the best thing to leave the animal where it is on the street (unless it is sick or injured) if you cannot offer him or her a lifetime's commitment. 'Rescuing' doesn't mean picking up litters of pups off the street that are with their mothers, unless you can offer them all a home. Because once you take them out of their natural environment they can never go back, and they are dependent on you for the rest of their life.

The best way you can help the dogs on the street is to participate in the sterilization drives that aim towards a happier, less fraught, more balanced life for all street dogs in the long run.

Kaju in the Sunlight

ORIJIT SEN

Kaju was born in a gutter behind my house in Saket, Delhi, in 2005. One day, when he was still a pup, he was viciously attacked by a large Doberman and suffered massive injuries. Some kids who were playing in the street called me downstairs and beseeched me to save him. When I saw him, he was heroically trying to drag himself back into the gutter for safety. Not screaming, not whimpering—just silently concentrating on the job at hand. I was sure he was about to die. But looking at the anguish in the kids' eyes, I felt compelled to do something. So I brought out a bedsheet, wrapped the pup's bleeding body in it, hailed a passing autorickshaw and rushed him to the nearest vet's clinic.

I didn't have a high opinion of the vet's abilities, having seen him cater only to the pedigreed dogs of posh folks. From the outside, his clinic looked more like a shop selling expensive dog shampoos and packaged snacks. I went in and asked him to put the little gasping creature out of his misery.

To my surprise, the vet examined the pup briefly, turned to me and said, 'He can be saved. Do you want to try saving him instead?

I can stitch him back together, but you will have to keep him with you for a couple of months to change his bandages and administer medications while he heals.'

I didn't know how to react. He had put me in a spot. In those days I was living in a small first-floor apartment and spending a lot of time away at work. I had no intention of adopting a sick dog. Seeing my hesitation, the vet pulled out his 'death dose' and broke the vial—warning me that it would cost me Rs 550.

But just as the needle touched the quivering paw, I had a vision of me carrying back a dead puppy to the kids waiting anxiously outside my house. 'Stop, stop! I want to save him!' I shouted out almost in reflex.

So he put away his syringe, and the stitching began. I stood by, passing along rags soaked in anaesthetic fluids, helping the vet as he stood there for two straight hours, sewing up muscles, tissues and skin. After what felt like an eternity, it was done. The little fellow was completely stitched up and bandaged—and sedated.

And so, Kaju came home. The kids had dispersed, for it was dinnertime by then, but news spread quickly, and they all came to welcome him back with elated smiles and laughter. My daughter was among the group, and she christened him officially now with the name they had already given to him before the incident.

Kaju lived the larger part of his life in Delhi, but eventually made a long and epic journey with me by train to our present home in Goa. He is now sixteen years old, and more than a little rickety in his legs. But he still roams the wooded paths of Goa as if they are the back streets of his native Saket.

May the light keep shining on Kaju.

Friends for Life

MARK TULLY

I was born the son of a Calcutta *burra sahib*, a senior partner of Gillanders Arbuthnot & Co., the largest and oldest of the managing agencies that controlled a vast number of commercial companies.

For the first nine years of my life, I lived in a *burra* bungalow in Calcutta. It had a big garden which included a tennis court. We children lived a very disciplined life, spending most of our time under the supervision of a strict British nanny. The one time during the day when we used to see our parents was for tea in the garden. This was also the time when Jane, our beloved black-and-white Spaniel, was released from the care of the house help and allowed to join us. In all my life, which has been lived with many different dogs, she was the only one I know who was so human that she drank tea with us. The tea would be served in a saucer to her so that it cooled quickly. The house help would carefully clip her long ears together over her head with a clothes peg to stop them from falling into the saucer.

I have tried giving tea to other dogs but sadly they all turned their noses up at it.

In time, Jane was joined by a Dachshund called Noodles, which was the title of a children's book of the time about a dog. My sister Prue, two years my senior, claimed ownership of Noodles and was very possessive of her. I can't recall how, but we managed to take Noodles with us on a winter holiday to Puri, travelling by train overnight. Prue and I would take Noodles for walks on the beach where Noodles had a habit of chasing crabs scuttling across the sand. Although the crabs always escaped, I thought this was very cruel, but my sister would hear nothing against her dog. We had an argument and—I remember with some shame—I got so angry that I burst into tears.

When we returned to Britain just at the end of World War II, we lived an unsettled life for some time because my father was looking for a job. Eventually he found one as a director of an engineering company in Manchester and we moved to another *burra* house in the Cheshire countryside, not far from the city. Immediately, we children, by then six in number, demanded a dog. So a brown-and-white Spaniel, a male this time, was purchased and we decided he should be called Pip, which was the name of a beloved pony we had in Calcutta. Pip had one feature: he was remarkably unwilling to accept discipline. This used to infuriate my father who was himself a very disciplined man, and a strict disciplinarian. Pip was particularly unruly on picnics when he would disappear, chasing rabbits or following the scent of other animals. When we eventually got him back, my father would give him a sharp slap, but that did no good.

From Pip we graduated to a delightful female Labrador who was described to us as cream-coloured. She was, like all Labradors, immensely sociable and very loving. She was so affectionate, and we loved her so much, that we indulged her other Labrador trait, the tendency to be greedy. As a result she became a stout lady. But when she was still young and slim, my father decided that this time he would have a disciplined dog. He sent poor Bess, as she was called, to the gamekeeper of the Conservative MP, Sir Walter Bromley Davenport, to be trained. Unlike my father, Sir Walter was very much a hunting and shooting man. His gamekeeper trained dogs to retrieve game birds that had been shot. But after a couple of days my father got a phone call from the gamekeeper, demanding he take Bess back, because she was 'vicious'. To this day I cannot imagine what our darling Bess, the most loving dog ever, might have done to be considered vicious. When father returned home with Bess, who was not the least chastened by her experience; she leapt out of the car, tail wagging ferociously, and ran madly from one member of her welcoming committee to the other, with Father looking on disapprovingly.

When Bess went to her heavenly resting place, a male black Labrador called Diver came into our lives. Like Bess, Diver was very loving and just as gluttonous. But unlike Bess, he was very active too and would disappear sometimes in search of female company. By this time, Father had given up on trying to discipline our dogs and accepted Diver's absences with resignation. My brother Bob somehow managed to establish ownership of Diver and would not allow him to sleep anywhere except on his bed. Bob used to delight in tickling Diver on his tummy so that one hind leg beat the air frantically as if to scratch. This he called 'diddling' Diver. My youngest brother, David, took to shooting but he never tried to train Diver to accompany him on his shoots, remembering Bess's failure. But Diver did often accompany us on our pony rides through the village. Being very keen on trains, I used to insist that David and our youngest sister, Felicity, ride with me to a bridge over the railway tracks when the crack Manchester–London express, The Mancunian, was due. As the magnificent steam engine hauling the train roared under the bridge at full speed, enveloping us in smoke and covering us in soot, the ponies would buck and neigh and try to bolt in terror, but Diver took it all in his stride and continued nonchalantly, investigating the possibilities of interesting smells.

Diver was the last dog of my childhood. As a young man I went through a period of doglessness because I never lived in a place big enough to have a dog. During my first spell in India working for the BBC, I didn't keep a dog because I realized that I would not be able to take him or her back to England with me. But on my second spell, which I hoped would last longer, I bought a Labrador as black and as loving as Diver. He had been bred by Field Marshal Sam Manekshaw, we were told, so we called him Bahadur, the Brave. He was even more of a wanderer than Diver. More than once he returned home badly mauled by other dogs competing for the same bitch.

Sadly, my time in India was made much shorter than I had expected by my being expelled from the country during the Emergency. The government had wanted me, and all other foreign correspondents, to sign a document agreeing not to report anything critical of the government. I, like most of my colleagues, refused to do so and was told to leave the country within twenty-four hours. My family followed shortly afterwards, leaving Bahadur in the kindly care of very close friends. When I came back to India eighteen months later, Bahadur almost knocked me over in the enthusiasm of his welcome. He had been beautifully looked after and we resumed our relationship as though there had never been a gap.

Since then, I have always had a Labrador to welcome me home after I've been away, with the love and loyalty that make a dog such a wonderful friend.

A Late Goodbye

AMITAVA KUMAR

My niece and her boyfriend, their dog in tow, came to stay with my sister during the coronavirus lockdown. No one was going out. But if anyone did, the dog kept an alert vigil, waiting.

We were all waiting. We were waiting for things to be all right.

I have had only one dog in my life. His name was Snoopy. A friend at school in Patna—I think I was in class eight then—had a dog that had a litter. This friend gave me a pup, white fur with black patches. Was Snoopy a terrier? I don't know. My father had bought us the ten-volume set of Arthur Mee's *Children's Encyclopedia*, and in one of them there were pictures identifying the different species of dogs. Snoopy had the pointed snout of a Collie, I remember deciding, but the small size of a terrier. From the local British Council library, closed for many years now, I brought a book that explained how to take care of dogs.

A year or so later, our family decided to go on a trip. As a government officer, my father was allowed to take his family on a Bharat-darshan, free second-class travel on trains. My older sister was reaching the age when she would become ineligible, so we went.

But what to do with the dog? We left Snoopy with my closest friend. This friend was the second of four brothers, the youngest being perhaps eight or nine years old. They liked Snoopy.

When we returned from our trip, my friend said that his youngest brother didn't want to part with Snoopy. Could the dog stay with them? This posed a problem, for I loved Snoopy. But in the end I decided I couldn't say no to the small boy. My mother was worried. She asked me, more than once, 'Are you sure?'

My friend and his brothers had lost their mother to cancer a few years earlier. The youngest brother was five when their mother, a schoolteacher, died. The death of a parent was the most catastrophic thing I could imagine at that time. I wasn't a particularly good or generous boy—I was even cruel to animals, trying to kill birds with an air gun someone had gifted me—but giving Snoopy to the motherless child seemed the right thing to do.

A year or two passed and my friend's family moved to Delhi. As it happened, I too got admission in a school in Delhi. Often, I was at my friend's house and I would see Snoopy. I would take the DTC bus to Sapna Cinema in Greater Kailash and when I entered the house, there Snoopy would be, welcoming me.

Only now, as I write these words, does it occur to me that I never wondered at the time what the dog made of all this. Did he think I had abandoned him? Or that I loved him less? There are so many mysteries that surround our memories of childhood. It strikes me now that there was very little discussion or debate among my sisters and me about Snoopy being given away. Why was this? It is entirely possible that we were all caught up in the pathos of our imagination, the sad story of the child whose mother had died and who now was in love with our dog.

Last month was my friend's birthday. I didn't call or email him. Although we aren't close any more, we have occasionally sent messages on each other's birthdays. And where is that boy now, his youngest brother? I just googled his name and found that he lives, or has lived, in California. He is a software engineer and there are photographs on the internet of him competing in ping-pong matches. I can still see the outline of the face he had as a boy in Patna more than forty years ago.

Within two years of my move to Delhi, my own family shifted there too. My father had an office in Udyog Bhavan. I joined Hindu College. One day there was a call from my friend's father. Snoopy had died. My mother was making sad noises. I remember wondering where the dog would be buried. My friend's father had a bad heart; I had heard that he had suffered a heart attack when the police summoned him to the local thana. My friend had met a woman at a college cultural festival. She was married but had decided to leave her husband and live with my friend. The husband had filed a police complaint. It is possible, then, that when my friend's father called to tell us about Snoopy, I also thought about his heart.

When all this was happening, I had already decided I was going to be a writer. While I was interested in the drama around me, I was living more and more in my head. A sense of distance had crept into me. I was just an observer of life, instead of being a participant.

But dogs are not like that. They are nothing if not active participants in our lives, pushing their empathetic noses, no, their entire beings, into whatever is going on. Their lives are shorter; they remember everything. So, this brief piece is about not forgetting. A delayed farewell to a dog I once had—Snoopy, from whom I was parted twice.

Editor's Editor

SUMITA MEHTA

E arly 2003. We were out on an evening walk when suddenly my
(late) husband, Vinod Mehta, said very casually, 'Let's keep
a dog.'

Having grown up with dogs as part of the family, I was quite
thrilled and wondered what breed we should consider. I was all for
adopting an Indian dog from a shelter but was somewhat uncertain
of Vinod's reaction. While his heart was with the *aam aadmi*,
Vinod's lifestyle preferences were often quite elitist. Somehow a
'pi dog' or '*nedi kutta*' did not quite fit into this picture. So my
thoughts went to breeds like a Lab, a Retriever or a Spaniel ... or
something else?

I consulted a relative, who was a dog lover, and before I could say
Jack Robinson, up popped this pup. 'Just for you!' she said. The pup
in her arms was a ball of fur and quite adorable. But it had a tail that
was a dead giveaway—he was unmistakably a 'pi'. She explained—
his mother, a 'stray', had given birth to a litter in a ditch in Gurgaon,
and she had picked this one for us. 'See, he even has socks,' she said,

pointing to his white paws. 'Baby, say hello to mama,' she cooed …
and gently put the pup into my arms. And left.

Awkwardly holding this ball of fur, I quickened my pace to
catch up with Vinod, who was out on his evening walk. He looked
at the pup and, to my surprise and joy, said, 'He's beautiful.' And
that's how Ed entered our lives. He soon became an integral
part of it—demanding, obstinate, stubborn and independent,
his unconditional love was impossible to resist, and he had us
completely captive.

Not given to an excessive display of emotions, Vinod wrote in his
column in *Outlook*, 'A stranger has come into my life and overtaken
it …' He chose the name Editor because 'he is disobedient, stubborn,
wilful and thinks he knows everything'.

Editor became Ed or Eddie. Vinod adored Eddie, and I could
see that he was quite fascinated by him. He wrote in his memoir
Lucknow Boy:

> Dogs who slobber all over you, do as they are told, are slightly timid,
> over-friendly, roll over to have their tummy tickled, are boring. Dogs
> like Editor may be infuriating, cause fights with neighbours … but
> they are much more engaging. Their unpredictability is their charm.

Early days. For the first few nights, Eddie cried a lot and seemed
unsettled in his little bed. I held him close, and he was asleep in
seconds. He grew from a lanky pup to a handsome adult with a
regal, majestic air. His 'teething' stage saw many things destroyed—
footwear, table legs, mobile phones, and a precious picture of Vinod
with Yasser Arafat! We caught him halfway, when Arafat was still
visible. As soon as he saw us, he gulped the remainder down, and
the rest is history.

He grew to be an exceptionally large dog—I guess his father was a hound. Perfect shape, with taut muscles; when he bounded across the park in front of our house, he was a pleasure to watch. His size was intimidating, and he was labelled *danger kutta* by all in the neighbourhood. And here are some 'Ed tales', many of which were recounted earlier in an article published in *Creature Companion*.

Coming back from work in the pouring rain one day, I received frantic calls from home. 'Come back fast, Ed's collar has slipped off and he's running around the colony.' Fear gripped me. Had he bitten anyone? Was he being attacked by strays? I asked the driver to press down on the pedal. When I reached home, there was not a soul in sight. All the drivers had locked themselves in their cars; the maids, the household help were inside the house, peering out of the windows—and the press-wallah had climbed on to his ironing table. '*Sher chhoot gaya*,' they said.

And where was Ed? Running in the rain, with me following in the car. Each time I drew close, he would look back with a wild expression and run faster still. Lazy Ed was running round and round the colony with the speed and grace of his youth. He just would not stop. I had to call my son Aditya (the only other person Ed adored) to help me. 'Eddie come,' Aditya said, and slowly, the huge, wet, muddy dog came quietly, licked his hand, and sat down while Aditya put on his collar; then he took him home.

Proprietorial at home, Ed was quite civil with dogs whom he liked. Like Bhola, the white-and-fawn male who guarded our lane. Dignified and gentle, Bhola never courted conflict. His sister/companion, Daisy, was just the opposite. Neutered when young, Daisy's persona was all-male—she was fierce, aggressive, and loved us with a passion. Both were children of a small, battered female, perhaps the ugliest I have ever known. We named her Funny.

Funny became part of the menagerie as well. One day, I found her
writhing in pain. Someone had hit her, and she had crawled into a
corner, bleeding. We took her to our vet, Dr Gandhi, and created a
small shelter next to the press-wallah's table for her. I remember, the
first day I took some food for her, she looked so happy in what was
perhaps the only 'home' she had known. Funny was with us only
briefly ... she succumbed to bodily decrepitude and years of neglect.

As Ed grew, so did his fame. He was photographed by Lord
Snowdon, appeared on Page 3 in publications, in high-end lifestyle
magazines, and of course, was frequently part of Vinod's columns.
Ed became fussy—he gave a photographer a hard time (much like
a petulant actor), he needed a full-time maid, and his culinary tastes
became more refined. He sniffed and left vegetarian meals—it had to
be meat or chicken—and he loved cheese! Yes, cheese ... We would
give him a bit of Amul cheese occasionally and he would gobble it
up. But later, when we returned from Italy, he had a bit of Parmesan
and Gouda, and from then on, he just would not touch Amul. So
Vinod, who never indulged anyone, made weekly trips to Khan
Market just to satisfy Eddie's demands. His minder thoughtfully
remarked, '*Rajah theyy pichhle janam mein, adatein vaisey hain* (He
must have been a king in his previous birth—his habits are such).'

But Ed was not just about engaging stories. He also brought
something very special to our lives. With Vinod, Ed opened a
floodgate of emotions—he became softer, gentler and much more
human. He put his face forward to be nuzzled and licked. I cooked
for Ed, fed him, took care of him, but it was Vinod whom he adored.
And the feeling was mutual.

Once, while on a trip to Mussoorie, we stopped at a hotel for
lunch and Vinod was happily taking Ed into the restaurant; when
we were stopped with 'No pets allowed, Sir,' he got so angry that he

walked off and we had lunch at an open-air café instead, one that offered a bowl of milk to Ed as well. Ed was always with Vinod and they both seemed to have found a silent language to communicate in. I asked Vinod one day, 'Who comes first, Ed or me?' to which he answered, 'Difficult question.' So I was considerably surprised and very touched to see that his last book, *Editor Unplugged*, was dedicated to me and to Editor, and in that order!

In 2014, when Ed was eleven, Vinod was hospitalized for almost three months. Ed who hated being cuddled and never slept with us, now stretched himself across the entire length of Vinod's bed, almost as if protecting it. He moaned often, grew sadder by the day, and slowly his body grew weak. The next year Vinod left us, and perhaps it was a combination of old age and grief, for Ed's body started giving way. His kidneys deteriorated rapidly, he developed cancer and grew frail and weak. But though his body was feeble, his face remained regal, giving a mistaken impression of strength. That gave me hope and I tried desperately to reverse the ravages to his body, but nature was stronger.

Weak as he was, he never left my side, almost as if he were conscious that he had to look after me. Each day when I returned home, Ed would rouse from his slumber and come to greet me. He was my son, but also a true friend who understood that in sad times, just being there is enough. Two years later, he left, leaving a gap that has never been filled.

But what he did leave has endured and is something special. Vinod wrote:

> I do not wish to get all sloppy and sentimental over what, finally, is a dog. Nevertheless, I feel Editor is God's gift to me. I must have done

some good karma to have found him. He has given me so much; I have given him so little. It is an unequal relationship.

Editor, I am convinced, has made me a better human being. I am more aware of the thoughtless cruelties I used to perpetrate, especially on those who have no power to respond. Moreover, thanks to Editor my appreciation of nature in all its forms—trees, flowers, peacocks, rabbits, tigers, mountains, streams—has grown by leaps and bounds. Editor has given me the strength to try and make ours a kinder, gentler world.

As the years progressed, I found Ed had changed me as well: awakened a consciousness that all forms of life are precious and should be allowed to live freely and with dignity. Not only did I really get to love and care about the strays in our colony, but I started feeding birds as well—pigeons and parrots and an occasional crow, all of whom were visitors to our home. As I watered the pots in our small veranda, there was a newfound feeling for plants and I felt so much closer and one with nature. And like Vinod, when I see injustice perpetrated on those who cannot fight back, often on those who have done nothing to provoke it, I feel compelled to respond.

Ed taught me many things, but primarily that the wonder of love is not conditional on what you could be, but for just the way you are.

Entries and Exits

GEETAN BATRA

Prologue: Bagheera

I was an insidious entry, a third-birthday gift to a dog-obsessed Cara from her dad. Memories of her cherubic face weeping into my dark-as-night coat every time she or I was reprimanded still make me smile. I was named Bagheera (what else would humans name a black Lab, especially when the kids watched *The Jungle Book* like a ritual every day) and was totally untrained. Road skiing was a constant event as I dragged Cara and her sister Tiya around the colony after me. I ate anything and begged for food non-stop.

I was the girls' first dog and, boy, was I loved. I was obsessed with their smell. They had to but drop a hair-tie somewhere or mistakenly leave their worn socks around and the next moment I would wolf it down (and promptly regurgitate it along with my last meal half an hour later). I just couldn't help myself. I have to admit I found the mother a bit schizoid, alternating between resentment at having to clean up after me, and being the one who remembered all my vaccines and held me tight as I shivered through every visit to the vet.

The children grew, as they are wont to do. Tiya was an emotional ball of energy—sometimes I thought she was even battier than I was. In an attempt to put a balm on her lonely, traumatized boyfriend's churning heart, she got a Beagle puppy that had been rescued from big pharma experiments and dispatched it to him as a birthday gift. An 'either that puppy lives here or I do' from his granny had the boyfriend scuttling back to our home with the creature, birthday bow and basket still intact. And that was how Astro, he of puppy breath and melting brown eyes, entered the household.

I-am-so-cute-I-can-get-away-with-anything was Astro's attitude—and he pretty much did! Whether it was because of the experiments done on his poor mom or because it was in his DNA, Astro was like the alien from *Men in Black*. He would sleep only once the girls covered him with his 'blankee' and only on this *one* particular sofa, no other spot would do. They were convinced he was the mutant who made the world go around from under there. Whatever he was, I did like the little fellow.

But now my time was up. I had lorded it over, lived a cushy life as the spoilt son of a loving family, and died easy. I know the woman lit a candle for me in an obscure church in Sweden; she was away travelling when I just didn't wake up one morning.

Astro

Where did the grouch go? His badass behaviour camouflaged some of my eccentricities, but then he went and left me. The girls just mothered me now. They combed me and kissed me and didn't get alarmed at all when I stared into the distance and let out barks for no reason, or jumped up from seemingly deep slumber and chomped on one of their friends' butts with no warning whatsoever. I sauntered through life being aggressive, randomly demanding and arrogant. And like Bagheera—god bless his soul—not one command did I obey. Is that an insight into the kind of dog parents we got? Humans are pretty whack—even the most terrible child has a special place in a mother's heart. Well, I was happy to be that terrible child.

One morning, I woke up to a small black puppy in the house. He was apparently a 'Bhutia', whatever that may be—and would grow up to be a magnificent big dog. They named him Baloo. (After Bagheera, Baloo. Sheesh, talk about lack of imagination! I mean— look at me: My name is Astro. Now that's a smart name.) But before I could even get used to having the new pup around, he went off to the hill house.

Once the puppy left, the humans shifted house. It was a most confounding experience. We ended up next to this place called Friendicoes. With both girls being soppy animal lovers and full of empathy—though they often left all their work to their mom—what could be more suitable? Frequent volunteering and fostering became routine. But between fostering forty rabbits in the front lawns because of an epidemic at the shelter, two civet kittens in the back, and a set of guinea pigs (Altu and Paltu) on the veranda along with half a dozen kittens within the house, they still made time for me. I barked occasionally at the blasted kittens who tried to scramble over me every chance they got.

But one foster really had me wonder at humanity. A ravaged, tawny Neapolitan Mastiff—Shaggy—who had been starved to the bone and had a maggot wound that was straight out of a horror movie was brought home. He weighed a mere twenty-seven kilos (instead of the average seventy that a Mastiff usually weighs). The stench of Himax filled our nostrils and the world condensed around helping him get better. I didn't begrudge Shaggy the attention; in fact, he mostly stayed out of everyone's way. The family thought they were doing quite well till, one night, his innards spilt out from the wound; he had managed to scratch away the dressing over the injury. I had to bark the place down to get everyone to come out and attend to him. After what I believe was a nerve-racking night at the vet's, the hound came back home. He tailed Cara like a shadow from then on. *I'll live if you're around*, his aura seemed to say. And then, a year later, as if he knew it was time to set her free (she had to leave for college), he gasped thrice and was gone. The gentle, if stinky, giant left a massive vacuum in my life. I had learnt a lot about humans from him. Yet another grave was added to our back garden now. Some people said that we lived in a pet cemetery and every time the power went off and it rained we could feel the spirit of the critters crawl all over us.

I was still getting over the Shaggy experience when two tan-and-black, high-energy Kani pups, Dharma and Karma, turned up, needing looking after. Both were frail and one was pigeon-toed. They were let in on the condition that they were to be 'outside' pups. I was okay with that. They ran around the back garden, barking at squirrels, pigeons and any shadow that dared to flit past. They licked and jumped at everyone (even me) as soon as the back door was opened. It was as if the garden had come alive. To my mind, they weren't dogs but graceful gazelles that could just levitate off the ground, up to about four feet. They had a grace and a feeling of belonging to the land—though they dug up every plant the woman tried to grow! When winter came, they crept into the inner sanctums of the house and there they stayed, much to my disgust.

And then there was heartbreak for the house again. A careless vendor left the gate open, and before anyone realized Dharma and Karma had sprinted out. Karma was hit by a car almost immediately and we lost him. Dharma went missing. Cara was distraught, but wouldn't give up. She spent hours wandering around, calling out to Dharma, hiring rickshaws to scour the gullies of the colony. Her strained face told the whole story. She even took me for a drive late into the night, within a five-kilometre radius, hoping I'd be able to trace Dharma. Then, thirty-six hours later, Cara found her sitting morosely on a trash dump. There was so much rejoicing! I was hugged non-stop too. I was a little emotional by the end of it, which was so unlike the pragmatic me.

A year later, when the news of two Bhutia pups up for adoption all the way in the Doon valley aroused memories of Baloo in Cara, she got them transported to the hill house. Sheru and Bijli were dream siblings who complemented each other perfectly. Sheru was a lovable doofus, whose mantra was loveme-loveme-loveme; he went and died on us, though: he foolishly went out exploring and was hit by a vehicle. Bijli on the other hand is wise and embodies the spirit of the mountains; there is a gentle timelessness to her, a grace and understanding. Apparently, the spirit of the ghost lady of the mountain who had built the old house resides in her. I've met her when I've gone up to the hill house.

Dharma and I were now in the house and, together with the five cats, played tag at different times of the day and night, daring the couple to get a full night's undisturbed sleep. Both girls were in college now and it was up to us to keep the oldies engaged. Locking us out would just make us hurl our bodies, big or small, against their door. We had learnt from each other and it was a trick we had mastered. A locked door was to be opened, period.

But there were yet more surprises in store. We animals do have a way of finding our way to the humans who are meant to be ours.

In the searing summer heat, two feisty puppies survived the death of their mother and four unfortunate siblings. The shelter was overflowing and we were the nearest port of call. Cara's plea— 'Please, Ma, just let them be under the tree, the whole back garden is empty'—left the woman with no option. So, greeted with indulgent exasperation, Lola and Begum, the two little misses, bounded in.

And all hell broke loose! Dharma couldn't stand them. Soon there was all-out war as the siblings grew and tried to protect their territory. The barks, yowls and cries that ensued each time their paths crossed had people running in from the streets to see what was going on. The six adults in the house weren't enough to get the marauding youngsters off Dharma; she lives with those scars till this day—a bifurcated ear, a furless patch on the rump and the tendency to see every dog as a potential Lola and Begum. All socializing stopped for Dharma after that.

The four of us were put on a merry-go-round. When Dharma and I had to go for a walk, Lola and Begum were seduced into the bathroom via the side door, and I dragged my old bones out through the main door with Dharma. There was much vicious scratching of the back garden by Lola and Begum to get our smell off 'their' territory.

Then I heard another story. Up in the mountains on a drive to the neighbouring hill, a mind-numbingly cruel act on a puppy had Cara bring home a little paralysed bundle of black fur. (Notice how black pups find a way to us? Bagheera, Baloo and now Badal.) The promise was that if Badal couldn't walk in three weeks, Cara would bring him down to the shelter and leave him there. (Like that would ever happen!) The staff in the house wasn't equipped to handle an immobile pup. But Badal did start walking, albeit a little crookedly at first. He is now this majestic creature who terrorizes any and every living being—two-legged or four—for even daring to be in his line of sight. But those he loves are blessed with his endearing, worshipful gaze that makes them feel like gods.

And as if there wasn't enough pandemonium in our home already, in came Delilah—much to the resigned exasperation of the woman. She was an abandoned senior Basset Hound who wouldn't have survived if left in the shelter. There was pain and despair written into every fold of her stinking jowls. She was a lady but what an offensive odour she had! Surprisingly, Lola and Begum, the fiery twosome outside didn't take too unkindly to her, so she was meant to be (which goes to show that even we animals are capable of empathizing with our fellow creatures).

I guess what started off as the intent to be cool, accepting parents nurturing the character traits of their child actually became a life of overwhelming emotion for the couple. Thank god for that!

The Ruff Art of Parenting

SHRUTKEERTI KHURANA

My daughter Krishnaa is a handful—a crazy bag of love with equal parts of wit and mischief. She has loved dogs since before she was born. How, you ask? Well, when she took temporary residence inside my belly for nine months, she frequently reacted whenever she heard a dog bark—almost as if she was trying to touch the source of the noise outside. She failed miserably, of course, and only ended up kicking my insides furiously.

A few months later she finally broke free, and I welcomed her into the world, even as I was thrown into the messy world of post-millennial parenting!

Despite being a newborn, she took to the family dog, a brown Dachshund named Poppins, quicker than she took to any human. Poppins returned the favour fervently and hovered around her like a mother hen, refusing to allow any visitors to hold her.

Days and weeks passed. Months went by. With my erratic sleep schedule and lack of naps, I barely paid any attention to Poppins, who was only too happy to be devoid of any supervision between meals and hung out with her 'friend' down the road. A few months later, we had an unexpected visit from the stork. I panicked and felt guilty about the 'neglect'. If I couldn't even keep an eye on the dog, how would I keep an eye on my child? I vowed to pay better attention to both Krishnaa and Poppins and be more responsible. It was my first lesson in the art of parenting.

Never again has a dog become pregnant on my watch!

Very soon, it was time for Poppins to give birth in my brother's cosy bedroom. A few hours of struggle went by and the first puppy emerged. We were horrified to see that he was stillborn, but we couldn't stop to think too much about it. We had to continue to focus on Poppins. She braved the labour for another hour and out came a little black pudgy fellow who looked a bit like a burger, with the biggest eyes and the cutest brown patches you will ever see! As soon as he took his first few breaths in the world, cheers and whistles filled the room at the announcement of the new arrival in the family.

Unanimously, the little boy was named Balram, in honour of the famous brother of Lord Krishna—also since he instantly became my daughter's sibling. As is the case in Punjabi families, he was quickly nicknamed, in a matter of days, and became Baloo thenceforth.

Often, Baloo was found rolled up in the blanket like a little burrito, with his little, long face sticking out and buried into Krishnaa's baby back. He refused to wake up until she did, and then insisted on eating when she did. Very quickly, the two had an ongoing schedule—she had milk and he had Cerelac; she played with toys and he chewed them; she listened to Bollywood music and he howled along at times completely out of tune.

For the two, it was the picture of an idyllic childhood. But for me, it was like living in a frat house—someone was always crying or screaming or barking, the house was always messy, and there was the occasional puddle of vomit for added excitement. The whole thing was a test of my tolerance, and learning to 'be patient' became my second lesson in parenting.

Soon, it was time for bathroom training, which of course tried that patience to the utmost. Baloo, unlike Krishnaa, was an absolute and complete disaster here. In an effort to train Baloo, I grudgingly began to take him for multiple long thirty-minute walks. He would smell the ground, eat the grass, watch passers-by with suspicion, and greet other dogs on the way. But during all those walks, he refused to go about his business. I cajoled him, scolded him and tried to bribe him with a treat, but there was no sign of the beautiful sunshine liquid that I eagerly hoped would emerge. Disappointed, we would walk back home, and within seconds of opening the door, Baloo would promptly pee on the carpet or on a mat nearby.

It would be months before Baloo and I could compromise and agree on a line of control. I accepted that he would never go about his business outside home, and he agreed to use the small garden area inside the compound wall, where we also housed two older Indies and had visiting squirrels, crows and parrots every day.

Both Baloo and Krishnaa grew up on a city street where they could see different animals and birds, and spend time near trees and plants. Krishnaa often fed and spoke to them and Baloo remained her constant companion, chasing little animals and insects he came across.

I noticed that Krishnaa's love for Baloo grew so deep that she began to mimic him in her own innocent way, in an effort to experience life as seen through his eyes. She was head over heels in puppy love. She walked on all fours like he did, she stared at him unflinchingly when she needed something from him, she slept with him on carpets and mats at odd hours of the day, and she even tried having food and water directly from the plate using only her mouth.

And she always, always found ways to spend more time with him. They were together every day, living in the present and celebrating life. Watching them live in the moment taught me my third important lesson in parenting.

Until one day …

Baloo began to vomit. No matter what we did, there was no relief. In a matter of hours, we discovered blood in his urine and knew that a trip to the vet was mandated. Within two days, our little boy was diagnosed with renal failure. Before I could even process the information, we had lost him.

It was a terrible shock to Krishnaa's young heart. That first day, she cried bitterly and was inconsolable for hours. To her, Baloo was her whole world—her friend, her companion, her brother. It was too early for her to learn about grief, I thought. I held her and spoke to her about the wonderful time we were given with him. It didn't matter. Teary-eyed, she sobbed, 'My brother is gone and I'll never keep another dog again. Never.'

I knew then that I had to go back and rely on the second lesson of parenting—patience. I had to let her little heart heal. She needed time, and we had plenty of it for now.

Occasionally, we looked at pictures of Baloo, recalled incidents of his mischief with fondness and treasured the bittersweet memories. Months went by and the tears flowed less often and the smile stayed on longer.

A little less than a year later, we received an important call around Christmas. It was a call that would change our lives forever.

'There's a pup up for adoption,' said the vet. 'She's weak and the runt of the litter. Nobody wants her.'

'So it's a girl?' I asked, stating the obvious.

'Yes, get back to me quickly,' he said, before disconnecting the call.

It is a well-known fact that girls rule the roost in our family. While it's a man's world, women shine in our family. My late grandmother was determined to make a life in India post the abandonment of the family home and all she owned in what is now Pakistan. She supported and stood by her husband as they struggled to grow their roots again in India and build a stable home for their family. Then came my mother who ruled the home, and my late father, whose talent she recognized and provided him with sound counsel in their life's journey. My sister-in-law, I am proud to say, is no different. She's the one in the family I run to when situations get dire. She's a master in the art of getting things done at lightning speed. And then there's me—a single parent who broke away from the norms of society for a better life. Today, I work in the fields of philanthropy and literature and actively encourage my young daughter to listen to her heart, to follow her instincts and to make her own choices.

When it comes to the dogs, the rules are no different! Girls are not just welcome, they are highly preferred.

I stopped and thought of Krishnaa, though: 'It will be a chance for her to reset and open her heart again. But will she agree?'

She didn't. Not at first. She was adamant about nobody taking the place of her departed brother.

So my mother and I took her to see the little doe-eyed, vertically challenged and scrawny brown pup. The moment the two laid eyes on each other, Krishnaa's eyes lit up and she gave such a loud high-squealed pitch of delight that people ran in from the other room to check on us. The puppy skipped in excitement too and ran towards her. One look at Krishnaa's face and I knew she was in love again. When the pup reached her, she picked her up and hugged her, turned around and promptly headed back to the car. Already, the pup was hers.

That is how Toffee joined the woman brigade and was welcomed into the family.

And I learnt what was perhaps my finest lesson in parenting yet: to give and receive love, time and again. Love in its purest and deepest form between souls. There's never, ever enough, and there's always room for more.

Today, Toffee and Krishnaa stay together in Bangalore—a dog and her little human, living happily ever after.

Yippee

MANU BHATTATHIRI

People say dogs adapt, and that's what keeps them happy. I don't believe adapting is even half the story. Let me explain.

We got Yippee about nine years ago—a beautiful 'Ooty-line' Labrador, white as an angel, naughty as the devil. But his naughtiness wasn't of the usual puppy type, which can at times get destructive and tiring. Six months with us and he was more subtly naughty, like he had developed a sense of humour which he needed to keep satisfying. Let me put it this way: If he was a little boy he wouldn't be breaking fishbowls or stealing sugar or falling off trees and howling. No, he would be the boy who hides your car keys or your spectacles and then quietly watches you search for them and fret, from behind his comic book, a glint in his eye.

Yippee had big, searching eyes that did not just go all the way into your soul but tickled it there and made you laugh.

He grew up in our home, soon hiding socks instead of making holes in them, barking suddenly when bored, only to ask for a treat when we came to investigate, and bullying, yes, bullying dogs older than him during our walks in the park. I remember, he once snatched an old Husky's leash out of its owner's hands and ran, dragging the grumbling bag of woe behind him, yapping and wagging his tail while everyone at the park clutched their tummies, laughing.

He was funny, he was warm, full of life. We used to joke that the only thing he liked more than us was his food. We had another, older dog at the time named Tuffy, and very often Yippee would help himself to Tuffy's food after quickly finishing his own. He would just go near the gate and bark vigorously at nothing. Tuffy was excitable and a little blind, and fell for the trick every time. He would think Yippee was barking at a squirrel or a cat, and he would sacrifice his bowl for a nice exuberant chase, only to come back a moment later to find Yippee busy at his extra meal.

Perhaps we did not notice the problem in this, so carried away were we at the fun of it all. Yippee was growing fat, tremendously fat. In the park some children called him 'food panda', because he never passed an abandoned chapati or piece of bread that might be lying around, and his figure had turned quite un-doglike. He had become this huge snow mountain, puffing his way around the track, his strain not showing on his smiling face. We could only see that he was big and fun! All of a sudden, we found one day in September 2016 that Yippee couldn't move his hind legs. He had a slipped disc and was paralysed waist-down. He was sixty-two kilos, and the vet hinted at putting him to sleep because paralysed dogs who were this obese were quite finished.

Thankfully, an MRI revealed that it was worth attempting to treat him. Only, we had to dedicatedly take him through his medication, diet, physiotherapy and laser treatment. Physiotherapy entailed rigorous swimming sessions for which the veterinary hospital had a pool, but it was doubtful that a dog as huge as Yippee, and as lazy and pampered, would indeed put in enough effort. Not to mention he only had his front limbs with which to flap about. His entire back apparatus—limbs, the massive gluteus, the lovely otter's tail—hung limp as rubber. The other thing was that he couldn't pass urine on his own, since his bladder, too, was paralysed. For all these reasons, the vet told us, it was best to admit Yippee at the hospital for a while.

That first evening of his hospital stay, I packed a bag with a bedsheet, an air pillow and my toothbrush and toothpaste, intending to request the doctors that I be accommodated in 'any corner' of the hospital for the night, because Yippee wasn't used to staying away from home and would most definitely be agitated. 'He will raise a din in the middle of the night, doctor,' I told the vet, hoping she'd see my very objective point, 'and then all your other dogs will be howling, too.' But the doctor gently told me that nothing like that would happen, that animals adapt, that Yippee would sleep peacefully in his new surroundings so long as he saw that there was nothing immediately threatening to him. Animals adapt, she repeated. After I made her promise that she would give him a sedative in case he was panicky, we left Yippee and came home.

In just a few days we discovered that Yippee was friends with most of the mild-mannered dogs in the hospital and indifferent to the grumpy ones. The vet, who was supposed to monitor his diet and make him lose weight, couldn't help but share her lunch with him, because he had melted her into compliance with his eyes. She began to bring low-carb food saying it was 'good for me and for Yippee'. We would visit every evening, and while our hearts broke to leave him after visiting hours, he would only look a little curiously as we left, as though to ask us why we needed to go from such a fun place. By the end of the first week the physiotherapist told us something remarkable—Yippee was one of the fattest dogs ever to swim there, but that wasn't his record. He did one hundred and forty laps in that pool each day: more than any other dog. His right leg moved a little by now, though his tail and left leg still hung limp. But we could see the way he was making that limp leg feel. He was clearly telling it to either get its act together or be satisfied with being dragged around like a dead cat.

But Yippee still couldn't pass urine on his own. We were asked to bring him back home after about ten days and were taught by the vet how to insert a catheter and remove urine from his bladder. So at home we had this new routine: We would be up by five in the morning, my wife, my daughter and I. We would lay Yippee in our midst while we squatted on the floor. My daughter would place his head on her lap and cuddle him and sometimes sing him a song, while my wife gently put the catheter in. I was more the peon or the nurse, handing things over, cleaning up if a little urine spilt and so on. Five in the morning, because the process took almost an hour, sometimes more, and everyone had to get to work early. We did this again in the evenings too.

On a wall in my mind there will always hang the picture of the three of us sitting in a huddle, Yippee in the middle, a tube with golden yellow urine snaking out of him and into a bottle. I also remember that I often used to look into his eyes at the time, to check for warmth and gratitude and love in return for all that we were doing for him. Instead I got back a stare that asked me to get on with it fast, and to cut the sissy stuff.

That was Yippee. Exactly a month after he was paralysed, he passed urine on his own. We held him up under a tree using a towel that passed under his belly, as the physiotherapist had taught us, and we heard the hiss of urine first, and then, as we looked down under him, saw the beautiful jet, with tears in our eyes, while he stood, his eyes amused at our relief. I wonder what a neighbour would have thought of us, standing on the road, crying with joy upon seeing a Labrador pee under a tree.

With swimming sessions every alternate day, laser treatment and a special diet, Yippee's right leg came back to almost normal, even as he shed more than twenty kilos. We began taking him to the park again. While we were gingerly and careful, he dragged us on, limping, though sometimes his left leg folded under him, in which case he just rolled over and made it seem like a new game.

And it was in the park that I completed the thoughts he had been making me think for a while now.

You will note that Yippee was by no means back to his old self yet. He had proved himself a fighter, but he still limped horribly, still fell very often, and was tired despite his enthusiasm, so that all he really did most of the time at the park was sit on the grass, smiling at the other dogs running about. And yet we were proud of him, my wife and I, as he sat bathed in the morning light as though the sun had climbed all the way up only to bathe him in light. Not one passer-by failed to look at him; most smiled at him, a few stopped to pet him—because he was white as satin and glowed like a jewel.

One day a new black-and-orange Rottweiler appeared. We hadn't seen her before, and she was extraordinarily graceful but rather stern and no-nonsense in appearance. You could say she looked a little grouchy, perhaps, and her sharp teeth glinted in an unfriendly manner. In her teeth she held a green ball. It was the kind that squeaked under pressure and glowed as it bounced. She played alone, while her owner, a middle-aged woman who looked rather serious herself, read a book. I thought the spectacles on the owner would look better on the dog.

We saw that Yippee had taken note of the Rottweiler. Slowly, heavily, he picked himself up and limped a little nearer to her. She smoothly picked the ball off the ground and shot arrows at him with her eyes. Completely polite and unconflicted, Yippee immediately sat down again, but every time she moved away, he limped over and closed the distance between them. My wife and I looked at each other, thinking the same thought: At the first instance, maybe even a little later this day itself, we would go to all the pet stores in the vicinity and rummage through their toys. We would find the very same ball for Yippee—perhaps two or three of them, in different colours.

'He wants to play with her,' said the Rottweiler's owner, folding her book. I thought that together dog and owner looked like the headmistress and assistant teacher of a very strict convent school. 'Bella, share the ball with this nice boy, darling. Come on, come on. Socialize, baby.'

Encouraged, Yippee dragged himself a little closer, but now Bella growled. It seemed like she would bite into the ball in her anger. Yippee wagged his tail, let his tongue hang almost to the ground, made his eyes large and dreamy. But Bella turned and faced away from him, still shuddering and letting out small growls. We smiled sheepishly, my wife and I, but in our hearts there was pain—there was a time, not so long ago, when our Yippee could stand tall against any Rottweiler, and not take growls with a wag of his tail. We would find him his toy later, but for now he would have to make do with sitting and watching Bella play with her ball.

But he wasn't about to do anything of the sort. The Rottie's owner asked us about Yippee, his name, what had happened to his leg. We fell to telling her the whole story of his paralysis and treatment, and when we turned around a little later, we found a curious new development. Yippee had moved right next to Bella, touching distance, as she stood, tense, baring all her teeth, biting her ball to breaking point. He swayed a little from weakness and fear, but he stood there, nonetheless, soon even leaning over to sniff her behind. Scandalized, Bella let out a fearsome growl, with which the ball in her tightened jaws squeaked too. We were about to yank our boy away, but Bella's owner suggested that maybe we should find out what would happen next. Well, what happened next was this: Yippee began to first sniff Bella all over with his wet nose, wagging his tail continuously, and then lick her here and there and then all over, even as her growls began to grow confused. Every time she bit into the ball in anger, the thing squeaked like a temper-management tool. he was obviously taking advantage of her possessiveness for the ball: he knew she wouldn't let go of it even for a pound of his flesh. He licked her on the side, on her paws, her ears, and even between her eyes! I saw that her owner, who had seemed so stern, had a lovely smile after all; a spontaneous smile that was infectious. We were all laughing, as Bella was rapidly covered in Yippee's drool. Her growls became small whines, as though she was at a loss.

'If you can't melt them, dissolve them,' the lady said, taking off her spectacles to wipe her eyes.

Stunningly, Yippee did not just get to play with that ball, which Bella soon let drop from her mouth. When it was time to return from the park, he had the ball in his mouth, and it wasn't like anyone could take it from him. When we tried, he turned his face downwards to hide what he held in his jaws and looked at us with upturned eyes. For the first time ever, he seemed in a hurry to come back from his walk. Bella's lady told us to please let Yippee keep the ball, that he had won it, clearly, and that she had never seen anything like it. As for Bella, I bet that girl would dream of Yippee for many days to come.

Now, that ball wasn't essential to his survival, was it? This was not merely coveting another's property, but going ahead, full force, and acquiring it. Through means that aren't entirely ethical. That's way beyond adapting. Adapting is about compromising and smiling while you are losing. Was Yippee cutting his own corners here to fit into the vault of fate, or was he kicking fate's behind and gifting himself what he wanted? The answer was clear. He wasn't just alive, just surviving—he was happy, as happy as any creature could be, because he could love himself without pitying himself, and make a grab for what his heart desired with the three limbs he had left. That goes a little further than adapting, you will agree.

Yippee left us in the summer of 2019. I'm sure at the rainbow bridge he stopped and demanded why it had just seven colours. A couple of Yippee colours have been added since for all posterity, I think, and he might have renamed it something less clichéd: just 'The Bridge' or something. And I'm also sure that when my time comes, I too shall not whimper and settle in. He has taught me that I must fight, tooth and nail, and then jump right into it, happily, because I know that there is furry warmth waiting for me on the other side.

The Dogs of Bhairava

DEVDUTT PATTANAIK

The world over, dogs are seen as loyal animals associated with unconditional love. However, in Hindu mythology, their representation is ambiguous. On the one hand, they are seen as auspicious, as guardians or as the symbol of the followers of Nath traditions—tantrics and hermits. On the other hand, they are known to be inauspicious, associated with death, attachment and neediness, and a metaphor for the ego. This metaphor stems from the fact that dogs are devoted to their masters. They follow their masters everywhere; wag their tails when they are happy and whine when their masters don't give them adequate attention and love. Thus they become a symbol of attachment and the gratification of the ego. They are also associated with refuse, and thus with impurity. In this respect, the dog is really located in opposition to the cow, which is seen as pure and holy. Of course, this is a very broad understanding.

Interestingly, the dog's rise to prominence in India is not recent. Indian mythology is peppered with fascinating tales featuring dogs.

The Korkus are a tribe scattered across Madhya Pradesh and Maharashtra, residing mainly in the Dharnagiri region. They consider themselves descendants of Ravana and believe that Shiva created their world. According to legend, once Ravana strayed into the scenic but unpopulated forests of the Vindhyachal and Satpura ranges. He prayed to Shiva to populate those forests with people. Shiva directed his messenger, the crow Kageshwar, to collect red soil from the hilly region between Bhavargadh and Savligadh (in the Betul district). Shiva then made two statues—of a man and a woman—from the soil and placed them in the forested region. However, before he could infuse them with life, Indra got his horses to destroy the statues. Enraged, Shiva proceeded to create two dogs out of the red soil. He infused them with life and had them drive Indra's horses away. He then remade the two human statues and bestowed life upon them. The man and the woman, named Moola and Moolai, respectively, are considered the ancestors of the Korku tribe. The Korku thus worship Shiva, Ravana and the dog.

Another story is of a community in Gujarat. Many of them were landless labourers. Some were cattle herders, some sold forest produce. They were also extremely talented artists, but were denied entry into temples. Therefore, they decided to create their own gods by painting their images on cloth. This led to a whole new art form of mobile temples on painted cloth. They worshipped their own goddess, Hadkai Mata, who rides a dog and protects people from measles.

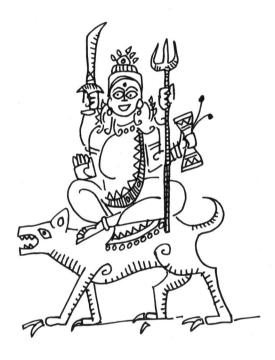

Further south, in Maharashtra and Telangana, the dog is associated with the warrior gods Khandoba and Mallanna, respectively, and with Revanta, the god of the hunt, in central India. A legend depicts Khandoba's wives futilely helping the deity collect the blood of the demon Mani, every drop of which was creating a new demon during battle. Finally, Khandoba's faithful dog swallows all the blood, thus helping him kill the demons.

Indra, the mighty god of the Rig Veda, has a female dog named Sarama. She is considered the mother of all dogs. Sarama has a long history in Hindu mythology. It is believed that Indra sent her out to find his cows, which had been stolen by people known as the Panis. In some stories, she not only found the cows, hidden in the cave of the Panis, but also negotiated their recovery. This earned her the love and affection of Indra.

In the Mahabharata, Sarama and her children visit a sacrificial site where King Janmejaya is performing a yagna to kill all the nagas. Sarama's children are accused of licking the pot of milk being used to prepare offerings to the gods. The king's brothers throw stones at them to stop them. Enraged, Sarama curses that the yagna will be unsuccessful—and that is exactly what happens.

According to the Puranas, Sarama is the mother of all creatures with claws, while Surabhi is the mother of all creatures with hooves. Thus, Sarama is the mother of the lion as well as the tiger, and is linked to the wolf and the fox.

Dogs, in general, are associated with the aggressive form of Shiva known as Bhairava. Shiva lived on a mountain covered with snow where there was nothing to eat. This did not matter, for Shiva taught the bull, his companion, the art of overcoming hunger. Shiva loved the bull, but sometimes, he took the form of Bhairava, who loved dark places. When Shiva became Bhairava, the dog became his friend. In art, Bhairava is visualized either as a ferocious alpha, riding a rabid dog, or as a child, also riding a dog. The former is called Kal Bhairava, or sometimes Kala Bhairava, associated with time, hence with death and destruction, and with darkness. The latter, the cherubic Bhairava, is called Batuk Bhairava, or Gora Bhairava, the childlike Bhairava, or the fair Bhairava.

The temple of Kilkari Bhairava is believed to have been established by the Pandavas at the entrance of Indraprastha (that now clings to the outer walls of Purana Qila in Delhi). Kilkari means squealing, the joyful cry of a child. Unlike the conventional temples of Shiva, there are no images of bulls here; only dogs which are the vahanas of Bhairava. The temple complex is full of dogs, who love the attention showered on them by devotees.

The Bhairava form of Shiva is kept outside the village and is associated with crematoriums. Dogs too are associated with crematoriums and the margins of society. Thus, the dogs of Bhairava may be associated with Sarama's children, the Sarameyas, who, according to later texts, are the four-eyed guardians of the Land of the Dead. This land is separated from the Land of the Living by the Vaitarini river. The dogs then become the companions of Yama. Thus, we find the dog associated with the wildest aspect of Shiva called Bhairava that essentially means 'the one who removes the fear of death'.

Bhairava's mildest form is the great teacher of teachers, Adinath Dattatreya. The Nath yogis are a special tradition of yogis that became popular over a thousand years ago. There are nine Naths, or Nav Naths, who wandered across India, Nepal and Southeast Asia, spreading their wisdom.

They all considered Dattatreya to be their guru. Dattatreya is imagined as a god accompanied by dogs and a cow. In art, he is shown with four mild-tempered dogs, often considered to be the embodiments of the four Vedas. They always walk in front of Dattatreya, frequently turning around, insecure and afraid that he will go away. Since Saraswati is the mother of the Vedas, some people argue that Sarama also represents the goddess Saraswati.

Illustrations by the author

Plum

VIKAS KHANNA

I always had a dog when I was growing up in Amritsar. Tiddy was my best favourite friend when I was a boy; she was also my tasting specialist in the kitchen as I conducted various culinary experiments. I was heartbroken when she left us at the age of twelve. I had never thought that I could feel so completely devastated.

That was back in 1998.

Twenty-three years later, in 2021, I still had not got over the pain.

One evening, my friend Julia Chatterly was having dinner at my place and started talking about her new pet, Romeo. Suddenly, it was like all the years had disappeared. The memories of the joyful and happy times I had had with Tiddy came rushing back, and I became aware once again of the emptiness I felt without her.

I just couldn't get the thought out of my head. The very next day, I decided to go to a pet shop in Brooklyn and look around.

A little two-month-old Maltese met my eyes, and I just couldn't look away. He was tiny, and I just had to bend down and pick him up. And then I couldn't let go. He had found me and I had found him.

And that's how, on 21 May 2021, Plum came into my life. And everything changed. Everything.

Why 'Plum'?

There's a story there. Soon after he and I found each other, I named my child after the flower Plumeria; it had been my father's favourite flower. Over time Plumeria got shortened to Plumie, Plumu and finally Plum.

Plum took to his new habitat very easily and made himself at home in my apartment. My sister Radhika and my friend Samir Shreshta were a huge help—they became Plum's guardian angels.

To be honest, I was little nervous at the start, because my life is like a workaholic's dream. I entertain almost every single night and have shoots virtually every day, and I thought the hectic schedule might disturb Plum. But as it turned out, Plum loved all the activity and all the people coming and going. He is a connecting force with all my friends and family members; he touches everyone's lives with his energy and love.

Pets bring a certain discipline and routine to life. Plum eats at regular hours, he goes for his walks at given times, he has a defined bedtime. That brings a rhythm to my day as well.

Plum is a young pup and it is such a joy to be with him and to see the world through his excited eyes. Our little trips in New York City are so much fun—I take him to my favourite spots and as I see him sniff and smell everything and take in the flavours of the place, I realize the importance of stopping, taking it all in, and living in the moment.

Recently, Plum took his first trip to the beach. He was so thrilled with the entire experience—he kept chasing the receding waves and then proceeded to excavate in the sand. As we drove back with the top down, his wonderful white fur flying in the breeze, I knew it was a day I'd remember with joy again and again in the future.

I often wonder how it was that I lived without a pet for twenty-three long years. They are the purest source of joy and unconditional love.

Every single night before he goes to sleep, I tell him, 'Thank you, Plum, for choosing me.'

And of course, I cook for Plum every so often. The recipe that appears below is one that he loves.

I also make things inspired by him. Cookies with a pawprint design on them is a favourite. The other day I made grilled mangoes with plum chutney—which Plum tasted. Just writing the word 'plum' makes me smile!

And when I'm in the kitchen with Plum by my side, it's like I'm back at home as a boy with my best favourite friend, cooking up the next new adventure.

Plum's Favourite Dish
A Recipe by Vikas Khanna

12 ounces minced chicken breasts
2 cups chicken stock, preferably low-sodium
1 medium carrot, peeled and grated
1 cup boiled brown rice
8 to 10 blueberries
2 boiled eggs, mashed

In a medium pan on high heat add the chicken with the chicken stock.

Let it cook, mashing it with the back of the spoon until the chicken is cooked and the mixture is dry (about 10 to 12 minutes).

Add the rice, carrot, blueberries and eggs.

Combine it well and serve with love.

(Do please consult your vet before preparing a meal for your pet.)

Kafka's Last Mango

ANINDITA GHOSE

When she came home in the end of February, it was time for the season's first *kul* (jujubes)—the first lick of spring.

I had carried her home on my lap in the front seat of my father's car, a warm heartbeat swaddled in an old sheet that smelt of her mother. We were quiet as we drove back home to my mother; she had steadfastly refused to have anything to do with a puppy being brought home.

I had never lived with a dog before. My father had grown up on an estate in Patna that always had impressive guard dogs. They were majestic creatures—Dalmatians, Dobermans, German Shepherds. His uncle would train them like police dogs. One had gone rabid and had to be shot in their front yard. The memory of Rana being shot—even though he had only heard the sound as a little boy—still haunted him.

It had taken a lot of convincing on my part for even my father to be an ally. The proposition had shown up without warning: a phone call from a friend. The heartbeat on my lap was born of incest.

Her mother—she was appropriately named Mischief—had seduced a son from her first litter to produce his younger siblings. There were nine of them, my friend told me over the phone. Five brown ones, three black ones and one black-and-white marvel, rare for English Cocker Spaniels. How soon could I come to see them?

I remember the scene when I first went to visit. The house wore the faintly acidic smell of urine and wet newspaper. The litter was in a large tub. As soon as the tub was tipped, the bleary-eyed creatures—they were about six weeks old—wet the floor one after the other like a circus routine. Then they proceeded to crowd around their mother, who pushed away the overfed of the lot with a wise paw. The lure of milk was soon trumped by new voices and smells and they came clumsily bounding towards where my friend and I knelt. All except one. She went the other way, towards uncharted ground, beyond the confines of her mother—tub—newspaper life.

'She's Caramel. Always the dreamer,' my friend said.

It wasn't long before Caramel metamorphosed into Kafka.

I was in university at the time, studying linguistics. The artifice of youth called for a name with more gravitas than an ice-cream flavour. Between the required classroom reading of Saussure and Lacan, Eco and Lévi-Strauss, I was enamoured by absurdist fiction. A line from Franz Kafka had lodged itself in my head: 'All knowledge, the totality of all questions and answers, is contained in the dog.'

'But Kafka was a man,' my father said. 'She's a baby girl.'

'Kafka is a family name … it bears no gender,' I argued.

My mother—who had managed to sit sullenly on the sofa for all of two minutes after I had put the new arrival down on the floor of our living room—used her vote to say Kafka Ghose had a phonetic ring to it.

Kafka herself, however, gave us no indication of her vocal cords for several weeks after she was home. She would whimper and squeak and make other noises in the base of her throat. When we had visitors, she would run under the bed. Barking was an alien word. Maybe she's just gentle, we thought. Maybe her incestuous conception is to blame. Or maybe she really is *boba*: she can't speak. It didn't matter. Her smells, her routine, her licks, her games had filled our days. Her presence was loud.

The crates of Alphonso arrived from Ratnagiri at their usual time in April. It was going to be a special weekend; we unpacked, fussed, pressed, chose, soaked, cut. Kafka had, by then, become the spoilt darling of the family. Everyone slipped slivers of fish or meat to her under the table all the time; everyone thought they were the only ones doing it. Devouring the first crate was a family celebration presided over by my grandmother, and Kafka was family. We gave her a tiny piece of fruit. Her first mango. It was when we turned back to our ambrosial platter that we heard her. Kafka's first bark. She wanted more.

As Kafka grew, so did her lust for food. All kinds of food. She was alert every time the door of the fridge opened. Pressure cooker whistles, the clanking of her dog bowl being washed in the sink before her next meal, and of course, the aroma of mangoes being sliced—her ears pricked up, her head cocked, her eyes coveted. Mutton stew with carrots was a special favourite. Curd was comfort. Cold, deseeded watermelon chunks were a treat. Bits of cheese made her go wild. We had to be all too careful not to leave a stray raisin or a bright pill fallen on the floor. If she didn't demand something from my mother at least once a day, my mother fretted that she was unwell. One day, she worried that Kafka was taking 'too long' to eat her small piece of mango. My grandmother was finishing her dinner at the time and said her mango didn't taste quite right. It was June, the crates were long gone, and even the Alphonsos in the market were running out.

'I got Kesar today,' my mother said. 'Please don't be difficult.'

My grandmother complied grudgingly. But Kafka left her mango half-nibbled. We were raising a snob.

We were also raising a woman, as we learnt all too painfully a few months later when Kafka adopted a red rubber dragon as her child. She snarled if anyone approached her or her dragon child. She slept and ate unlike herself. She didn't even want to go for her walks. A visit to the vet revealed she was having a pseudo-pregnancy, a remnant from the days in the wild when all the female dogs in a pack showed symptoms of pregnancy at the same time so a motherless pup would have teats to nourish it.

She would have to be spayed. There would be an operation. 'With general anaesthesia!' my mother screamed at regular intervals in the days leading up to it. Kafka was still very groggy from her anaesthesia when we brought her back home. Her head lolled, her eyes didn't focus. She was asleep, but my mother and I cried for hours. When she woke up, she moved slowly, refused her food, and went back to sleep. None of us had eaten a full meal. Our cook brought in a plate of chopped watermelon for the family. We saw Kafka's nose twitch. She was up again. She chased a piece of watermelon around the house.

In a few weeks, when she regained her strength, Kafka learnt to stand on two legs for a piece of watermelon. My father had started the terrible practice of giving her vitamins and other medicines wrapped in a thin layer of cheese, so she did some roll-on-the-floor tricks for that as well.

When Kafka was two years old, I left for graduate school in New York. I carried her paw prints with me on the flight. It was July; classes started in August. Kafka had come to the airport on that wet, rainy Mumbai evening and said goodbye to me in the only way she knew how, with her paws on my light-blue jeans, jeans I didn't wash for days. I was going away from home for the first time, away from my first boyfriend, leaving my parents and my grandmother behind. But I could always speak to them over the phone. They could visit me. How could I explain to Kafka that I wasn't going away because I didn't love her? Where was the linguistic theory to communicate that?

American linguist Charles Hockett's Design Features lays down a list of things that characterizes human language and sets it apart from animal communication. A primary distinguishing feature of human language is the ability to lie. In a world of shifting truths and unreliable narrators, a dog's love is the most honest thing I've known.

I was back in India two years later, but Kafka and I never stayed in the same house together again. I lived in Delhi for a few years, and even when I moved back to Mumbai, I lived with a friend, not with family. I would visit Kafka. And on weekends Kafka would visit me. It was not enough; you only know it was not enough afterwards. You know it when your dog is ill and it hurts her to move. You know it when she is lying around all day with dull eyes and you tell yourself that you would give anything for her to get back to the ways that you chastised her for: dashing out of doors, running inside the house, chasing crows on the veranda like a demented fool, waking up too early on a Sunday when you wanted to sleep in. Why doesn't anyone tell you these things: that you should call your grandfather more while he still remembers your name; that your first love can end just as soon as it began; that you will never read the last page of your favourite novel again.

When she was ten, Kafka fell sick, for the first time in any serious way. She was peeing blood, she had sores on her body. She was put on a strict hypoallergenic diet that made her sad. A dignified grand dame, she now wet the floor all around the house. We gathered there was a tumour in her bladder. She was given pain relief. There was some reprieve in homeopathy, and so I started to believe in homeopathy—and god. My parents had to travel abroad. I moved back home. From a visit to her vet for a growth in her paw, and an X-ray right after, it was confirmed that Kafka had cancer and that it had metastasized to her bones. The vet said she was too weak for surgery or chemo. While my parents were still away, she became violently ill, very fast. They cut their trip short to return.

My beloved grandmother, whom Kafka spent her days with while my parents were at work, unable to see her youngest grandchild in pain, fell ill. In the final stages of her own sickness, Kafka was a picture of gentleness and consideration. She had almost lost the function of a paw, and couldn't go down for her walks, but she dragged herself to the bathroom floor every time she had to go, which was often.

The vet said they could do nothing beyond pain relief, but the homeopath said he could cure her. I put my faith in white sugar pills; I stared at the glass vials, hoping to learn some magic from them. In this period, Kafka never whimpered, she just slept all the time. She was *boba* once again, she didn't bark even when the doorbell rang. The doctors, and friends, asked if she was eating well, if her appetite was good. That was a good sign, they said. Yes, she was always eating well. Even when she was peeing blood, being carried for X-rays, being given injections, having her sores cleaned, she was always eating well.

When even the homeopath gave up, we switched Kafka back from the insipid hypoallergenic German fare to the food she loved. It was April again, mangoes were in season. By the end of her life, Kafka ate like a Bengali zamindar—rice and fish, mango and *mishti doi*, and Marie biscuits dipped in tea to give my grandmother company. (She had eaten vet-prescribed food throughout her life before that.)

The vet said we should put her to sleep. It was the kinder thing to do, she assured us.

'Why did you ever bring her home and do this to me?' my mother cried every night.

Kafka's full life had been a fraction of ours—a fact that dog owners must wilfully forget every time they bring a dog home.

Over the next two months, my family couldn't reach a decision on euthanasia. There were arguments in the family about who was being sentimental and who was being practical. We raged, we cried, we blamed each other. My internet search history remains overrun with searches for 'signs your dog is in pain' and 'best practices for pet euthanasia'—which I learnt most Indian vets do not follow. They inject one heavy dose of barbiturates to stop the heart.

A friend told me her dog had howled all night for a month before she passed away in great agony; they just couldn't get themselves to put her to sleep. We couldn't set a date either. We needed a sign.

The day before we put her to rest, she refused mango.

It was July. The Alphonsos were no longer in the market. My father drove a long way out to get them, as succour for a family in low spirits, for Kafka. We chose the best few, sliced them, and held out pieces for her. She took one in her mouth. We took deep breaths. But then she spat it out and stared at it, confused by this thing that once gave her great joy. We stared at Kafka staring at the mango for hours.

We knew it was time.

Stay

SIDDHARTH DHANVANT SHANGHVI

The window in the room where I stayed in Nottingham overlooked a bend in the Trent; beyond it was a dusty old manor home which in the summer of 1992 was being refurbished into a set of apartments. I was fourteen, I had flown from Bombay to England to work on a farm where I would learn more about dogs, chiefly Lakeland Terriers and Boxers. Barbara and Philip Greenway owned Rayfos Kennels; they had bred Rayfos Cockrobin, an influential sire and for many years a record holder for championship certificates. The Greenways had read my letter in *Boxer Quarterly* —I had written to the editor saying that I was a teenager from India who wanted experience raising dogs and was prepared to work as a kennel boy or a farmhand. Barbara wrote me a card inviting me to stay with them at their farm and to learn from them by working at their kennels. On the cover of this card was a photograph of her house: Obscured by autumn ivy, tones of yellow and rust leaves was a red brick country house with a gravel stone driveway.

To impress Barbara of my credentials I had written of exhibiting a neighbour's Boxer at the Bombay Presidency Kennel Club's shows held at the grounds of a school in Bandra. I had done this also as I was in thrall of the Kennel Club's secretary, Sheila Naharwar, who was half Scot; gruff and lovely, she loved her Whippets, miniature Pinschers and Dachshunds. A formidable figure with a thick accent, Sheila was original, fearless, charming, an aesthete with deep reserves for compassion. (When Sheila passed away this July, I thought to myself it was her, this tough, wry eagle of a person who had been my doorway into the world of Bombay dog shows, which attracted a miscellany of madcaps and dandies.)

A white picket-fence gate separated the Greenways' main red brick listed house from the barns with the dogs in large, heated kennels—there were thirty-four dogs in all. Adjacent to the barn was a row of outdoor kennels where the Terriers were allowed the run during the day. The Boxers, meanwhile, had access to the house or to a paddock of around an acre, the length of which ran alongside the river. The nearest shops were miles away but there was a petrol station I walked to in the evenings, after work, to get a bar of Snickers—I nearly got run over by a truck one time. I was properly a teenager so I sat in the barns at dusk, listened to Sheryl Crow, drank and wept for people who didn't even know that I existed; I often threatened to drown myself in the river. Once, Tessa, the obese brindle Boxer bitch, chased me through the paddock (which helped me realize that, in fact, I wanted very much to live, my nihilism had been superficial, I was wired to endure). In an effort to escape Tessa, I hurled myself over the paddock fence and landed on the ground right next to the Terrier pens—they all went crazy, yapping wildly, running circles in the run. As I looked up at their barking faces I thought: *They could probably eat me.*

My fears about dog attacks were not unfounded. When I was nine, a Doberman who belonged to a family friend gave me a bit of a chase through the house. I had accompanied my mother to Mrs Chandaben Patel's house on 12th Road, where the incident occurred in the late morning. The large, muscular dog chased me down a long, narrow garden path, on either side of which grew large elephant-ear palms. This border of palms furthered the impression of a fairy tale, one in which I would probably end up in a witch's stew. It was only a nip, but the real scare was tumbling over after the Doberman had lunged at me. I felt small, and grew instantly terrified of dogs. When my mother took me to see Baby Mashi in Prabhadevi I would go along but wait it out in the car below. Baby Mashi had a black Pomeranian mix, with a white flash between his eyes, and he was best described as 'temperamental' or 'unpredictable'. Of course, I was wrong—he was the sweetest little thing for the most part, I told Claire, who also worked at Rayfos Kennels the summer that I had showed up in Nottingham. 'He wouldn't hurt a fly,' but I was terrified after the incident with the Doberman and came to view all dogs as potential attackers.

'How did you go from being terrified of dogs to working with them?' Claire was short, white, blonde. She was an expert trimmer who suffered from bursts of uncontrollable flatulence; she often fantasized about the possibility of roping in her husband for a three-way with the farm's handyman. I told Claire that to correct my manic fear of dogs, I had joined the Aquarius Man Dog Training Academy, located in a penthouse flat at the top of a hill in Breach Candy. Vijay Multani trained people to train their own dogs; he had made an exception by agreeing to teach me—then twelve—how to train dogs. His large green terrace, overlooking the Arabian Sea in the distance, was impossibly glamorous to a suburban hick like me;

a wealthy Gujarati lady with her problem Beagle eyed me nervously,
perhaps wondering if I was too young to be around here.

'But I don't understand it,' Claire said to me. 'The jump from
your fear of dogs to learning how to handle them. How'd you go
to the extreme?' I did not understand this either, but it was an
experience akin to getting married—it was eventually so painful
that one simply doesn't recall going through with it.

Over the two years of my certificate course I learnt how to teach
a dog to sit, stay, speak, along with other basic obedience commands.
I also learnt to show dogs—to handle them in a ring—and in the last
month of my course I handled a Doberman. In the only surviving
image from my days at the Aquarius Man Dog Training Academy,
I am prepping the dog as one would at a show, spreading his right
paw to land him the correct posture, adjusting his cropped ears, my
right hand is under his head even as I squat behind him. I look like
an elf behind a beast. And yet, something had changed in me in
the year I spent at the academy: In my soft, steely eyes, one can see
that I would fight the dog to the ground if it did something silly with
me—this was excellent practice for a writer's life.

My education at the academy came in handy at the farm, where
most dogs were show dogs—they worked. Every weekend, Philip
loaded a big red van and drove it up and down the length of the
country, attending various shows; I would accompany him, loading
the dog boxes, setting up grooming tables at the showground. I learnt
a great deal about handling dogs from Philip, who was one of the
best. He taught me how to treat the hounds with a piece of liver;
how to turn when you showed off their gait to the judge. At the time,
it seemed valuable practice, but later I came to detest the culture of
dog shows, their artificial, strained constructs of beauty, and how
this harmed dogs. Dogs are dogs, pi dogs, show dogs, cross-breeds,

the dogs with a foot missing—it doesn't matter, they are perfect as they are.

I came to see this more acutely after I began to help out at Welfare for Animals (WAG), an animal shelter in north Goa where I had moved in my thirties, and where I continue to live. At the shelter, in the village of Siolim, I saw all kinds of dogs, the ones who skulked around you in fear, the lean ones, the pretty ones, the one-eyed rescues, the ones who growled and drooled, the silent nippers, the puppies who dissolved to a word of kindness, and the slightly stupid mutts too. All the dogs were perfect because they had figured out the secret to love, which was to dispense it without either caution or expectation.

'Take the two bitches,' said Atul Sarin, founder of WAG. 'They're sisters. You'll never be lonely.' I was a few weeks into my forty-second year, in 2019. Thirty years had gone by since I went to my first dog-training class in south Mumbai, when bus number 84 had brought me to Breach Candy. 'I don't need dogs,' I said to Atul. I had stopped by the shelter on my way back from Morjim beach—I passed the shelter often during the week. 'I'm too solitary. They won't last around me.'

'You'll be a happy man,' he insisted.

On my drive to the beach I always saw Atul working on the grounds of the shelter, tending to an injured calf, cleaning up the bird pen. His dedication and grace were staggering, and unmatched. He had a bad hip after an incident with a bull. He remained undaunted.

I named the two black bitches Kora and Lila; they threw up all over the car on the drive from Siolim to Moira. I had changed my mind and gone and got them a few months after my conversation with Atul. The hornbills in the mango tree went a bit nuts that evening, freaking out the dogs even more. They were limber, black with sooty eyes, hunter's dogs with fine paws. Lila looked like an apprentice witch. Her sister was a tad more inscrutable—she was hiding a scandal, it looked like. Actually, there *had* been a scandal— they had been adopted as puppies, then given up, and then adopted again by a sketchy woman. The watchman in her building beat them with a stick—they went from full confidence to cowering fear. I took them on because it seemed unlikely that they would find another home; they were mostly terrified.

Three days after I brought them home I got a call that Lila and Kora had run away from home—they had escaped the pen. I was driving back from a work appointment. As the car pulled into the lane I saw Lila given a run by a pack of the neighbourhood dogs—a scene out of a classical painting as the slim black cur tore down the road with a pack of bloodthirsty hounds chasing after her. I stopped the car outside the cottage into whose porch Lila had run. I opened the car door. She saw me and jumped into the car—it was a miracle of timing. During the brief ride home she threw up in the car—she looked traumatized again. The next morning, Kora showed up.

Just as once I had been terrified of dogs, there were dogs who lived in some terror of me—even without meaning to be, or knowing it fully, I had been a source of great anxiety. I guess we all are, in so many ways, and I wonder if there's a way to make up for this, you know, with everyone, but especially the dogs—they bruise more deeply, more easily. Luckily, a few days after that night, Lila and Kora settled into the house and more recently I saw them gamely chase the same gang of strays that had gone after them on the night they ran away from home. They have a lay of the land now; they know how to be boss.

I hope they never run away again.

I hope they stay.

About the Authors

AANCHAL MALHOTRA is a Delhi-based oral historian and writer. She is also the co-founder of the Museum of Material Memory, a crowd-sourced digital repository tracing family histories and social ethnography through heirlooms, collectibles and antiques from the Indian subcontinent.

ABHISHEK JOSHI is the founder of Dog with Blog (https://dogwithblog.in), a niche community that aims at finding homes for stray and abandoned dogs across India. They have organized 900+ free adoptions, and counting.

AMITAVA KUMAR is the author of several books of fiction and non-fiction. His two children want him to get them a dog.

ANANYA VAJPEYI is a fellow and associate professor at the Centre for the Study of Developing Societies, New Delhi. She works at the intersection of intellectual history, political theory and critical philology.

ANINDITA GHOSE is a writer and journalist. She was previously the editor of *Mint Lounge* and the features director of *Vogue India*. In 2019, she was a Hawthornden writing fellow. Her debut novel, *The Illuminated*, was published in 2021.

ANITA NAIR is an award-winning novelist, poet and playwright. Her latest book is the novel *Eating Wasps*. Anita is also the founder of the creative writing and mentorship programme Anita's Attic.

ANUJA CHAUHAN worked in advertising for over seventeen years and is the author of several bestselling novels. She lives outside Bangalore with her husband, their three children and a varying number of dogs and cats.

TINGMO is a poet and a Golden Retriever, owner of ARUNAVA SINHA, a translator and teacher of creative writing.

ASHOK FERREY writes books and designs houses. His latest book, *The Ceaseless Chatter of Demons*, was nominated for the DSC Prize, and his last house, The Cricket Club Café in Colombo, for a Geoffrey Bawa Award.

ASHWIN SANGHI is one of India's highest-selling English fiction authors. He has also co-authored two *New York Times* bestselling crime thrillers with James Patterson. He lives in Mumbai.

ATUL SARIN is the founder of Welfare for Animals in Goa (WAG), which rescues and rehabilitates as many stray animals as possible. Atul also pioneers new programmes towards enhancing animal welfare, which include free sterilization and ensuring sustainability.

BULBUL SHARMA has published some twenty books and has been translated into French, Italian and Chinese. She likes to add a dog in every story she writes for adults or for children.

CYRUS BROACHA is a theatre personality, comedian, political satirist, columnist, podcaster and author. He was the host of the popular TV show *Bakra* (MTV) and currently anchors *The Week That Wasn't* (CNN News18).

DEVDUTT PATTANAIK writes on the relevance of mythology in modern times. He is the author of more than fifty books and over 1,000 columns.

DIVYA DUGAR is a documentary producer and freelance journalist, and a former correspondent for the French television channel France 2. She also writes for various publications about travelling with dogs and a toddler.

FIONA FERNANDEZ, retrophile, heritage nut and senior journalist, frequently scouts for hidden stories in Mumbai's corners and contours, and while on these adventures she almost always spots or befriends an Indie or two.

GEETAN BATRA has been a journalist, worked on renovating old buildings, run boutique resorts and set up craft bazaars while playing mom to two strong-willed daughters and fostering creatures big and small. She lives in Delhi.

GILLIAN WRIGHT is a Delhi-based author and translator. Her works include a delightful account of her adventures with her dog Mishti, titled *Mishti the Mirzapuri Labrador*.

GULZAR, one of India's leading poets, is also a renowned scriptwriter, film director and lyricist. He has been awarded the Sahitya Akademi Award, the Padma Bhushan, the Dadasaheb Phalke Award, an Oscar and a Grammy. He lives and works in Mumbai.

JAI ARJUN SINGH is a Delhi-based journalist and writer. He writes on books and films, but also on many other subjects such as evil water tanks, Delhi traffic and dogs.

JERRY PINTO is a Bombay-based writer of poetry, prose, non-fiction and children's fiction. He is the award-winning author of *Helen: The Life and Times of an H-Bomb* and *Em and the Big Hoom*.

KESHAVA GUHA is a writer of fiction as well as literary and political journalism. His novel *Accidental Magic* is set in a community of adult Harry Potter obsessives.

MAHESH RAO's debut novel, *The Smoke Is Rising*, won the Tata Lit Live! First Book Award for fiction. He is the author of *One Point Two Billion*, a collection of short stories, and *Polite Society*, a novel.

MANEKA GANDHI is a politician, writer, environmentalist and animal rights activist. In 1992 she founded People for Animals, one of India's largest animal welfare organizations.

MANJULA NARAYAN enjoys reading books and riding motorbikes. She is Books Editor at *Hindustan Times* and hosts Books&Authors, a weekly podcast on www.htsmartcast.com. She is @utterflea on Twitter and Instagram.

MANU BHATTATHIRI is the author of *Savithri's Special Room*, *The Town That Laughed* and *The Oracle of Karuthupuzha*. He lives in Bangalore with his parents, wife, daughter and no less than three dogs.

MARK TULLY was a correspondent for the BBC in South Asia for twenty-two years and host of the popular BBC Radio 4 programme *Something Understood*. He is the author of several well-known books.

MEENAKSHI ALIMCHANDANI is a Toronto-based literary consultant who specializes in South Asian literature. She consults for Canadian publishers and promotes several well-known authors. She is also an ardent dog lover.

NAOMI BARTON works as a digital sheep-wrangler at *The Wire*, where she also occasionally writes. In her free time, she takes her dog to visit priceless ancient monuments, which she appreciates with due respect, and her dog sometimes pees on.

NILANJANA S. ROY is a novelist, columnist and editor who lives in New Delhi. She writes a regular column for *Financial Times* on the reading life. She is the author of several books, including *The Wildings*; her third novel, *Black River*, will be out in 2022.

ORIJIT SEN is a graphic artist, muralist, cartoonist and designer. He is the chief editor of *Comixense*, a magazine for young adults. In 1990, he co-founded People Tree, a collaborative studio and store for artists, designers and craftspeople.

PARO ANAND has written books for children, young adults and adults, and is a Sahitya Akademi Bal Sahitya Award winner for her book *Wild Child*. She has spoken and written extensively on children's literature.

PRERNA SINGH BINDRA has been at the forefront of the battle to conserve India's wildlife. She is the author of several books, including *The Vanishing*. Prerna lives in Gurgaon but her heart, she says, resides in the forest.

RAJDEEP SARDESAI is an award-winning senior journalist and TV anchor. He is the author of the bestselling *2019: How Modi Won India* and *Democracy's Eleven: The Great Story of Indian Cricket*.

RUSKIN BOND is one of India's best-loved writers, with numerous short stories, essays, novels and books to his credit. He received the Padma Bhushan in 2014. He lives in Landour, Mussoorie.

SARNATH BANERJEE is the author of the graphic novels *Corridor*, *The Barn Owl's Wondrous Capers*, *The Harappa Files*, *All Quiet in Vikaspuri* and *Doab Dil*.

SHOBHAA DÉ is a bestselling author and columnist, and one of India's most respected opinion shapers. She lives in Mumbai with her family.

SHRUTKEERTI KHURANA is programme director at Infosys Foundation and an independent editor who has worked with various authors, including Sudha Murty and APJ Abdul Kalam. She lives in Bangalore with her family and three goofy dogs.

SIAN MORTON lives in the UK and is an animal lover and ethical vegan. She campaigns for changes to the law concerning 'dangerous dogs' by volunteering with DDA Watch, a not-for-profit organization.

SIDDHARTH DHANVANT SHANGHVI is the author of *The Last Song of Dusk*, *The Lost Flamingoes of Bombay*, *The Rabbit & the Squirrel* and *Loss*. He lives in north Goa.

SOONI TARAPOREVALA is a photographer, filmmaker and screenwriter of films such as *The Namesake* and *Salaam Bombay!*. Her directorial debut, *Little Zizou*, won the National Award for Best Film on Family Values in 2010.

SUMITA MEHTA, a journalist for several decades, continues to write, and works with development agencies. A follower of Nichiren Daishonin's Buddhist philosophy, her love for animals and nature stems from a deeply felt sense of interconnectedness.

TANDRALI KULI has been wildly passionate about animals since a young age. After graduating from Delhi University in 2003, she began volunteering at Friendicoes. She now heads the adoption programme at the rescue organization.

TISHANI DOSHI publishes poetry, essays and fiction. Her most recent books are the novel *Small Days and Nights* and *A God at the Door*, her fourth full-length collection of poems. She lives in a small village on the beach in Tamil Nadu.

VIKAS KHANNA is a Michelin Star chef, restaurateur, cookbook writer, filmmaker, TV host and humanitarian. He is the host of *MasterChef India*, *Twist of Taste* and *Mega Kitchens* on National Geographic. He lives in New York.

About the Editor

HEMALI SODHI is the founder of A Suitable Agency, which represents writers, and advises on communications and brand strategy. A dog person and a pet parent, Hemali describes her best days as those spent in the company of dogs. She is passionate about books and travel, and lives in Gurgaon with her husband—and three of the most wonderful dogs on the planet.

Hemali can be reached at sodhi.hemali@gmail.com.

Hemali's Simba

Clockwise from top right: Gulzar with Pali, Maneka with Goofy, Rajdeep's Nemo, Naomi's Melo, Tishani's Buggy and Zelda, Anindita with Kafka, Manu's Yippee, and Ananya with Rufus and Laika.

Clockwise from top right: Ashok's Fritz, Lucky and Jools, Aanchal's Juno and Keats, Keshava with Pumba, Abhishek with Kaali, Sian's Alex at home and in a muzzle, Anuja with Chhabbis, Atul and the dogs of WAG, and Geetan's Begum and Lola.

Clockwise from top right: Ashwin's Simba, Gillian's Soni, Anita's Sunderapandi and Nachimuthu, Cyrus with Opo and Ginny, Meenakshi with EcVee, Fiona's Cocoa (the new Jim Brown), Jai's Chameli, Siddharth's Lila, Arunava with Tingmo, Shobhaa with Gong Li, and Tandrali with Lara.

Clockwise from top right: Prerna with Doginder, Shrutkeerti's daughter Krishnaa with Toffee, Vinod with Editor, Vikas with Plum (photo courtesy Ylva Erevall), Paro with Nadia and Gia, Manjula's Kondhi, Biskut and Kuro, and Jerry with a pup.